AIC 36 Course Guide

Liability Claim Practices
3rd Edition

The Institutes
720 Providence Road, Suite 100
Malvern, Pennsylvania 19355-3433

3rd Edition • 6th Printing • January 2011

ISBN 978-0-89463-369-0

Contents

 ## Study Materials Available for AIC 36

James R. Jones, *Liability Claim Practices*, 1st ed., 2001, AICPCU.

AIC 36 *Course Guide*, 3rd ed., 2008, AICPCU (includes access code for SMART Online Practice Exams).

AIC 36 SMART Study Aids—Review Notes and Flash Cards, 2nd ed.

Student Resources

Catalog A complete listing of our offerings can be found in *Succeed,* The Institutes' professional development catalog, including information about:

- Current programs and courses
- Current textbooks, course guides, SMART Study Aids, and online offerings
- Program completion requirements
- Exam registration

To obtain a copy of the catalog, visit our Web site at www.TheInstitutes.org or contact Customer Service at (800) 644-2101.

How to Prepare for Institutes Exams This free handbook is designed to help you by:

- Giving you ideas on how to use textbooks and course guides as effective learning tools
- Providing steps for answering exam questions effectively
- Recommending exam-day strategies

The handbook is printable from the Student Services Center on The Institutes' Web site at www.TheInstitutes.org, or available by calling Customer Service at (800) 644-2101.

Educational Counseling Services To ensure that you take courses matching both your needs and your skills, you can obtain free counseling from The Institutes by:

- E-mailing your questions to advising@TheInstitutes.org
- Calling an Institutes' counselor directly at (610) 644-2100, ext. 7601
- Obtaining and completing a self-inventory form, available on our Web site at www.TheInstitutes.org or by contacting Customer Service at (800) 644-2101

Exam Registration Information As you proceed with your studies, be sure to arrange for your exam.

- Visit our Web site at www.TheInstitutes.org/forms to access and print the Registration Booklet, which contains information and forms needed to register for your exam.
- Plan to register with The Institutes well in advance of your exam.

How to Contact The Institutes For more information on any of these publications and services:

- Visit our Web site at www.TheInstitutes.org
- Call us at (800) 644-2101 or (610) 644-2100 outside the U.S.
- E-mail us at customerservice@TheInstitutes.org
- Fax us at (610) 640-9576
- Write to us at The Institutes, Customer Service, 720 Providence Road, Suite 100, Malvern, PA 19355-3433

Using This Course Guide

This course guide will help you learn the course content and prepare for the exam.

Each assignment in this course guide typically includes the following components:

Educational Objectives These are the most important study tools in the course guide. Because all of the questions on the exam are based on the Educational Objectives, the best way to study for the exam is to focus on these objectives.

Each Educational Objective typically begins with one of the following action words, which indicate the level of understanding required for the exam:

Analyze—Determine the nature and the relationship of the parts.

Apply—Put to use for a practical purpose.

Associate—Bring together into relationship.

Calculate—Determine numeric values by mathematical process.

Classify—Arrange or organize according to class or category.

Compare—Show similarities and differences.

Contrast—Show only differences.

Define—Give a clear, concise meaning.

Describe—Represent or give an account.

Determine—Settle or decide.

Evaluate—Determine the value or merit.

Explain—Relate the importance or application.

Identify or list—Name or make a list.

Illustrate—Give an example.

Justify—Show to be right or reasonable.

Paraphrase—Restate in your own words.

Recommend—Suggest or endorse something to be used.

Summarize—Concisely state the main points.

Outline The outline lists the topics in the assignment. Read the outline before the required reading to become familiar with the assignment content and the relationships of topics.

Key Words and Phrases These words and phrases are fundamental to understanding the assignment and have a common meaning for those working in insurance. After completing the required reading, test your understanding of the assignment's Key Words and Phrases by writing their definitions.

Review Questions The review questions test your understanding of what you have read. Review the Educational Objectives and required reading, then answer the questions to the best of your ability. When you are finished, check the answers at the end of the assignment to evaluate your comprehension.

Application Questions These questions continue to test your knowledge of the required reading by applying what you've studied to "hypothetical" real-life situations. Again, check the suggested answers at the end of the assignment to review your progress.

Sample Exam Your course guide includes a sample exam (located at the back) or a code for accessing SMART Online Practice Exams (which appears on the inside back cover). Use the option available for the course you're taking to become familiar with the test format.

For courses that offer SMART Online Practice Exams, you can either download and print a sample credentialing exam or take full practice exams using questions like those that will appear on your credentialing exam. SMART Online Practice Exams are as close as you can get to experiencing an actual exam before taking one.

More Study Aids

The Institutes also produce supplemental study tools, called SMART Study Aids, for many of our courses. When SMART Study Aids are available for a course, they are listed on page iii of the course guide. SMART Study Aids include Review Notes and Flash Cards and are excellent tools to help you learn and retain the information in each assignment.

AIC Advisory Committee

Elise M. Farnham, CPCU, ARM, AIM
Illumine Consulting

James A. Franz, AIC, ARM, CPCU
United Farm Family Mutual Ins. Co.
Farm Bureau Insurance

James Jones, CPCU, AIC, ARM
Katie School of Insurance & Financial Services
Illinois State University

Douglas J. Kent, Esq.
Marshall, Dennehey, Warner, Coleman & Goggin

William McCullough, CPCU, CLU, AIC
State Farm Insurance

Kevin M. Quinley, CPCU, ARM, AIC
Medmarc Insurance Group

James Sherlock, CPCU, CLU, ARM
ACE USA

Robert D. Stevens, Sr., CPCU, CLU, AIC
Crawford & Co.

William C. Stewart, Jr., CPCU, AIC, RPA
Claims Training Services

Christine A. Sullivan, CPCU, AIM
Allstate Insurance Company

Assignments

1. Overview of Liability Claims
2. Coverage Issues for Automobile Insurance
3. Coverage Issues With Homeowners and Commercial Liability Policies
4. Avoiding and Handling Coverage Disputes

Segment A is the first of three segments in the AIC 36 course.
These segments are designed to help structure your study.

Direct Your Learning

Overview of Liability Claims

Educational Objectives

After learning the content of this assignment, you should be able to:

1. Describe the legal relationship among the three parties involved in liability claims.

2. Identify and describe various types of liability claims, such as:
   - Auto liability
   - Premises liability
   - Product liability
   - Professional liability
   - Employer liability
   - Directors and officers liability
   - Personal and advertising liability
   - Intellectual property rights claims
   - Environmental liability

3. Explain the legal basis of employment practices liability and identify employer conduct that could lead to an employment practice liability claim.

4. Describe the liability claim process.

5. Explain how to analyze liability coverage.

6. Describe the competencies and characteristics of effective liability claim representatives.

7. Explain some of the major issues that affect changes in the role and responsibilities of liability claim representatives, such as:
   - Technology
   - Dynamic legal environment
   - Managed care
   - Ethical issues

8. Explain how to identify, avoid, and resolve ethical dilemmas in claims.

9. Describe the various parts, and insuring agreements, found in an automobile insurance policy.

10. Define or describe each of the Key Words and Phrases for this assignment.

Study Materials

Required Reading:
▶ Liability Claim Practices
  • Chapter 1

Study Aids:
▶ SMART Online Practice Exams
▶ SMART Study Aids
  • Review Notes and Flash Cards— Assignment 1

Outline

▶ **Introduction to Liability Claims**
- A. Liability Claims Basics
  1. Parties Involved in Liability Claims

▶ **Types of Liability Claims**
- A. Auto Liability Claims
- B. Premises Liability Claims
- C. Product Liability Claims
- D. Professional Liability Claims
- E. Employer Liability Claims
  1. Injury Claims Outside of Workers Compensation
  2. Employment Practices Liability
- F. Directors and Officers Liability Claims
- G. Personal and Advertising Injury Claims
- H. Intellectual Property Rights Claims
- I. Environmental Liability Claims

▶ **The Liability Claim Process**
- A. Determining Coverage
  1. Who Is Covered?
  2. Are the Activities Causing the Injury or Damages Covered?
  3. Are the Damages Covered?
  4. Do Any Policy Exclusions Apply to the Claim?
  5. Did the Covered Damages Occur Within the Policy's Time Period?
  6. Is the Location of the Loss Covered?
  7. Did Insured and Insurer Meet Their Obligations Before and After the Loss?
  8. What Limitations Exist on Liability?
  9. Do Any Laws or Regulations Affect Coverage?
- B. Investigating Liability
  1. Good Faith Duty To Investigate
  2. Information Needed for Proper Evaluation
- C. Evaluating Damages

- D. Settling Liability Claims
  1. Methods
  2. Concluding a Claim

▶ **Competencies and Characteristics of Effective Liability Claim Professionals**
- A. Skills and Knowledge of Effective Claim Representatives
- B. Characteristics of Effective Claim Representatives

▶ **Issues in Liability Claims**
- A. Technology in Claims
  1. Computerized Evaluation and Negotiation
- B. Dynamic Legal Environment
- C. Managed Care
- D. Ethical Issues
  1. Identifying Ethical Issues in Claims
  2. Resolving Ethical Dilemmas

▶ **Liability Insurance Policy Basics**
- A. Auto Insurance Policy Basics
  1. Declarations
  2. Definitions
  3. Insuring Agreements
  4. Exclusions
  5. Conditions
  6. Miscellaneous Provisions and Endorsements

▶ **Conclusion**

Don't spend time on material you have already mastered. The SMART Review Notes are organized by the Educational Objectives found in each course guide assignment to help you track your study.

Key Words and Phrases

Define or describe each of the words and phrases listed below.

Claimant (p. 1.2)

Third-party claim (p. 1.3)

Professional liability (p. 1.4)

Consent to settle clause (p. 1.5)

Employment practices liability (EPL) (p. 1.5)

Sexual harassment (p. 1.6)

Quid pro quo ("something for something") (p. 1.6)

Hostile work environment (p. 1.6)

Occurrence-based policy (p. 1.12)

Claims-made policy (p. 1.12)

Conditions precedent (p. 1.13)

Conditions subsequent (p. 1.13)

Declarations (p. 1.28)

Definitions (p. 1.29)

Insuring agreement (p. 1.30)

Liability Coverage (p. 1.30)

Medical Payments Coverage (p. 1.31)

Uninsured Motorists Coverage (p. 1.31)

Underinsured Motorists Coverage (p. 1.31)

Collision Coverage (p. 1.31)

Other Than Collision Coverage (Comprehensive Coverage) (p. 1.31)

Exclusions (p. 1.32)

Named Driver Exclusion (p. 1.34)

Conditions (p. 1.35)

Review Questions

1. Identify the three parties involved in a liability claim. (p. 1.2)

2. Auto liability, premises liability, and product liability are types of liability claims. Identify and describe three other types of liability claims. (pp. 1.4–1.8)

3. What unique policy provision is found in professional liability policies? Explain why some professionals prefer this unique provision. (pp 1.4–1.5)

4. Give three examples of employer conduct that could lead to an employment practices liability claim. (pp. 1.5–1.7)

5. Describe the main duties that a liability claim representative must perform from the beginning to the end of a liability claim. (pp. 1.8–1.9)

6. What are at least five questions that claim representatives must ask to determine whether liability coverage applies? (p. 1.10)

7. Describe two reasons an investigation is needed in liability claims.
   (p. 1.14)

8. Identify three skills, three kinds of knowledge, and three
   characteristics effective liability claim representatives possess.
   (pp. 1.17–1.20)
   a. Skills:

   b. Knowledge:

   c. Characteristics:

9. Identify two key issues causing changes in the role and responsibilities of liability claim representatives, and describe their effect
   on that role. (pp. 1.20–1.25)

10. Describe three common situations that can create ethical dilemmas
    for liability claim representatives, and explain how these dilemmas
    could be avoided or resolved. (pp. 1.25–1.27)
    (1)

    (2)

    (3)

11. Identify five key parts of any liability insurance policy. (p. 1.28)

12. Identify five common insuring agreements found in auto liability
    policies. (p. 1.30)

13. Describe four reasons for the existence of exclusions in liability insurance policies. (p. 1.32)

14. Give three examples of conditions found in a typical auto liability policy. (p. 1.35)

Application Questions

1. The CEO for Conglomerate Motors decides to cut costs by reducing salary expenses. To accomplish this, the CEO mandates that all men over the age of fifty-nine should be fired. Conglomerate does this. What two illegal employment practices did Conglomerate commit?

2. Becky is a claim representative with Premium American Insurance company. She receives a loss notice for an automobile claim involving the insured's fifteen-year-old nephew, who borrowed the insured's car in San Diego, California, and drove to Tijuana, Mexico, with his fourteen-year-old cousin (the named insured's son). While driving through Mexico, the driver of the car collided with and injured a T-shirt vendor. The Mexican authorities arrested the boys, put them in jail, and impounded the insured's car. In addition to the injury claim, the authorities demand a $1,000 fee for the insured to recover the car. The insured turns the claim over to his insurance company. What are four questions that Becky should ask regarding this claim that would help her identify potential coverage problems *in this claim*?

3. Statistics show that the percentage of soft tissue injuries in auto accidents has risen over time. Now, more treatments involve chiropractors and physical therapists. Describe how managed care might be used to address this trend.

4. Big Country Insurance Company begins an aggressive marketing campaign to try to get claimants to shift their insurance to Big Country. To help with this effort, Big Country's auto appraisers are asked to obtain information from the claimants about their current policy with their existing insurer. Included in this information are expiration dates of the claimants' policies. This helps Big Country identify when to contact the claimant for policy renewals. Appraisers are given incentive awards for gathering this information. Consequently, appraisers become somewhat surly when, during the course of a damage appraisal, a claimant refuses to provide this policy information.

   a.   Explain the ethical dilemma of this practice.

   b.   Identify questions that claim representatives could ask to assist in determining whether this practice is ethical.

   c.   How might this ethical dilemma be avoided while obtaining the same marketing goal?

Answers to Assignment 1 Questions

NOTE: These answers are provided to give students a basic understanding of acceptable types of responses. They often are not the only valid answers and are not intended to provide an exhaustive response to the questions.

Review Questions

1. Insured (first party); insurer (second party); claimant (third party)

2. Professional liability; employer liability; directors and officers liability; personal and advertising injury; intellectual property rights claims; environmental liability

3. The consent to settle clause is included in professional liability policies because claim settlements can affect a professional's reputation.

4. • Sexual harassment (*quid pro quo* or hostile work environment)
    • Discrimination based on race, color, gender, religion, or national origin
    • Age discrimination
    • Discrimination against people with disabilities
    • Unequal payment of men and women holding the same level job

5. • Determine coverage
    • Set reserves
    • Investigate and determine liability
    • Evaluate damages
    • Negotiate and settle claims
    • Manage litigation

6. • Who is covered?
    • Are the activities causing the injury or damages covered?
    • Are the damages covered?
    • Do any policy exclusions apply?
    • Did covered damage occur during the policy period?
    • Is the location of the loss covered?
    • What limitations exist on liability?
    • Do any laws or regulations affect coverage?

7. To fulfill good faith duty to insured to investigate and to provide needed information to evaluate liability and damages

8. a. Skills: Liability claim representatives should have the ability to:
    • Read and interpret contracts
    • Assess credibility of people
    • Communicate
    • Negotiate

- Develop rapport
- Interview people (take statements)

b. Knowledge: Liability claim representatives should understand the following:
- The law affecting liability claims
- Medical and damage issues
- Human nature
- Technology and its uses

c. Characteristics: Claim representatives should:
- Be adaptable
- Enjoy learning
- Be inquisitive
- Be analytical
- Have strong self-esteem
- Be able to handle stress
- Have a positive attitude
- Be trustworthy

9.
- Technology is changing the way claims are processed, evaluated, and settled.
- The dynamic legal environment affects coverage interpretation, creates and expands new areas of liability, and changes the types and amounts of damages allowable and awarded by courts.
- Managed care is being used increasingly in all types of injury claims, including liability claims.

10. Possible answers include:

(1) The relationship among insureds, insurers, and defense counsel can give rise to potential conflicts when coverage issues exist. Using separate legal counsel can help resolve this conflict.

(2) Making unreasonably low offers to claimants. This practice can be overcome by using objective, established guidelines for valuing and settling claims and by treating claimants in a manner that claim representatives would want to be treated.

(3) Accepting gifts from people who do business with the claim representative. This can be resolved by setting reasonable guidelines on what gifts may be accepted.

11. Declarations, definitions, insuring agreements, exclusions, conditions, endorsements

12. Liability, medical payments, uninsured motorists, underinsured motorists, damage to insured autos

13.
- Eliminate coverage for uninsurable losses
- Assist in managing moral hazards
- Reduce the likelihood of coverage duplications
- Eliminate coverages that the typical purchaser does not need
- Eliminate coverages requiring special treatment

14. Pay premiums, report losses promptly, provide documentation for losses, cooperate with the insurer, and refrain from jeopardizing the insurer's right to recovery from third parties (protect subrogation rights).

Application Questions

1. Age discrimination and gender discrimination

2. Who is insured? Is the accident location covered? Are the damages covered (such as impound fee for car)? Do any exclusions apply (such as lack of reasonable belief to use the car)?

3. Utilization reviews, case management (especially in PIP states), review of bills to make sure they meet proper guidelines

4. a. It could give the appearance that claimants must provide marketing information in order to get paid (or at least paid fairly).

   b. Questions to ask might be:

      Are there laws to guide such practices?

      If not, what would be the result if every claim representative did this? (Probably increased regulation)

   c. Perhaps asking for information after the claim has been paid might eliminate the conflict.

Direct Your Learning

Coverage Issues for Automobile Insurance

Educational Objectives

After learning the content of this assignment, you should be able to:

1. Identify auto insurance policy provisions that are complex or commonly subject to different legal interpretations.

2. Explain why a given policy provision might be subject to contradictory interpretations.

3. Describe specific "claim representative solutions" for determining issues related to the following coverage questions:

    a. Whether a person is a resident of a household

    b. Whether a person is "occupying" a vehicle

    c. Whether emotional (purely nonphysical) injuries are covered

    d. How coverage is determined for damages resulting from "intentional or expected acts"

    e. How a "reasonable belief to use an auto" is determined

    f. Whether a car is "furnished or available for regular use"

    g. Whether injuries caused by a "phantom" vehicle are covered by uninsured motorists insurance

    h. How coverage applies for the business use of a personal auto

    i. How coverage applies when the insured borrows a vehicle from a repair facility or an auto dealership

    j. How coverage applies with insureds using rental cars

4. Given the factual circumstances of a claim, explain the most likely coverage interpretation.

5. Define or describe each of the Key Words and Phrases for this assignment.

Study Materials

Required Reading:
▶ Liability Claim Practices
  • Chapter 2

Study Aids:
▶ SMART Online Practice Exams
▶ SMART Study Aids
  • Review Notes and Flash Cards—Assignment 2

Outline

▶ **How Court Decisions Affect Coverage**

▶ **Definitions in Auto Policies**

   A. Who Is a "Family Member"?

     1. Factors To Consider in Determining Whether a Person Is a Resident of a Household

     2. Temporary Residents

     3. Children Away at School

     4. Children in the Military

     5. Emancipated Children

     6. Children of Divorced Parents

   B. "Occupying" a Vehicle

     1. The Physical Contact Test

     2. Sufficient Proximity and Vehicle Orientation

   C. Bodily Injury

     1. Emotional Injury Claims Without Any Physical Injury

     2. Is an Emotional Injury a Bodily Injury?

   D. Employees

▶ **Liability Coverage Insuring Agreement**

   A. Co-Owner and Co-Insured Liability

   B. What Is an Auto?

   C. What Does "Use" of the Auto Mean?

   D. The Duty To Defend

▶ **Exclusions in the Liability Coverage**

   A. Intentional Injury

   B. Care, Custody, or Control

   C. Business Use of a Personal Auto

     1. Business Exclusions

     2. Exceptions to Business Use

     3. Material Misrepresentations

   D. Unauthorized Use of an Insured Vehicle

     1. Underage, Unlicensed Drivers

   E. Cars Owned or Available for the Regular Use of Insureds

   F. Exclusionary Endorsements

▶ **Limit of Liability for the Liability Coverage**

   A. Per Person Limit

     1. Derivative Claims Versus Separate Injury Claims

   B. Duplicate Payments (Offsets)

   C. Out-of-State Coverage Limits

▶ **Other Insurance**

   A. State Laws Contrary to the Policy Wording

     1. Contribution by Equal Shares

     2. Pro Rata Contribution

   B. Applying the Other Insurance Provision to Dealer or Repair Shop Autos

   C. Insureds Driving Rental Cars

     1. Effect of State Laws on Which Policy Is Primary

     2. Conduct of the Insured

     3. Vicarious Liability

     4. Which State's Law Applies

     5. States With No Statute or Case Law

     6. Supplemental Liability Insurance

     7. Rented Vehicles That Are Substitutes or Replacement Vehicles

     8. Damage to the Rented Vehicle

     9. Special Vehicle Rental Laws

     10. Vehicles "Loaned" to the Insured by an Auto Dealer or a Service Shop

     11. Self-Insured Rental Car Companies

▶ **Medical Payments Coverage Insuring Agreement**

   A. Coverage in No-Fault States

   B. Other Insurance

   C. Subrogation

Reduce the number of Key Words and Phrases that you must review. SMART Flash Cards contain the Key Words and Phrases and their definitions, allowing you to set aside those cards that you have mastered.

PERSONAL AUTO
PP 00 01 06 98

PERSONAL AUTO POLICY

AGREEMENT

In return for payment of the premium and subject to all the terms of this policy, we agree with you as follows:

DEFINITIONS

A. Throughout this policy, "you" and "your" refer to:

1. The "named insured" shown in the Declarations; and

2. The spouse if a resident of the same household.

If the spouse ceases to be a resident of the same household during the policy period or prior to the inception of this policy, the spouse will be considered "you" and "your" under this policy but only until the earlier of:

1. The end of 90 days following the spouse's change of residency;

2. The effective date of another policy listing the spouse as a named insured; or

3. The end of the policy period.

B. "We", "us" and "our" refer to the Company providing this insurance.

C. For purposes of this policy, a private passenger type auto, pickup or van shall be deemed to be owned by a person if leased:

1. Under a written agreement to that person; and

2. For a continuous period of at least 6 months.

Other words and phrases are defined. They are in quotation marks when used.

D. "Bodily injury" means bodily harm, sickness or disease, including death that results.

E. "Business" includes trade, profession or occupation.

F. "Family member" means a person related to you by blood, marriage or adoption who is a resident of your household. This includes a ward or foster child.

G. "Occupying" means in, upon, getting in, on, out or off.

H. "Property damage" means physical injury to, destruction of or loss of use of tangible property.

I. "Trailer" means a vehicle designed to be pulled by a:

1. Private passenger auto; or

2. Pickup or van.

It also means a farm wagon or farm implement while towed by a vehicle listed in **1.** or **2.** above.

J. "Your covered auto" means:

1. Any vehicle shown in the Declarations.

2. A "newly acquired auto".

3. Any "trailer" you own.

4. Any auto or "trailer" you do not own while used as a temporary substitute for any other vehicle described in this definition which is out of normal use because of its:

a. Breakdown;

b. Repair;

c. Servicing;

d. Loss; or

e. Destruction.

This Provision (**J.4.**) does not apply to Coverage For Damage To Your Auto.

K. "Newly acquired auto":

1. "Newly acquired auto" means any of the following types of vehicles you become the owner of during the policy period:

a. A private passenger auto; or

b. A pickup or van, for which no other insurance policy provides coverage, that:

(1) Has a Gross Vehicle Weight of less than 10,000 lbs.; and

(2) Is not used for the delivery or transportation of goods and materials unless such use is:

(a) Incidental to your "business" of installing, maintaining or repairing furnishings or equipment; or

(b) For farming or ranching.

2. Coverage for a "newly acquired auto" is provided as described below. If you ask us to insure a "newly acquired auto" after a specified time period described below has elapsed, any coverage we provide for a "newly acquired auto" will begin at the time you request the coverage.

a. For any coverage provided in this policy except Coverage For Damage To Your Auto, a "newly acquired auto" will have the broadest coverage we now provide for any vehicle shown in the Declarations. Coverage begins on the date you become the owner. However, for this coverage to apply to a "newly acquired auto" which is in addition to any vehicle shown in the Declarations, you must ask us to insure it within 14 days after you become the owner.

If a "newly acquired auto" replaces a vehicle shown in the Declarations, coverage is provided for this vehicle without your having to ask us to insure it.

b. Collision Coverage for a "newly acquired auto" begins on the date you become the owner. However, for this coverage to apply, you must ask us to insure it within:

(1) 14 days after you become the owner if the Declarations indicate that Collision Coverage applies to at least one auto. In this case, the "newly acquired auto" will have the broadest coverage we now provide for any auto shown in the Declarations.

(2) Four days after you become the owner if the Declarations do not indicate that Collision Coverage applies to at least one auto. If you comply with the 4 day requirement and a loss occurred before you asked us to insure the "newly acquired auto", a Collision deductible of $500 will apply.

c. Other Than Collision Coverage for a "newly acquired auto" begins on the date you become the owner. However, for this coverage to apply, you must ask us to insure it within:

(1) 14 days after you become the owner if the Declarations indicate that Other Than Collision Coverage applies to at least one auto. In this case, the "newly acquired auto" will have the broadest coverage we now provide for any auto shown in the Declarations.

(2) Four days after you become the owner if the Declarations do not indicate that Other Than Collision Coverage applies to at least one auto. If you comply with the 4 day requirement and a loss occurred before you asked us to insure the "newly acquired auto", an Other Than Collision deductible of $500 will apply.

PART A – LIABILITY COVERAGE

INSURING AGREEMENT

A. We will pay damages for "bodily injury" or "property damage" for which any "insured" becomes legally responsible because of an auto accident. Damages include prejudgment interest awarded against the "insured". We will settle or defend, as we consider appropriate, any claim or suit asking for these damages. In addition to our limit of liability, we will pay all defense costs we incur. Our duty to settle or defend ends when our limit of liability for this coverage has been exhausted by payment of judgments or settlements. We have no duty to defend any suit or settle any claim for "bodily injury" or "property damage" not covered under this policy.

B. "Insured" as used in this Part means:

1. You or any "family member" for the ownership, maintenance or use of any auto or "trailer".

2. Any person using "your covered auto".

3. For "your covered auto", any person or organization but only with respect to legal responsibility for acts or omissions of a person for whom coverage is afforded under this Part.

4. For any auto or "trailer", other than "your covered auto", any other person or organization but only with respect to legal responsibility for acts or omissions of you or any "family member" for whom coverage is afforded under this Part. This Provision (**B.4.**) applies only if the person or organization does not own or hire the auto or "trailer".

SUPPLEMENTARY PAYMENTS

In addition to our limit of liability, we will pay on behalf of an "insured":

1. Up to $250 for the cost of bail bonds required because of an accident, including related traffic law violations. The accident must result in "bodily injury" or "property damage" covered under this policy.

2. Premiums on appeal bonds and bonds to release attachments in any suit we defend.

3. Interest accruing after a judgment is entered in any suit we defend. Our duty to pay interest ends when we offer to pay that part of the judgment which does not exceed our limit of liability for this coverage.

4. Up to $200 a day for loss of earnings, but not other income, because of attendance at hearings or trials at our request.

5. Other reasonable expenses incurred at our request.

EXCLUSIONS

A. We do not provide Liability Coverage for any "insured":

1. Who intentionally causes "bodily injury" or "property damage".

2. For "property damage" to property owned or being transported by that "insured".

       PP 00 01 06 98

3. For "property damage" to property:
   a. Rented to;
   b. Used by; or
   c. In the care of;
   that "insured".

   This Exclusion (**A.3.**) does not apply to "property damage" to a residence or private garage.

4. For "bodily injury" to an employee of that "insured" during the course of employment. This Exclusion (**A.4.**) does not apply to "bodily injury" to a domestic employee unless workers' compensation benefits are required or available for that domestic employee.

5. For that "insured's" liability arising out of the ownership or operation of a vehicle while it is being used as a public or livery conveyance. This Exclusion (**A.5.**) does not apply to a share-the-expense car pool.

6. While employed or otherwise engaged in the "business" of:
   a. Selling;
   b. Repairing;
   c. Servicing;
   d. Storing; or
   e. Parking;

   vehicles designed for use mainly on public highways. This includes road testing and delivery. This Exclusion (**A.6.**) does not apply to the ownership, maintenance or use of "your covered auto" by:
   a. You;
   b. Any "family member"; or
   c. Any partner, agent or employee of you or any "family member".

7. Maintaining or using any vehicle while that "insured" is employed or otherwise engaged in any "business" (other than farming or ranching) not described in Exclusion **A.6.**

   This Exclusion (**A.7.**) does not apply to the maintenance or use of a:
   a. Private passenger auto;
   b. Pickup or van; or
   c. "Trailer" used with a vehicle described in **a.** or **b.** above.

8. Using a vehicle without a reasonable belief that that "insured" is entitled to do so. This Exclusion (**A.8.**) does not apply to a "family member" using "your covered auto" which is owned by you.

9. For "bodily injury" or "property damage" for which that "insured":
   a. Is an insured under a nuclear energy liability policy; or
   b. Would be an insured under a nuclear energy liability policy but for its termination upon exhaustion of its limit of liability.

   A nuclear energy liability policy is a policy issued by any of the following or their successors:
   a. Nuclear Energy Liability Insurance Association;
   b. Mutual Atomic Energy Liability Underwriters; or
   c. Nuclear Insurance Association of Canada.

B. We do not provide Liability Coverage for the ownership, maintenance or use of:

1. Any vehicle which:
   a. Has fewer than four wheels; or
   b. Is designed mainly for use off public roads.

   This Exclusion (**B.1.**) does not apply:
   a. While such vehicle is being used by an "insured" in a medical emergency;
   b. To any "trailer"; or
   c. To any non-owned golf cart.

2. Any vehicle, other than "your covered auto", which is:
   a. Owned by you; or
   b. Furnished or available for your regular use.

3. Any vehicle, other than "your covered auto", which is:
   a. Owned by any "family member"; or
   b. Furnished or available for the regular use of any "family member".

   However, this Exclusion (**B.3.**) does not apply to you while you are maintaining or "occupying" any vehicle which is:
   a. Owned by a "family member"; or
   b. Furnished or available for the regular use of a "family member".

4. Any vehicle, located inside a facility designed for racing, for the purpose of:
   a. Competing in; or
   b. Practicing or preparing for;

   any prearranged or organized racing or speed contest.

LIMIT OF LIABILITY

A. The limit of liability shown in the Declarations for each person for Bodily Injury Liability is our maximum limit of liability for all damages, including damages for care, loss of services or death, arising out of "bodily injury" sustained by any one person in any one auto accident. Subject to this limit for each person, the limit of liability shown in the Declarations for each accident for Bodily Injury Liability is our maximum limit of liability for all damages for "bodily injury" resulting from any one auto accident.

The limit of liability shown in the Declarations for each accident for Property Damage Liability is our maximum limit of liability for all "property damage" resulting from any one auto accident.

This is the most we will pay regardless of the number of:

1. "Insureds";

2. Claims made;

3. Vehicles or premiums shown in the Declarations; or

4. Vehicles involved in the auto accident.

B. No one will be entitled to receive duplicate payments for the same elements of loss under this coverage and:

1. Part **B** or Part **C** of this policy; or

2. Any Underinsured Motorists Coverage provided by this policy.

OUT OF STATE COVERAGE

If an auto accident to which this policy applies occurs in any state or province other than the one in which "your covered auto" is principally garaged, we will interpret your policy for that accident as follows:

A. If the state or province has:

1. A financial responsibility or similar law specifying limits of liability for "bodily injury" or "property damage" higher than the limit shown in the Declarations, your policy will provide the higher specified limit.

2. A compulsory insurance or similar law requiring a nonresident to maintain insurance whenever the nonresident uses a vehicle in that state or province, your policy will provide at least the required minimum amounts and types of coverage.

B. No one will be entitled to duplicate payments for the same elements of loss.

FINANCIAL RESPONSIBILITY

When this policy is certified as future proof of financial responsibility, this policy shall comply with the law to the extent required.

OTHER INSURANCE

If there is other applicable liability insurance we will pay only our share of the loss. Our share is the proportion that our limit of liability bears to the total of all applicable limits. However, any insurance we provide for a vehicle you do not own shall be excess over any other collectible insurance.

PART B – MEDICAL PAYMENTS COVERAGE

INSURING AGREEMENT

A. We will pay reasonable expenses incurred for necessary medical and funeral services because of "bodily injury":

1. Caused by accident; and

2. Sustained by an "insured".

We will pay only those expenses incurred for services rendered within 3 years from the date of the accident.

B. "Insured" as used in this Part means:

1. You or any "family member":

   a. While "occupying"; or

   b. As a pedestrian when struck by;

   a motor vehicle designed for use mainly on public roads or a trailer of any type.

2. Any other person while "occupying" "your covered auto".

EXCLUSIONS

We do not provide Medical Payments Coverage for any "insured" for "bodily injury":

1. Sustained while "occupying" any motorized vehicle having fewer than four wheels.

2. Sustained while "occupying" "your covered auto" when it is being used as a public or livery conveyance. This Exclusion **(2.)** does not apply to a share-the-expense car pool.

3. Sustained while "occupying" any vehicle located for use as a residence or premises.

4. Occurring during the course of employment if workers' compensation benefits are required or available for the "bodily injury".

5. Sustained while "occupying", or when struck by, any vehicle (other than "your covered auto") which is:

   a. Owned by you; or

   b. Furnished or available for your regular use.

6. Sustained while "occupying", or when struck by, any vehicle (other than "your covered auto") which is:

   a. Owned by any "family member"; or

   b. Furnished or available for the regular use of any "family member".

However, this Exclusion **(6.)** does not apply to you.

7. Sustained while "occupying" a vehicle without a reasonable belief that that "insured" is entitled to do so. This Exclusion **(7.)** does not apply to a "family member" using "your covered auto" which is owned by you.

8. Sustained while "occupying" a vehicle when it is being used in the "business" of an "insured". This Exclusion **(8.)** does not apply to "bodily injury" sustained while "occupying" a:

   a. Private passenger auto;

   b. Pickup or van that you own; or

   c. "Trailer" used with a vehicle described in **a.** or **b.** above.

9. Caused by or as a consequence of:

   a. Discharge of a nuclear weapon (even if accidental);

   b. War (declared or undeclared);

   c. Civil war;

   d. Insurrection; or

   e. Rebellion or revolution.

10. From or as a consequence of the following, whether controlled or uncontrolled or however caused:

    a. Nuclear reaction;

    b. Radiation; or

    c. Radioactive contamination.

11. Sustained while "occupying" any vehicle located inside a facility designed for racing, for the purpose of:

    a. Competing in; or

    b. Practicing or preparing for;

    any prearranged or organized racing or speed contest.

LIMIT OF LIABILITY

A. The limit of liability shown in the Declarations for this coverage is our maximum limit of liability for each person injured in any one accident. This is the most we will pay regardless of the number of:

1. "Insureds";

2. Claims made;

3. Vehicles or premiums shown in the Declarations; or

4. Vehicles involved in the accident.

B. No one will be entitled to receive duplicate payments for the same elements of loss under this coverage and:

1. Part **A** or Part **C** of this policy; or

2. Any Underinsured Motorists Coverage provided by this policy.

OTHER INSURANCE

If there is other applicable auto medical payments insurance we will pay only our share of the loss. Our share is the proportion that our limit of liability bears to the total of all applicable limits. However, any insurance we provide with respect to a vehicle you do not own shall be excess over any other collectible auto insurance providing payments for medical or funeral expenses.

PART C – UNINSURED MOTORISTS COVERAGE

INSURING AGREEMENT

A. We will pay compensatory damages which an "insured" is legally entitled to recover from the owner or operator of an "uninsured motor vehicle" because of "bodily injury":

1. Sustained by an "insured"; and

2. Caused by an accident.

The owner's or operator's liability for these damages must arise out of the ownership, maintenance or use of the "uninsured motor vehicle".

Any judgment for damages arising out of a suit brought without our written consent is not binding on us.

B. "Insured" as used in this Part means:

1. You or any "family member".

2. Any other person "occupying" "your covered auto".

3. Any person for damages that person is entitled to recover because of "bodily injury" to which this coverage applies sustained by a person described in **1.** or **2.** above.

C. "Uninsured motor vehicle" means a land motor vehicle or trailer of any type:

1. To which no bodily injury liability bond or policy applies at the time of the accident.

2. To which a bodily injury liability bond or policy applies at the time of the accident. In this case its limit for bodily injury liability must be less than the minimum limit for bodily injury liability specified by the financial responsibility law of the state in which "your covered auto" is principally garaged.

3. Which is a hit-and-run vehicle whose operator or owner cannot be identified and which hits:

   a. You or any "family member";

   b. A vehicle which you or any "family member" are "occupying"; or

   c. "Your covered auto".

4. To which a bodily injury liability bond or policy applies at the time of the accident but the bonding or insuring company:

   a. Denies coverage; or

   b. Is or becomes insolvent.

However, "uninsured motor vehicle" does not include any vehicle or equipment:

1. Owned by or furnished or available for the regular use of you or any "family member".

2. Owned or operated by a self-insurer under any applicable motor vehicle law, except a self-insurer which is or becomes insolvent.

3. Owned by any governmental unit or agency.

4. Operated on rails or crawler treads.

5. Designed mainly for use off public roads while not on public roads.

6. While located for use as a residence or premises.

EXCLUSIONS

A. We do not provide Uninsured Motorists Coverage for "bodily injury" sustained:

1. By an "insured" while "occupying", or when struck by, any motor vehicle owned by that "insured" which is not insured for this coverage under this policy. This includes a trailer of any type used with that vehicle.

2. By any "family member" while "occupying", or when struck by, any motor vehicle you own which is insured for this coverage on a primary basis under any other policy.

B. We do not provide Uninsured Motorists Coverage for "bodily injury" sustained by any "insured":

1. If that "insured" or the legal representative settles the "bodily injury" claim without our consent.

2. While "occupying" "your covered auto" when it is being used as a public or livery conveyance. This Exclusion (**B.2.**) does not apply to a share-the-expense car pool.

3. Using a vehicle without a reasonable belief that that "insured" is entitled to do so. This Exclusion (**B.3.**) does not apply to a "family member" using "your covered auto" which is owned by you.

C. This coverage shall not apply directly or indirectly to benefit any insurer or self-insurer under any of the following or similar law:

1. Workers' compensation law; or

2. Disability benefits law.

D. We do not provide Uninsured Motorists Coverage for punitive or exemplary damages.

LIMIT OF LIABILITY

A. The limit of liability shown in the Declarations for each person for Uninsured Motorists Coverage is our maximum limit of liability for all damages, including damages for care, loss of services or death, arising out of "bodily injury" sustained by any one person in any one accident. Subject to this limit for each person, the limit of liability shown in the Declarations for each accident for Uninsured Motorists Coverage is our maximum limit of liability for all damages for "bodily injury" resulting from any one accident.

This is the most we will pay regardless of the number of:

1. "Insureds";

2. Claims made;

3. Vehicles or premiums shown in the Declarations; or

4. Vehicles involved in the accident.

B. No one will be entitled to receive duplicate payments for the same elements of loss under this coverage and:

1. Part **A.** or Part **B.** of this policy; or

2. Any Underinsured Motorists Coverage provided by this policy.

C. We will not make a duplicate payment under this coverage for any element of loss for which payment has been made by or on behalf of persons or organizations who may be legally responsible.

D. We will not pay for any element of loss if a person is entitled to receive payment for the same element of loss under any of the following or similar law:

1. Workers' compensation law; or

2. Disability benefits law.

OTHER INSURANCE

If there is other applicable insurance available under one or more policies or provisions of coverage that is similar to the insurance provided under this Part of the policy:

1. Any recovery for damages under all such policies or provisions of coverage may equal but not exceed the highest applicable limit for any one vehicle under any insurance providing coverage on either a primary or excess basis.

2. Any insurance we provide with respect to a vehicle you do not own shall be excess over any collectible insurance providing such coverage on a primary basis.

       PP 00 01 06 98

3. If the coverage under this policy is provided:

   a. On a primary basis, we will pay only our share of the loss that must be paid under insurance providing coverage on a primary basis. Our share is the proportion that our limit of liability bears to the total of all applicable limits of liability for coverage provided on a primary basis.

   b. On an excess basis, we will pay only our share of the loss that must be paid under insurance providing coverage on an excess basis. Our share is the proportion that our limit of liability bears to the total of all applicable limits of liability for coverage provided on an excess basis.

ARBITRATION

A. If we and an "insured" do not agree:

   1. Whether that "insured" is legally entitled to recover damages; or

   2. As to the amount of damages which are recoverable by that "insured";

   from the owner or operator of an "uninsured motor vehicle", then the matter may be arbitrated. However, disputes concerning coverage under this Part may not be arbitrated.

Both parties must agree to arbitration. If so agreed, each party will select an arbitrator. The two arbitrators will select a third. If they cannot agree within 30 days, either may request that selection be made by a judge of a court having jurisdiction.

B. Each party will:

   1. Pay the expenses it incurs; and

   2. Bear the expenses of the third arbitrator equally.

C. Unless both parties agree otherwise, arbitration will take place in the county in which the "insured" lives. Local rules of law as to procedure and evidence will apply. A decision agreed to by two of the arbitrators will be binding as to:

   1. Whether the "insured" is legally entitled to recover damages; and

   2. The amount of damages. This applies only if the amount does not exceed the minimum limit for bodily injury liability specified by the financial responsibility law of the state in which "your covered auto" is principally garaged. If the amount exceeds that limit, either party may demand the right to a trial. This demand must be made within 60 days of the arbitrators' decision. If this demand is not made, the amount of damages agreed to by the arbitrators will be binding.

PART D – COVERAGE FOR DAMAGE TO YOUR AUTO

INSURING AGREEMENT

A. We will pay for direct and accidental loss to "your covered auto" or any "non-owned auto", including their equipment, minus any applicable deductible shown in the Declarations. If loss to more than one "your covered auto" or "non-owned auto" results from the same "collision", only the highest applicable deductible will apply. We will pay for loss to "your covered auto" caused by:

   1. Other than "collision" only if the Declarations indicate that Other Than Collision Coverage is provided for that auto.

   2. "Collision" only if the Declarations indicate that Collision Coverage is provided for that auto.

   If there is a loss to a "non-owned auto", we will provide the broadest coverage applicable to any "your covered auto" shown in the Declarations.

B. "Collision" means the upset of "your covered auto" or a "non-owned auto" or their impact with another vehicle or object.

   Loss caused by the following is considered other than "collision":

   1. Missiles or falling objects;

   2. Fire;

   3. Theft or larceny;

   4. Explosion or earthquake;

   5. Windstorm;

   6. Hail, water or flood;

   7. Malicious mischief or vandalism;

   8. Riot or civil commotion;

   9. Contact with bird or animal; or

   10. Breakage of glass.

   If breakage of glass is caused by a "collision", you may elect to have it considered a loss caused by "collision".

C. "Non-owned auto" means:

   1. Any private passenger auto, pickup, van or "trailer" not owned by or furnished or available for the regular use of you or any "family member" while in the custody of or being operated by you or any "family member"; or

   2. Any auto or "trailer" you do not own while used as a temporary substitute for "your covered auto" which is out of normal use because of its:

      a. Breakdown;

      b. Repair;

      c. Servicing;

      d. Loss; or

      e. Destruction.

TRANSPORTATION EXPENSES

A. In addition, we will pay, without application of a deductible, up to a maximum of $600 for:

1. Temporary transportation expenses not exceeding $20 per day incurred by you in the event of a loss to "your covered auto". We will pay for such expenses if the loss is caused by:

   a. Other than "collision" only if the Declarations indicate that Other Than Collision Coverage is provided for that auto.

   b. "Collision" only if the Declarations indicate that Collision Coverage is provided for that auto.

2. Expenses for which you become legally responsible in the event of loss to a "non-owned auto". We will pay for such expenses if the loss is caused by:

   a. Other than "collision" only if the Declarations indicate that Other Than Collision Coverage is provided for any "your covered auto".

   b. "Collision" only if the Declarations indicate that Collision Coverage is provided for any "your covered auto".

   However, the most we will pay for any expenses for loss of use is $20 per day.

B. If the loss is caused by:

1. A total theft of "your covered auto" or a "non-owned auto", we will pay only expenses incurred during the period:

   a. Beginning 48 hours after the theft; and

   b. Ending when "your covered auto" or the "non-owned auto" is returned to use or we pay for its loss.

2. Other than theft of a "your covered auto" or a "non-owned auto", we will pay only expenses beginning when the auto is withdrawn from use for more than 24 hours.

C. Our payment will be limited to that period of time reasonably required to repair or replace the "your covered auto" or the "non-owned auto".

EXCLUSIONS

We will not pay for:

1. Loss to "your covered auto" or any "non-owned auto" which occurs while it is being used as a public or livery conveyance. This Exclusion **(1.)** does not apply to a share-the-expense car pool.

2. Damage due and confined to:

   a. Wear and tear;

   b. Freezing;

   c. Mechanical or electrical breakdown or failure; or

   d. Road damage to tires.

This Exclusion **(2.)** does not apply if the damage results from the total theft of "your covered auto" or any "non-owned auto".

3. Loss due to or as a consequence of:

   a. Radioactive contamination;

   b. Discharge of any nuclear weapon (even if accidental);

   c. War (declared or undeclared);

   d. Civil war;

   e. Insurrection; or

   f. Rebellion or revolution.

4. Loss to any electronic equipment designed for the reproduction of sound and any accessories used with such equipment. This includes but is not limited to:

   a. Radios and stereos;

   b. Tape decks; or

   c. Compact disc players.

This Exclusion **(4.)** does not apply to equipment designed solely for the reproduction of sound and accessories used with such equipment, provided:

   a. The equipment is permanently installed in "your covered auto" or any "non-owned auto"; or

   b. The equipment is:

   (1) Removable from a housing unit which is permanently installed in the auto;

   (2) Designed to be solely operated by use of the power from the auto's electrical system; and

   (3) In or upon "your covered auto" or any "non-owned auto" at the time of loss.

5. Loss to any electronic equipment that receives or transmits audio, visual or data signals and any accessories used with such equipment. This includes but is not limited to:

   a. Citizens band radios;

   b. Telephones;

   c. Two-way mobile radios;

   d. Scanning monitor receivers;

   e. Television monitor receivers;

   f. Video cassette recorders;

   g. Audio cassette recorders; or

   h. Personal computers.

This Exclusion **(5.)** does not apply to:

   a. Any electronic equipment that is necessary for the normal operation of the auto or the monitoring of the auto's operating systems; or

       PP 00 01 06 98

b. A permanently installed telephone designed to be operated by use of the power from the auto's electrical system and any accessories used with the telephone.

6. Loss to tapes, records, discs or other media used with equipment described in Exclusions **4.** and **5.**

7. A total loss to "your covered auto" or any "non-owned auto" due to destruction or confiscation by governmental or civil authorities.

This Exclusion **(7.)** does not apply to the interests of Loss Payees in "your covered auto".

8. Loss to:

a. A "trailer", camper body, or motor home, which is not shown in the Declarations; or

b. Facilities or equipment used with such "trailer", camper body or motor home. Facilities or equipment include but are not limited to:

(1) Cooking, dining, plumbing or refrigeration facilities;

(2) Awnings or cabanas; or

(3) Any other facilities or equipment used with a "trailer", camper body, or motor home.

This Exclusion **(8.)** does not apply to a:

a. "Trailer", and its facilities or equipment, which you do not own; or

b. "Trailer", camper body, or the facilities or equipment in or attached to the "trailer" or camper body, which you:

(1) Acquire during the policy period; and

(2) Ask us to insure within 14 days after you become the owner.

9. Loss to any "non-owned auto" when used by you or any "family member" without a reasonable belief that you or that "family member" are entitled to do so.

10. Loss to equipment designed or used for the detection or location of radar or laser.

11. Loss to any custom furnishings or equipment in or upon any pickup or van. Custom furnishings or equipment include but are not limited to:

a. Special carpeting or insulation;

b. Furniture or bars;

c. Height-extending roofs; or

d. Custom murals, paintings or other decals or graphics.

This Exclusion **(11.)** does not apply to a cap, cover or bedliner in or upon any "your covered auto" which is a pickup.

12. Loss to any "non-owned auto" being maintained or used by any person while employed or otherwise engaged in the "business" of:

a. Selling;

b. Repairing;

c. Servicing;

d. Storing; or

e. Parking;

vehicles designed for use on public highways. This includes road testing and delivery.

13. Loss to "your covered auto" or any "non-owned auto", located inside a facility designed for racing, for the purpose of:

a. Competing in; or

b. Practicing or preparing for;

any prearranged or organized racing or speed contest.

14. Loss to, or loss of use of, a "non-owned auto" rented by:

a. You; or

b. Any "family member";

if a rental vehicle company is precluded from recovering such loss or loss of use, from you or that "family member", pursuant to the provisions of any applicable rental agreement or state law.

LIMIT OF LIABILITY

A. Our limit of liability for loss will be the lesser of the:

1. Actual cash value of the stolen or damaged property; or

2. Amount necessary to repair or replace the property with other property of like kind and quality.

However, the most we will pay for loss to:

1. Any "non-owned auto" which is a trailer is $500.

2. Equipment designed solely for the reproduction of sound, including any accessories used with such equipment, which is installed in locations not used by the auto manufacturer for installation of such equipment or accessories, is $1,000.

B. An adjustment for depreciation and physical condition will be made in determining actual cash value in the event of a total loss.

C. If a repair or replacement results in better than like kind or quality, we will not pay for the amount of the betterment.

PAYMENT OF LOSS

We may pay for loss in money or repair or replace the damaged or stolen property. We may, at our expense, return any stolen property to:

1. You; or

2. The address shown in this policy.

If we return stolen property we will pay for any damage resulting from the theft. We may keep all or part of the property at an agreed or appraised value.

If we pay for loss in money, our payment will include the applicable sales tax for the damaged or stolen property.

NO BENEFIT TO BAILEE

This insurance shall not directly or indirectly benefit any carrier or other bailee for hire.

OTHER SOURCES OF RECOVERY

If other sources of recovery also cover the loss, we will pay only our share of the loss. Our share is the proportion that our limit of liability bears to the total of all applicable limits. However, any insurance we provide with respect to a "non-owned auto" shall be excess over any other collectible source of recovery including, but not limited to:

1. Any coverage provided by the owner of the "non-owned auto";

2. Any other applicable physical damage insurance;

3. Any other source of recovery applicable to the loss.

APPRAISAL

A. If we and you do not agree on the amount of loss, either may demand an appraisal of the loss. In this event, each party will select a competent appraiser. The two appraisers will select an umpire. The appraisers will state separately the actual cash value and the amount of loss. If they fail to agree, they will submit their differences to the umpire. A decision agreed to by any two will be binding. Each party will:

1. Pay its chosen appraiser; and

2. Bear the expenses of the appraisal and umpire equally.

B. We do not waive any of our rights under this policy by agreeing to an appraisal.

PART E – DUTIES AFTER AN ACCIDENT OR LOSS

We have no duty to provide coverage under this policy unless there has been full compliance with the following duties:

A. We must be notified promptly of how, when and where the accident or loss happened. Notice should also include the names and addresses of any injured persons and of any witnesses.

B. A person seeking any coverage must:

1. Cooperate with us in the investigation, settlement or defense of any claim or suit.

2. Promptly send us copies of any notices or legal papers received in connection with the accident or loss.

3. Submit, as often as we reasonably require:

   a. To physical exams by physicians we select. We will pay for these exams.

   b. To examination under oath and subscribe the same.

4. Authorize us to obtain:

   a. Medical reports; and

   b. Other pertinent records.

5. Submit a proof of loss when required by us.

C. A person seeking Uninsured Motorists Coverage must also:

1. Promptly notify the police if a hit-and-run driver is involved.

2. Promptly send us copies of the legal papers if a suit is brought.

D. A person seeking Coverage For Damage To Your Auto must also:

1. Take reasonable steps after loss to protect "your covered auto" or any "non-owned auto" and their equipment from further loss. We will pay reasonable expenses incurred to do this.

2. Promptly notify the police if "your covered auto" or any "non-owned auto" is stolen.

3. Permit us to inspect and appraise the damaged property before its repair or disposal.

PART F – GENERAL PROVISIONS

BANKRUPTCY

Bankruptcy or insolvency of the "insured" shall not relieve us of any obligations under this policy.

CHANGES

A. This policy contains all the agreements between you and us. Its terms may not be changed or waived except by endorsement issued by us.

B. If there is a change to the information used to develop the policy premium, we may adjust your premium. Changes during the policy term that may result in a premium increase or decrease include, but are not limited to, changes in:

1. The number, type or use classification of insured vehicles;

2. Operators using insured vehicles;

3. The place of principal garaging of insured vehicles;

4. Coverage, deductible or limits.

If a change resulting from **A.** or **B.** requires a premium adjustment, we will make the premium adjustment in accordance with our manual rules.

C. If we make a change which broadens coverage under this edition of your policy without additional premium charge, that change will automatically apply to your policy as of the date we implement the change in your state. This Paragraph **(C.)** does not apply to changes implemented with a general program revision that includes both broadenings and restrictions in coverage, whether that general program revision is implemented through introduction of:

1. A subsequent edition of your policy; or

2. An Amendatory Endorsement.

FRAUD

We do not provide coverage for any "insured" who has made fraudulent statements or engaged in fraudulent conduct in connection with any accident or loss for which coverage is sought under this policy.

LEGAL ACTION AGAINST US

A. No legal action may be brought against us until there has been full compliance with all the terms of this policy. In addition, under Part **A,** no legal action may be brought against us until:

1. We agree in writing that the "insured" has an obligation to pay; or

2. The amount of that obligation has been finally determined by judgment after trial.

B. No person or organization has any right under this policy to bring us into any action to determine the liability of an "insured".

OUR RIGHT TO RECOVER PAYMENT

A. If we make a payment under this policy and the person to or for whom payment was made has a right to recover damages from another we shall be subrogated to that right. That person shall do:

1. Whatever is necessary to enable us to exercise our rights; and

2. Nothing after loss to prejudice them.

However, our rights in this Paragraph **(A.)** do not apply under Part **D,** against any person using "your covered auto" with a reasonable belief that that person is entitled to do so.

B. If we make a payment under this policy and the person to or for whom payment is made recovers damages from another, that person shall:

1. Hold in trust for us the proceeds of the recovery; and

2. Reimburse us to the extent of our payment.

POLICY PERIOD AND TERRITORY

A. This policy applies only to accidents and losses which occur:

1. During the policy period as shown in the Declarations; and

2. Within the policy territory.

B. The policy territory is:

1. The United States of America, its territories or possessions;

2. Puerto Rico; or

3. Canada.

This policy also applies to loss to, or accidents involving, "your covered auto" while being transported between their ports.

TERMINATION

A. Cancellation

This policy may be cancelled during the policy period as follows:

1. The named insured shown in the Declarations may cancel by:

   a. Returning this policy to us; or

   b. Giving us advance written notice of the date cancellation is to take effect.

2. We may cancel by mailing to the named insured shown in the Declarations at the address shown in this policy:

   a. At least 10 days notice:

   (1) If cancellation is for nonpayment of premium; or

(2) If notice is mailed during the first 60 days this policy is in effect and this is not a renewal or continuation policy; or

b. At least 20 days notice in all other cases.

3. After this policy is in effect for 60 days, or if this is a renewal or continuation policy, we will cancel only:

a. For nonpayment of premium; or

b. If your driver's license or that of:

(1) Any driver who lives with you; or

(2) Any driver who customarily uses "your covered auto";

has been suspended or revoked. This must have occurred:

(1) During the policy period; or

(2) Since the last anniversary of the original effective date if the policy period is other than 1 year; or

c. If the policy was obtained through material misrepresentation.

B. Nonrenewal

If we decide not to renew or continue this policy, we will mail notice to the named insured shown in the Declarations at the address shown in this policy. Notice will be mailed at least 20 days before the end of the policy period. Subject to this notice requirement, if the policy period is:

1. Less than 6 months, we will have the right not to renew or continue this policy every 6 months, beginning 6 months after its original effective date.

2. 6 months or longer, but less than one year, we will have the right not to renew or continue this policy at the end of the policy period.

3. 1 year or longer, we will have the right not to renew or continue this policy at each anniversary of its original effective date.

C. Automatic Termination

If we offer to renew or continue and you or your representative do not accept, this policy will automatically terminate at the end of the current policy period. Failure to pay the required renewal or continuation premium when due shall mean that you have not accepted our offer.

If you obtain other insurance on "your covered auto", any similar insurance provided by this policy will terminate as to that auto on the effective date of the other insurance.

D. Other Termination Provisions

1. We may deliver any notice instead of mailing it. Proof of mailing of any notice shall be sufficient proof of notice.

2. If this policy is cancelled, you may be entitled to a premium refund. If so, we will send you the refund. The premium refund, if any, will be computed according to our manuals. However, making or offering to make the refund is not a condition of cancellation.

3. The effective date of cancellation stated in the notice shall become the end of the policy period.

TRANSFER OF YOUR INTEREST IN THIS POLICY

A. Your rights and duties under this policy may not be assigned without our written consent. However, if a named insured shown in the Declarations dies, coverage will be provided for:

1. The surviving spouse if resident in the same household at the time of death. Coverage applies to the spouse as if a named insured shown in the Declarations; and

2. The legal representative of the deceased person as if a named insured shown in the Declarations. This applies only with respect to the representative's legal responsibility to maintain or use "your covered auto".

B. Coverage will only be provided until the end of the policy period.

TWO OR MORE AUTO POLICIES

If this policy and any other auto insurance policy issued to you by us apply to the same accident, the maximum limit of our liability under all the policies shall not exceed the highest applicable limit of liability under any one policy.

Key Words and Phrases

Define or describe each of the words and phrases listed below.

Jurisdiction (p. 2.1)

Doctrine of reasonable expectations (p. 2.4)

Public policy (p. 2.4)

Family member (p. 2.5)

Resident (p. 2.5)

Occupying a vehicle (p. 2.10)

Sufficient geographic proximity (p. 2.11)

Emotional injury (p. 2.13)

Co-owner liability (p. 2.16)

Use of auto (p. 2.18)

Duty to defend (p. 2.19)

Material misrepresentation (p. 2.24)

Derivative claim (p. 2.31)

Contribution by equal shares (p. 2.35)

Mutually repugnant (p. 2.35)

Pro rata contribution (p. 2.36)

Escape clause (p. 2.38)

"Hit-and-run vehicle" (p. 2.47)

Phantom vehicle (p. 2.47)

Corroborative evidence (p. 2.47)

Arbitration clause (p. 2.50)

Stacking (p. 2.54)

Premium rule (p. 2.56)

Damages trigger (p. 2.59)

Limits trigger (p. 2.59)

Concealment (p. 2.62)

Review Questions

1. Give an example of how public policy could affect auto coverage interpretation. (pp. 2.4–2.5)

2. Identify five factors that should be considered in determining whether a person is a resident of a household. (p. 2.7)

3. Explain how the residency issue of children away at school is
usually viewed by the courts. (p. 2.7)

4. Identify five factors that courts consider when determining the
residency of children. (pp. 2.9–2.10)

5. Which of the following circumstances could (depending on the
state) be considered "occupying" a vehicle? Explain. (pp. 2.10–2.12)

   a.   Sitting on the hood of a car.

   b.   Changing the tire on a car.

   c.   Standing next to a car waiting for the door to be unlocked.

d.   Standing six inches away from an unknown person's car smoking a cigarette.

6. Explain how the wording in the 1994 ISO Personal Auto Policy (PAP) and the 1998 PAP differ with respect to when an insurer's duty to defend ends. (p. 2.19)

7. Identify four activities a claim representative should perform when encountering a claim involving a potentially intentional injury. (pp. 2.20–2.21)

8. Describe how coverage might be affected by state statutes regulating the coverage of vehicles loaned to insureds by repair facilities or automobile dealerships. (p. 2.21)

9. Explain the PAP coverage issues involving underaged, unlicensed drivers. (pp. 2.25–2.26)

10. What is the purpose of the named driver exclusion, and why might insurance regulators favor its use in today's insurance environment? (p. 2.29)

11. Explain the problems associated with reducing liability claim payments for duplicate payments made under the medical payments section of the PAP. (pp. 2.32–2.34)

12. Explain why it is sometimes incorrect to apply the Other Insurance provision according to the policy wording. (pp. 2.34–2.39)

13. Describe four issues that claim representatives should consider when handling claims involving an insured's accident with a rental car. (p. 2.41)

14. What are some coverage issues related to uninsured motorists coverage for "phantom vehicles"? (pp. 2.47–2.49)

15. Give two reasons courts in some states have permitted stacking of uninsured motorists coverage liability limits, even when the policy wording prohibits stacking. (pp. 2.55–2.56)

16. What are some issues that can be resolved by the arbitration clause found in the uninsured motorists coverage section? (pp. 2.52–2.53)

17. Can a claim representative deduct the amounts paid under the medical payments coverage from the amount owed for an uninsured motorist claim? Explain. (pp. 2.56–2.57)

18. The PAP requires prompt notice of loss by the insured to the insurer. How might late notice of loss adversely affect an insurer? (pp. 2.60–2.61)

19. What general provisions of the PAP might apply to suspicious injury claims? (p. 2.61)

Application Questions

1. A mother is standing on a sidewalk with her four-year-old daughter. The insured accidentally runs over the daughter, who was standing on the curb next to the sidewalk. The mother is physically uninjured but is making a claim against the insured for emotional trauma related to watching the event.

   What are four important issues that claim representatives must address in this claim?

2. A person walking past a car is bitten by a dog that leaned out the car window. Explain how the wording in the PAP insuring agreement might be used by an insurer to deny coverage.

3. The insured's eighteen-year-old son delivers pizza in the family minivan insured under a PAP.
   a.   Under what circumstances would this business use be covered?

   b.   When would it not be covered?

4. Bill Hanson is the named insured under a PAP. His son, Pete, is home for three weeks on leave from the military. Bill's mother is staying with Bill because of her declining health. Her car has been parked in his driveway for six months. Bill has permission to use her car, but he used it only once to have some maintenance work performed on it. While Pete was at home, he borrowed his grandmother's car and was involved in an accident. Unfortunately, Bill and Pete discover that coverage has lapsed on her auto policy. Pete does not have a policy of his own. Would Pete's accident be covered under Bill's PAP? (Hint: Use the Decision Tree on p. 2.27 to help determine coverage.)

5. Karen is driving down a country road when a car pulls in front of her and forces her to stop. Passengers in the other car begin shooting at her car. Karen speeds away but is injured by gunfire from the unidentified vehicle. Karen makes a UM claim under her PAP.

   a.   Describe three possible auto coverage defenses to this claim.

   b.   Explain one argument that courts have used in the past to provide coverage for this type of claim.

6. Clarence is driving home at 1:30 AM on a Saturday morning when he fails to negotiate a sharp curve and runs into a guardrail. Clarence claims that he was forced off the road by a pickup truck. Clarence suffered serious injuries and was taken to the emergency room by ambulance. He is now making a UM claim under his PAP.

a. What are some important issues that a claim representative should investigate in this claim?

b. Could the issues in this claim be resolved through application of the arbitration clause?

7. Mary is struck by a motorist who has $50,000/$100,000 liability limits on his auto. Mary suffers $75,000 in bodily injury damages. Mary has an underinsured motorists (UIM) policy that has $50,000/$100,000 limits of liability. What amount should Mary's underinsured motorists carrier pay in a state that recognizes

a. A damages trigger for underinsured motorists coverage?

b. A limits trigger for underinsured motorists coverage?

8. Hometown Insurance Company decides that it is going to outsource its subrogation to an independent adjusting company. To avoid making any initial cash outlay, Hometown wants to base its contract on a percentage of subrogation returns. Hometown is seeking subrogation returns on numerous medical payments and uninsured motorists claims it has paid nationwide.

Terrie is the general manager of an independent adjusting company that is considering contracting with Hometown for this work. What are some subrogation issues that Terrie should consider before accepting a percentage-type contract with Hometown?

Answers to Assignment 2 Questions

NOTE: These answers are provided to give students a basic understanding of acceptable types of responses. They often are not the only valid answers and are not intended to provide an exhaustive response to the questions.

Review Questions

1. When statutes (such as those mandating liability or uninsured motorists coverage) conflict with policy wording, courts use the public policy argument to override policy wording in favor of the coverage that is mandated by law.

2. Factors include:
   - How frequently and how long the person stayed at the residence
   - The person's intent to stay
   - The permanent connection the person has to the residence in terms of mailing address, voter registration, tax payments, and vehicle registration
   - The type and nature of personal belongings at the residence
   - The nature of the person's relationship to other members of the household

3. The courts consider the child's and parent's intent. Normally, they will permit some transitional period for children, unless the child has specifically expressed the intent to become emancipated from the parents and establish a residency elsewhere.

4. Child factors include:
   - The child's age
   - The child's and parent's intent
   - How financially dependent the child is on the parents
   - Is the child in college or the military?
   - Does the child have his or her own room?
   - If parents are divorced, which parent has custody? Does the state law permit children to have the dual residencies?

5. a. Yes, by definition.
   b. Yes, most likely. The person is in sufficient proximity, is vehicle oriented, and may even be considered in physical contact.
   c. Yes, most likely, especially in states that recognize sufficient proximity.
   d. No, probably not. The person is close but not vehicle oriented. The car is just there by happenstance.

6. The new wording states that the duty to defend ends once there has been a judgment or settlement. This differs from the old wording that stated that the duty to defend ended when the policy limits had been exhausted.

7. • Reserve the rights of the company.
   - Promptly take detailed statements from insureds, claimants, and witnesses (this investigation should probe into issues of the motive of the insured and the insured's ability to form intent).

- Determine whether the incident involved "use" of the vehicle as interpreted by courts in the state where the incident occurred.
- Consider the jurisdictional interpretation of the term "accident."

8. State statutes often require the insured's PAP liability coverage to provide primary coverage notwithstanding the policy wording. Also, some statutes require the liability section of the PAP to apply to the damage to the loaned car, which is contrary to the "care, custody, or control" exclusion.

9. The issue of whether the driver had reasonable belief might apply for underaged, unlicensed drivers who do not qualify as "family members."

10. The purpose of the named driver exclusion is to exclude insurance coverage for the operation of a vehicle by a specified person (who has an exceptionally poor driving record). Regulators might prefer that companies use this exclusionary endorsement rather than reject an entire family because of one person's driving record. The named driver exclusionary endorsement might reduce the overall number of people who must go to the high-risk (assigned risk) pool to obtain insurance.

11. One problem is that it is sometimes difficult to conclude that the liability payment has a duplicate element because of the nature of general damage evaluations in liability payments. Also, some states do not permit offsets because liability coverage is a mandated coverage.

12. Some states have statutory wording that contradicts the Other Insurance provision.

13.
- Check the rental agreement to determine whether the insured renter opted for additional coverages that should have been primary.
- Check the rental contract wording to see how it is intended to work with Other Insurance.
- Determine how the state interprets "escape clauses" in rental contracts.
- Find out what kind of insurance the rental car company has for its rental cars.

14.
- Did the "phantom vehicle" cause the accident (or was it the insured's own negligence?)?
- Does the state UM statute (or case law) require physical contact for the UM coverage to apply?
- Does the state UM statute (or case law) require corroborative evidence of a phantom vehicle (evidence other than the insured's statement)?

15. Stacking of UM coverage has been permitted because:
- The coverage is state mandated, and insurers cannot reduce coverage from that provided by a state's statute.
- The insured pays a separate premium for each UM coverage and should therefore be entitled to collect for the coverage under each.

16. UM arbitration is appropriate for all disputes except those concerning UM coverage. The percentage of liability or the amounts of damages are appropriately resolved with UM arbitration. Beyond those two issues, coverage-related issues may or may not be resolved by arbitration depending on state law.

17. First there is the issue of whether a state statute permits deductions from statutorily mandated coverages (such as UM). If, for example, the state law requires vehicle owners to purchase a minimum of $25,000 uninsured motorists coverage, a deduction from this coverage limit for amounts paid under the medical payments coverage might be seen as contrary to the statute.

Determining whether a payment is truly duplicative can also be challenging.

18. Late notice of loss may be a problem because memories fade, the opportunity to examine physical surroundings and document them with photographs may be lost, the ability to locate and interview witnesses is hampered, and securing an early settlement and avoiding litigation become more difficult.

19. The General Provisions have a section that precludes coverage for fraud. This includes fraudulent statements made by insureds. Concealment and misrepresentation may also obviate coverage.

Application Questions

1. Issues:
   - Do the courts in the jurisdiction where the accident occurred recognize purely nonphysical injury claims? Does the jurisdiction require the person to be within the "zone of danger" (which the mother probably was)?
   - Do the courts in the jurisdiction where the accident occurred consider purely emotional injury claims to be covered as a "bodily injury"?
   - If the answer to the above question is no, then did the mother develop any physical symptoms that could be considered "bodily injury," such as headaches, high blood pressure, sleeplessness, nausea, diarrhea, or ulcers?
   - Did the mother actually witness the event?

2. The insuring agreement applies to the "use" of the auto. Depending on the state, the dog bite might not be considered "using" the auto.

3. a. Under most circumstances, this would be covered as the exception to the business exclusion for a private passenger car or van owned by the insured.

   b. If the van was owned by someone else, if the vehicle was a truck rather than a van, or if the insured had lied about this business usage on the application for coverage (perhaps a material misrepresentation), then coverage would not apply.

4. With the use of the decision tree, the first coverage hurdle is whether the car is furnished or available for Bill's use. This is questionable because the grandmother's car is available for Bill's use, and this might make it not covered. Assuming that Pete gets past this hurdle, Pete must qualify as any other insured under Bill's PAP. That means he must be a resident of Bill's household. His military leave would probably not exclude him from residency if Pete intended to come back home after his military service had been completed. The final issue is whether Bill's mother is now a "family member" because she lives with Bill. Most likely, she would be considered a family member, and therefore coverage would be excluded.

   Courts might consider the purpose of this exclusion in making their decision. A conflict of intents is found in the policy, and courts might seize on this conflict to come to different conclusions. First, the "regularly furnished" exclusion is intended to preclude free insurance. This is a good reason not to cover this loss. But on the other hand, the intent of the PAP is to provide nonownership coverage for an insured for whom the auto is not regularly furnished. This second intent might logically operate to provide coverage for Pete. He is not around enough for the grandmother's car to be regularly furnished to Pete. And if Pete had borrowed a car from the elderly lady next door, Pete would have been covered (if he were truly a resident).

   According to the policy language, if the car is regularly furnished to Bill by a family member, then Pete has no coverage while using it. This is the most likely coverage interpretation.

▶▶

5. a. Coverage defenses would include:

   - This incident does not meet the definition of an accident. This is probably not a strong defense.

   - This incident was not related to the use of the vehicle. This is a stronger defense. The car might be considered incidental to her injury.

   - This was not caused by an uninsured motorist. The facts indicate that passengers in the car were doing the shooting. The passengers could just as easily have been standing on the shoulder of the road.

   b. • Arguments in favor of coverage would include: The nexus of the accident involved the use of a car. The unidentified car was used to get her to stop.

   - According to public policy, UM is mandated coverage, and Karen is an innocent victim.

6. a. A complete statement from Clarence is obviously required, along with a police report.

   - Did Clarence tell the police or emergency medical team/ambulance attendants the story about the pickup, or was this a later invention?

   - Does the state in which this accident occurred have an uninsured motorists statute that requires physical contact?

   - Have court decisions in the state addressed the coverage issue of "phantom vehicles"?

   - Is there corroborative evidence of Clarence's story, such as physical damage to his car caused by another vehicle?

     A reconstruction engineer might be required to make this determination. Also, the reconstruction engineer could help assess the speed at which Clarence was traveling. A UM claim is based on the negligence of a UM driver. Even if a UM driver existed, the UM claim would be diminished if Clarence's own speeding was the proximate cause of the accident. Another issue to consider is whether Clarence had been drinking. The time of the accident is suspect. An authorization to obtain medical records should also include the lab results of Clarence's blood alcohol content. This would be a standard test conducted at the hospital emergency room for someone presented to the staff with serious injuries from an automobile accident. An examination under oath may be in order if the evidence is unconvincing for or against the UM claim.

   b. Depending on the state, some of these issues may not be able to be arbitrated. The existence of coverage is one issue that many states allow the courts to decide. The negligence of the UM driver and the amount of damages are certainly items that can be arbitrated.

     Another issue to consider is whether arbitration results are binding. Some states will not permit enforcement of arbitration results. A small number of states still allow the parties to decline to arbitrate, even though the policy wording indicates otherwise.

7. a. The per person limit of liability of the adverse party is $50,000. This is inadequate to cover Mary's claim. She therefore has a $25,000 underinsured motorist claim based on the damages trigger.

b. Because the limit of liability of the tortfeasor matches the limit of liability of Mary's own UIM coverage, the vehicle does not meet the definition of an underinsured motorist. Mary's UIM carrier would therefore pay nothing under the limits trigger.

Note: Policy wording and state laws vary widely, and this issue is in a constant state of flux. Claim representatives should always seek management or legal counsel when an insured's damages are significant enough to potentially trigger the UIM coverage.

8. Subrogation of these claims might be against state laws that do not permit assignment of injury claims. However, many states have uninsured motorists statutes that specifically permit subrogation of these claims. States that have no-fault laws may not permit subrogation of medical payments claims. Terrie needs to find out which states Hometown is seeking recovery in and make sure that the laws in those states permit subrogation of medical payments or uninsured motorists claims.

Direct Your Learning

Coverage Issues With Homeowners and Commercial Liability Policies

Educational Objectives

After learning the content of this assignment, you should be able to:

1. Explain and provide examples of the difficulties associated with the application of coverage to claims as a result of the controversial nature of:
   a. The definition of an "occurrence"
      - What constitutes an "occurrence"
      - How courts determine whether a series of related claims constitutes one single occurrence or multiple occurrences.
      - When an "occurrence" takes place
   b. The definition of "property damage"
   c. Coverage for punitive damages
   d. The broad nature of the duty to defend under the CGL and homeowners Section II coverage
2. Explain the coverage concerns and investigative issues involved in the "intentional acts" exclusion.
3. Explain the coverage concerns and investigative issues involved in the "business pursuits" exclusion, found in the homeowners policy.
4. Given a claim situation, identify any exclusion in the homeowners policy that could potentially apply.
5. Identify a claim situation in which the Section II—Additional Coverages would apply.

With respect to the CGL policy:

6. Explain coverages A, B, and C provided by the CGL, and identify examples of claims that fall within the insuring agreements of each.
7. Give examples of claims with which the definition of "property damage" could be disputed.
8. Given a claim situation involving "loading and unloading," determine whether the CGL or the business auto policy would apply.
9. Given a claim situation involving an insured's premises, operations, or products, recognize exclusions that could potentially apply.
10. Given a claim involving a hold harmless or an indemnity agreement, determine the CGL coverage for liability under these agreements.
11. Describe the application of the individual and aggregate limits of liability of the CGL policy for claims involving:
    - Fire legal liability (Damage to Premises Rented)
    - Personal and advertising injury
    - Product liability
    - Other liability covered under the CGL
12. Given a claim situation involving personal or advertising injury offenses, identify acts that could potentially be covered under the CGL policy.
13. Define or describe each of the Key Words and Phrases for this assignment.

Outline

▶ **Coverage Issues Common to the CGL and Homeowners Policies**

  A. "Occurrence"

    1. What Constitutes an Occurrence?

    2. Determining the Number of Occurrences

    3. Determining When an Occurrence Takes Place

  B. Property Damage

  C. Duty To Defend Against a Suit

  D. Punitive Damages

▶ **Homeowners Section II—Liability Coverages**

  A. Section II Coverage E—The Personal Liability Insuring Agreement

  B. Section II Coverage F—The Medical Payments to Others Insuring Agreement

▶ **Homeowners Section II—Exclusions**

  A. Motor Vehicles, Watercraft, Aircraft, and Hovercraft Liability Exclusions

    1. Expected or Intended Injury Exclusion

    2. Business Exclusion

    3. Professional Services Exclusion

    4. "Insured's Premises Not an Insured Location" Exclusion

    5. War

    6. Communicable Disease

    7. Sexual Molestation, Corporal Punishment, or Physical or Mental Abuse

    8. Controlled Substances

    9. Exclusions Only for Personal Liability—Coverage E

  B. Exclusions Applicable Only to Coverage F

  C. Homeowners Section II—Additional Coverages

    1. Claim Expenses

    2. First-Aid Expenses

    3. Damage to the Property of Others

    4. Loss Assessment

▶ **Conditions Applying to Liability Coverages**

  A. Limits of Liability

  B. Severability of Interests

  C. Duties After Occurrence

  D. Suit Against the Insurance Company

  E. Bankruptcy of an Insured

  F. Other Insurance

  G. Policy Period

  H. Concealment and Fraud

  I. Summary of Homeowners Policy

▶ **Overview of the CGL Form**

▶ **Coverage A—Bodily Injury and Property Damage Liability**

  A. Premises and Operations Liability Coverage

  B. Contractual Liability Coverage

  C. Fire Legal Liability (Damage to Rented Property) Coverage

  D. Products and Completed Operations

▶ **Coverage A Exclusions**

  A. Expected or Intended Injury

  B. Contractual Liability

    1. Insured Contracts

  C. Liquor Liability

  D. Workers Compensation and Similar Laws

  E. Employers Liability

  F. Pollution

  G. Aircraft, Auto, or Watercraft

    1. "Auto" Versus "Mobile Equipment"

    2. Negligent Entrustment

    3. Loading and Unloading

  H. Mobile Equipment

  I. War

  J. Damage to Property

  K. Damage to Your Product

  L. Damage to Your Work

  M. Damage to Impaired Property or Property Not Physically Injured

  N. Recall of Products, Work, or Impaired Property

  O. CGL Limits of Liability

▶ **Coverage B—Personal and Advertising Injury Liability**

  A. Coverage B—Coverage Offenses and Practical Concerns

  B. Coverage B—Exclusions

▶ **Coverage C—Medical Payments**

▶ **Summary**

Reading 3-1

2001 CGL Changes[1]

The 2001 revision of the CGL coverage forms is aimed mainly at defining coverage for Internet-related loss exposures. The following summaries of the ISO changes include excerpts from ISO Circular LI-GL-2001-176, "Advisory Guide to Broadenings, Restrictions and Clarification of Coverage for the 2001 General Liability Multistate Forms Revision Is Furnished."

Broadenings of Coverage

In CG 00 01 and CG 00 02, the definition of "coverage territory" is expanded to include personal and advertising injury offenses that take place via the Internet or other electronic means of communication, limited to some extent by the location where the suit is filed.

Restrictions in Coverage

In CG 00 01 and CG 00 02, as well as other general liability coverage forms, the definition of "property damage" is amended to state that electronic data is not tangible property. (This change affects the definition of property damage discussed in Chapter 3 of the text.) As a result of this amendment, the 2001 CGL forms do not cover claims alleging that the insured is legally liable for loss of electronic data. In most states, the question of whether electronic data is tangible has not been finally decided by the courts in the context of the prior policy language.

The 2001 editions of CG 00 01 and CG 00 02 are revised to exclude coverage for "personal and advertising injury" for Web site designers, Internet access and service providers (with an exception for mere placing of links, frames, or borders), and electronic chatrooms or bulletin boards.

Clarifications in Coverage

ISO made various amendments to CGL coverage forms CG 00 01 and CG 00 02 in order to clarify coverage for personal and advertising injury. For example, ISO modified the definition of "personal and advertising injury" offenses such as slander, libel, and invasion of privacy by specifically applying the word "publication" to include all types of publication, including those that are electronic. Similarly, the definition of "advertisement" has also been amended to include notices that are published via the Internet and other forms of electronic communication.

Broadenings of "Who Is an Insured"

The 2001 CGL coverage forms broaden the "Who Is an Insured" section of the forms in two ways:

- When designated in the policy declarations as named insureds, trusts are included as insureds.

- Volunteer workers (as defined in the forms) are automatically included as insureds, but only while performing duties related to the conduct of the insured's business.

Reading Note

1. Adapted from Reading 5-1 of the Commercial Liability Insurance and Risk Management Course Guide, 1st ed. by Donald Malecki and Arthur Flitner.

HOMEOWNERS
HO 00 03 10 00

HOMEOWNERS 3 – SPECIAL FORM

AGREEMENT

We will provide the insurance described in this policy in return for the premium and compliance with all applicable provisions of this policy.

DEFINITIONS

A. In this policy, "you" and "your" refer to the "named insured" shown in the Declarations and the spouse if a resident of the same household. "We", "us" and "our" refer to the Company providing this insurance.

B. In addition, certain words and phrases are defined as follows:

1. "Aircraft Liability", "Hovercraft Liability", "Motor Vehicle Liability" and "Watercraft Liability", subject to the provisions in **b.** below, mean the following:

a. Liability for "bodily injury" or "property damage" arising out of the:

(1) Ownership of such vehicle or craft by an "insured";

(2) Maintenance, occupancy, operation, use, loading or unloading of such vehicle or craft by any person;

(3) Entrustment of such vehicle or craft by an "insured" to any person;

(4) Failure to supervise or negligent supervision of any person involving such vehicle or craft by an "insured"; or

(5) Vicarious liability, whether or not imposed by law, for the actions of a child or minor involving such vehicle or craft.

b. For the purpose of this definition:

(1) Aircraft means any contrivance used or designed for flight except model or hobby aircraft not used or designed to carry people or cargo;

(2) Hovercraft means a self-propelled motorized ground effect vehicle and includes, but is not limited to, flarecraft and air cushion vehicles;

(3) Watercraft means a craft principally designed to be propelled on or in water by wind, engine power or electric motor; and

(4) Motor vehicle means a "motor vehicle" as defined in **7.** below.

2. "Bodily injury" means bodily harm, sickness or disease, including required care, loss of services and death that results.

3. "Business" means:

a. A trade, profession or occupation engaged in on a full-time, part-time or occasional basis; or

b. Any other activity engaged in for money or other compensation, except the following:

(1) One or more activities, not described in **(2)** through **(4)** below, for which no "insured" receives more than $2,000 in total compensation for the 12 months before the beginning of the policy period;

(2) Volunteer activities for which no money is received other than payment for expenses incurred to perform the activity;

(3) Providing home day care services for which no compensation is received, other than the mutual exchange of such services; or

(4) The rendering of home day care services to a relative of an "insured".

4. "Employee" means an employee of an "insured", or an employee leased to an "insured" by a labor leasing firm under an agreement between an "insured" and the labor leasing firm, whose duties are other than those performed by a "residence employee".

5. "Insured" means:

a. You and residents of your household who are:

(1) Your relatives; or

(2) Other persons under the age of 21 and in the care of any person named above;

b. A student enrolled in school full time, as defined by the school, who was a resident of your household before moving out to attend school, provided the student is under the age of:

(1) 24 and your relative; or

(2) 21 and in your care or the care of a person described in **a.(1)** above; or

c. Under Section **II:**

  (1) With respect to animals or watercraft to which this policy applies, any person or organization legally responsible for these animals or watercraft which are owned by you or any person included in **a.** or **b.** above. "Insured" does not mean a person or organization using or having custody of these animals or watercraft in the course of any "business" or without consent of the owner; or

  (2) With respect to a "motor vehicle" to which this policy applies:

    (a) Persons while engaged in your employ or that of any person included in **a.** or **b.** above; or

    (b) Other persons using the vehicle on an "insured location" with your consent.

Under both Sections **I** and **II,** when the word an immediately precedes the word "insured", the words an "insured" together mean one or more "insureds".

6. "Insured location" means:

  a. The "residence premises";

  b. The part of other premises, other structures and grounds used by you as a residence; and

    (1) Which is shown in the Declarations; or

    (2) Which is acquired by you during the policy period for your use as a residence;

  c. Any premises used by you in connection with a premises described in **a.** and **b.** above;

  d. Any part of a premises:

    (1) Not owned by an "insured"; and

    (2) Where an "insured" is temporarily residing;

  e. Vacant land, other than farm land, owned by or rented to an "insured";

  f. Land owned by or rented to an "insured" on which a one, two, three or four family dwelling is being built as a residence for an "insured";

  g. Individual or family cemetery plots or burial vaults of an "insured"; or

  h. Any part of a premises occasionally rented to an "insured" for other than "business" use.

7. "Motor vehicle" means:

  a. A self-propelled land or amphibious vehicle; or

  b. Any trailer or semitrailer which is being carried on, towed by or hitched for towing by a vehicle described in **a.** above.

8. "Occurrence" means an accident, including continuous or repeated exposure to substantially the same general harmful conditions, which results, during the policy period, in:

  a. "Bodily injury"; or

  b. "Property damage".

9. "Property damage" means physical injury to, destruction of, or loss of use of tangible property.

10. "Residence employee" means:

  a. An employee of an "insured", or an employee leased to an "insured" by a labor leasing firm, under an agreement between an "insured" and the labor leasing firm, whose duties are related to the maintenance or use of the "residence premises", including household or domestic services; or

  b. One who performs similar duties elsewhere not related to the "business" of an "insured".

A "residence employee" does not include a temporary employee who is furnished to an "insured" to substitute for a permanent "residence employee" on leave or to meet seasonal or short-term workload conditions.

11. "Residence premises" means:

  a. The one family dwelling where you reside;

  b. The two, three or four family dwelling where you reside in at least one of the family units; or

  c. That part of any other building where you reside;

and which is shown as the "residence premises" in the Declarations.

"Residence premises" also includes other structures and grounds at that location.

   HO 00 03 10 00

DEDUCTIBLE

Unless otherwise noted in this policy, the following deductible provision applies:

Subject to the policy limits that apply, we will pay only that part of the total of all loss payable under Section **I** that exceeds the deductible amount shown in the Declarations.

SECTION I – PROPERTY COVERAGES

A. Coverage A – Dwelling

1. We cover:

    a. The dwelling on the "residence premises" shown in the Declarations, including structures attached to the dwelling; and

    b. Materials and supplies located on or next to the "residence premises" used to construct, alter or repair the dwelling or other structures on the "residence premises".

2. We do not cover land, including land on which the dwelling is located.

B. Coverage B – Other Structures

1. We cover other structures on the "residence premises" set apart from the dwelling by clear space. This includes structures connected to the dwelling by only a fence, utility line, or similar connection.

2. We do not cover:

    a. Land, including land on which the other structures are located;

    b. Other structures rented or held for rental to any person not a tenant of the dwelling, unless used solely as a private garage;

    c. Other structures from which any "business" is conducted; or

    d. Other structures used to store "business" property. However, we do cover a structure that contains "business" property solely owned by an "insured" or a tenant of the dwelling provided that "business" property does not include gaseous or liquid fuel, other than fuel in a permanently installed fuel tank of a vehicle or craft parked or stored in the structure.

3. The limit of liability for this coverage will not be more than 10% of the limit of liability that applies to Coverage **A**. Use of this coverage does not reduce the Coverage **A** limit of liability.

C. Coverage C – Personal Property

1. **Covered Property**

    We cover personal property owned or used by an "insured" while it is anywhere in the world. After a loss and at your request, we will cover personal property owned by:

    a. Others while the property is on the part of the "residence premises" occupied by an "insured"; or

    b. A guest or a "residence employee", while the property is in any residence occupied by an "insured".

2. **Limit For Property At Other Residences**

    Our limit of liability for personal property usually located at an "insured's" residence, other than the "residence premises", is 10% of the limit of liability for Coverage **C**, or $1,000, whichever is greater. However, this limitation does not apply to personal property:

    a. Moved from the "residence premises" because it is being repaired, renovated or rebuilt and is not fit to live in or store property in; or

    b. In a newly acquired principal residence for 30 days from the time you begin to move the property there.

3. **Special Limits Of Liability**

    The special limit for each category shown below is the total limit for each loss for all property in that category. These special limits do not increase the Coverage **C** limit of liability.

    a. $200 on money, bank notes, bullion, gold other than goldware, silver other than silverware, platinum other than platinumware, coins, medals, scrip, stored value cards and smart cards.

    b. $1,500 on securities, accounts, deeds, evidences of debt, letters of credit, notes other than bank notes, manuscripts, personal records, passports, tickets and stamps. This dollar limit applies to these categories regardless of the medium (such as paper or computer software) on which the material exists.

    This limit includes the cost to research, replace or restore the information from the lost or damaged material.

c. $1,500 on watercraft of all types, including their trailers, furnishings, equipment and outboard engines or motors.

d. $1,500 on trailers or semitrailers not used with watercraft of all types.

e. $1,500 for loss by theft of jewelry, watches, furs, precious and semiprecious stones.

f. $2,500 for loss by theft of firearms and related equipment.

g. $2,500 for loss by theft of silverware, silver-plated ware, goldware, gold-plated ware, platinumware, platinum-plated ware and pewterware. This includes flatware, hollowware, tea sets, trays and trophies made of or including silver, gold or pewter.

h. $2,500 on property, on the "residence premises", used primarily for "business" purposes.

i. $500 on property, away from the "residence premises", used primarily for "business" purposes. However, this limit does not apply to loss to electronic apparatus and other property described in Categories **j.** and **k.** below.

j. $1,500 on electronic apparatus and accessories, while in or upon a "motor vehicle", but only if the apparatus is equipped to be operated by power from the "motor vehicle's" electrical system while still capable of being operated by other power sources.

Accessories include antennas, tapes, wires, records, discs or other media that can be used with any apparatus described in this Category **j.**

k. $1,500 on electronic apparatus and accessories used primarily for "business" while away from the "residence premises" and not in or upon a "motor vehicle". The apparatus must be equipped to be operated by power from the "motor vehicle's" electrical system while still capable of being operated by other power sources.

Accessories include antennas, tapes, wires, records, discs or other media that can be used with any apparatus described in this Category **k.**

4. Property Not Covered

We do not cover:

a. Articles separately described and specifically insured, regardless of the limit for which they are insured, in this or other insurance;

b. Animals, birds or fish;

c. "Motor vehicles".

  (1) This includes:

    (a) Their accessories, equipment and parts; or

    (b) Electronic apparatus and accessories designed to be operated solely by power from the electrical system of the "motor vehicle". Accessories include antennas, tapes, wires, records, discs or other media that can be used with any apparatus described above.

  The exclusion of property described in **(a)** and **(b)** above applies only while such property is in or upon the "motor vehicle".

  (2) We do cover "motor vehicles" not required to be registered for use on public roads or property which are:

    (a) Used solely to service an "insured's" residence; or

    (b) Designed to assist the handicapped;

d. Aircraft meaning any contrivance used or designed for flight including any parts whether or not attached to the aircraft.

We do cover model or hobby aircraft not used or designed to carry people or cargo;

e. Hovercraft and parts. Hovercraft means a self-propelled motorized ground effect vehicle and includes, but is not limited to, flarecraft and air cushion vehicles;

f. Property of roomers, boarders and other tenants, except property of roomers and boarders related to an "insured";

g. Property in an apartment regularly rented or held for rental to others by an "insured", except as provided in **E.10.** Landlord's Furnishings under Section I – Property Coverages;

h. Property rented or held for rental to others off the "residence premises";

i. "Business" data, including such data stored in:

  (1) Books of account, drawings or other paper records; or

  (2) Computers and related equipment.

We do cover the cost of blank recording or storage media, and of prerecorded computer programs available on the retail market;

     HO 00 03 10 00

j. Credit cards, electronic fund transfer cards or access devices used solely for deposit, withdrawal or transfer of funds except as provided in **E.6.** Credit Card, Electronic Fund Transfer Card Or Access Device, Forgery And Counterfeit Money under Section **I** – Property Coverages; or

k. Water or steam.

D. Coverage D – Loss Of Use

The limit of liability for Coverage **D** is the total limit for the coverages in **1.** Additional Living Expense, **2.** Fair Rental Value and **3.** Civil Authority Prohibits Use below.

1. Additional Living Expense

If a loss covered under Section **I** makes that part of the "residence premises" where you reside not fit to live in, we cover any necessary increase in living expenses incurred by you so that your household can maintain its normal standard of living.

Payment will be for the shortest time required to repair or replace the damage or, if you permanently relocate, the shortest time required for your household to settle elsewhere.

2. Fair Rental Value

If a loss covered under Section **I** makes that part of the "residence premises" rented to others or held for rental by you not fit to live in, we cover the fair rental value of such premises less any expenses that do not continue while it is not fit to live in.

Payment will be for the shortest time required to repair or replace such premises.

3. Civil Authority Prohibits Use

If a civil authority prohibits you from use of the "residence premises" as a result of direct damage to neighboring premises by a Peril Insured Against, we cover the loss as provided in **1.** Additional Living Expense and **2.** Fair Rental Value above for no more than two weeks.

4. Loss Or Expense Not Covered

We do not cover loss or expense due to cancellation of a lease or agreement.

The periods of time under **1.** Additional Living Expense, **2.** Fair Rental Value and **3.** Civil Authority Prohibits Use above are not limited by expiration of this policy.

E. Additional Coverages

1. Debris Removal

a. We will pay your reasonable expense for the removal of:

(1) Debris of covered property if a Peril Insured Against that applies to the damaged property causes the loss; or

(2) Ash, dust or particles from a volcanic eruption that has caused direct loss to a building or property contained in a building.

This expense is included in the limit of liability that applies to the damaged property. If the amount to be paid for the actual damage to the property plus the debris removal expense is more than the limit of liability for the damaged property, an additional 5% of that limit is available for such expense.

b. We will also pay your reasonable expense, up to $1,000, for the removal from the "residence premises" of:

(1) Your tree(s) felled by the peril of Windstorm or Hail or Weight of Ice, Snow or Sleet; or

(2) A neighbor's tree(s) felled by a Peril Insured Against under Coverage **C**;

provided the tree(s):

(3) Damage(s) a covered structure; or

(4) Does not damage a covered structure, but:

(a) Block(s) a driveway on the "residence premises" which prevent(s) a "motor vehicle", that is registered for use on public roads or property, from entering or leaving the "residence premises"; or

(b) Block(s) a ramp or other fixture designed to assist a handicapped person to enter or leave the dwelling building.

The $1,000 limit is the most we will pay in any one loss regardless of the number of fallen trees. No more than $500 of this limit will be paid for the removal of any one tree.

This coverage is additional insurance.

2. Reasonable Repairs

a. We will pay the reasonable cost incurred by you for the necessary measures taken solely to protect covered property that is damaged by a Peril Insured Against from further damage.

b. If the measures taken involve repair to other damaged property, we will only pay if that property is covered under this policy and the damage is caused by a Peril Insured Against. This coverage does not:

(1) Increase the limit of liability that applies to the covered property; or

(2) Relieve you of your duties, in case of a loss to covered property, described in **B.4.** under Section **I** – Conditions.

3. Trees, Shrubs And Other Plants

We cover trees, shrubs, plants or lawns, on the "residence premises", for loss caused by the following Perils Insured Against:

a. Fire or Lightning;

b. Explosion;

c. Riot or Civil Commotion;

d. Aircraft;

e. Vehicles not owned or operated by a resident of the "residence premises";

f. Vandalism or Malicious Mischief; or

g. Theft.

We will pay up to 5% of the limit of liability that applies to the dwelling for all trees, shrubs, plants or lawns. No more than $500 of this limit will be paid for any one tree, shrub or plant. We do not cover property grown for "business" purposes.

This coverage is additional insurance.

4. Fire Department Service Charge

We will pay up to $500 for your liability assumed by contract or agreement for fire department charges incurred when the fire department is called to save or protect covered property from a Peril Insured Against. We do not cover fire department service charges if the property is located within the limits of the city, municipality or protection district furnishing the fire department response.

This coverage is additional insurance. No deductible applies to this coverage.

5. Property Removed

We insure covered property against direct loss from any cause while being removed from a premises endangered by a Peril Insured Against and for no more than 30 days while removed.

This coverage does not change the limit of liability that applies to the property being removed.

6. Credit Card, Electronic Fund Transfer Card Or Access Device, Forgery And Counterfeit Money

a. We will pay up to $500 for:

(1) The legal obligation of an "insured" to pay because of the theft or unauthorized use of credit cards issued to or registered in an "insured's" name;

(2) Loss resulting from theft or unauthorized use of an electronic fund transfer card or access device used for deposit, withdrawal or transfer of funds, issued to or registered in an "insured's" name;

(3) Loss to an "insured" caused by forgery or alteration of any check or negotiable instrument; and

(4) Loss to an "insured" through acceptance in good faith of counterfeit United States or Canadian paper currency.

All loss resulting from a series of acts committed by any one person or in which any one person is concerned or implicated is considered to be one loss.

This coverage is additional insurance. No deductible applies to this coverage.

b. We do not cover:

(1) Use of a credit card, electronic fund transfer card or access device:

(a) By a resident of your household;

(b) By a person who has been entrusted with either type of card or access device; or

(c) If an "insured" has not complied with all terms and conditions under which the cards are issued or the devices accessed; or

(2) Loss arising out of "business" use or dishonesty of an "insured".

c. If the coverage in **a.** above applies, the following defense provisions also apply:

(1) We may investigate and settle any claim or suit that we decide is appropriate. Our duty to defend a claim or suit ends when the amount we pay for the loss equals our limit of liability.

(2) If a suit is brought against an "insured" for liability under **a.(1)** or **(2)** above, we will provide a defense at our expense by counsel of our choice.

(3) We have the option to defend at our expense an "insured" or an "insured's" bank against any suit for the enforcement of payment under **a.(3)** above.

       HO 00 03 10 00

7. Loss Assessment

a. We will pay up to $1,000 for your share of loss assessment charged during the policy period against you, as owner or tenant of the "residence premises", by a corporation or association of property owners. The assessment must be made as a result of direct loss to property, owned by all members collectively, of the type that would be covered by this policy if owned by you, caused by a Peril Insured Against under Coverage **A**, other than:

(1) Earthquake; or

(2) Land shock waves or tremors before, during or after a volcanic eruption.

The limit of $1,000 is the most we will pay with respect to any one loss, regardless of the number of assessments. We will only apply one deductible, per unit, to the total amount of any one loss to the property described above, regardless of the number of assessments.

b. We do not cover assessments charged against you or a corporation or association of property owners by any governmental body.

c. Paragraph **P.** Policy Period under Section **I** – Conditions does not apply to this coverage.

This coverage is additional insurance.

8. Collapse

a. With respect to this Additional Coverage:

(1) Collapse means an abrupt falling down or caving in of a building or any part of a building with the result that the building or part of the building cannot be occupied for its current intended purpose.

(2) A building or any part of a building that is in danger of falling down or caving in is not considered to be in a state of collapse.

(3) A part of a building that is standing is not considered to be in a state of collapse even if it has separated from another part of the building.

(4) A building or any part of a building that is standing is not considered to be in a state of collapse even if it shows evidence of cracking, bulging, sagging, bending, leaning, settling, shrinkage or expansion.

b. We insure for direct physical loss to covered property involving collapse of a building or any part of a building if the collapse was caused by one or more of the following:

(1) The Perils Insured Against named under Coverage **C**;

(2) Decay that is hidden from view, unless the presence of such decay is known to an "insured" prior to collapse;

(3) Insect or vermin damage that is hidden from view, unless the presence of such damage is known to an "insured" prior to collapse;

(4) Weight of contents, equipment, animals or people;

(5) Weight of rain which collects on a roof; or

(6) Use of defective material or methods in construction, remodeling or renovation if the collapse occurs during the course of the construction, remodeling or renovation.

c. Loss to an awning, fence, patio, deck, pavement, swimming pool, underground pipe, flue, drain, cesspool, septic tank, foundation, retaining wall, bulkhead, pier, wharf or dock is not included under **b.(2)** through **(6)** above, unless the loss is a direct result of the collapse of a building or any part of a building.

d. This coverage does not increase the limit of liability that applies to the damaged covered property.

9. Glass Or Safety Glazing Material

a. We cover:

(1) The breakage of glass or safety glazing material which is part of a covered building, storm door or storm window;

(2) The breakage of glass or safety glazing material which is part of a covered building, storm door or storm window when caused directly by earth movement; and

(3) The direct physical loss to covered property caused solely by the pieces, fragments or splinters of broken glass or safety glazing material which is part of a building, storm door or storm window.

b. This coverage does not include loss:

   (1) To covered property which results because the glass or safety glazing material has been broken, except as provided in **a.(3)** above; or

   (2) On the "residence premises" if the dwelling has been vacant for more than 60 consecutive days immediately before the loss, except when the breakage results directly from earth movement as provided in **a.(2)** above. A dwelling being constructed is not considered vacant.

c. This coverage does not increase the limit of liability that applies to the damaged property.

10. Landlord's Furnishings

We will pay up to $2,500 for your appliances, carpeting and other household furnishings, in each apartment on the "residence premises" regularly rented or held for rental to others by an "insured", for loss caused by a Peril Insured Against in Coverage **C,** other than Theft.

This limit is the most we will pay in any one loss regardless of the number of appliances, carpeting or other household furnishings involved in the loss.

This coverage does not increase the limit of liability applying to the damaged property.

11. Ordinance Or Law

a. You may use up to 10% of the limit of liability that applies to Coverage **A** for the increased costs you incur due to the enforcement of any ordinance or law which requires or regulates:

   (1) The construction, demolition, remodeling, renovation or repair of that part of a covered building or other structure damaged by a Peril Insured Against;

   (2) The demolition and reconstruction of the undamaged part of a covered building or other structure, when that building or other structure must be totally demolished because of damage by a Peril Insured Against to another part of that covered building or other structure; or

   (3) The remodeling, removal or replacement of the portion of the undamaged part of a covered building or other structure necessary to complete the remodeling, repair or replacement of that part of the covered building or other structure damaged by a Peril Insured Against.

b. You may use all or part of this ordinance or law coverage to pay for the increased costs you incur to remove debris resulting from the construction, demolition, remodeling, renovation, repair or replacement of property as stated in **a.** above.

c. We do not cover:

   (1) The loss in value to any covered building or other structure due to the requirements of any ordinance or law; or

   (2) The costs to comply with any ordinance or law which requires any "insured" or others to test for, monitor, clean up, remove, contain, treat, detoxify or neutralize, or in any way respond to, or assess the effects of, pollutants in or on any covered building or other structure.

   Pollutants means any solid, liquid, gaseous or thermal irritant or contaminant, including smoke, vapor, soot, fumes, acids, alkalis, chemicals and waste. Waste includes materials to be recycled, reconditioned or reclaimed.

This coverage is additional insurance.

12. Grave Markers

We will pay up to $5,000 for grave markers, including mausoleums, on or away from the "residence premises" for loss caused by a Peril Insured Against under Coverage **C.**

This coverage does not increase the limits of liability that apply to the damaged covered property.

SECTION I – PERILS INSURED AGAINST

A. Coverage A – Dwelling And Coverage B – Other Structures

  1. We insure against risk of direct physical loss to property described in Coverages **A** and **B.**

  2. We do not insure, however, for loss:

   a. Excluded under Section I – Exclusions;

   b. Involving collapse, except as provided in **E.8.** Collapse under Section I – Property Coverages; or

   c. Caused by:

    (1) Freezing of a plumbing, heating, air conditioning or automatic fire protective sprinkler system or of a household appliance, or by discharge, leakage or overflow from within the system or appliance caused by freezing. This provision does not apply if you have used reasonable care to:

     (a) Maintain heat in the building; or

(b) Shut off the water supply and drain all systems and appliances of water.

However, if the building is protected by an automatic fire protective sprinkler system, you must use reasonable care to continue the water supply and maintain heat in the building for coverage to apply.

For purposes of this provision a plumbing system or household appliance does not include a sump, sump pump or related equipment or a roof drain, gutter, downspout or similar fixtures or equipment;

(2) Freezing, thawing, pressure or weight of water or ice, whether driven by wind or not, to a:

(a) Fence, pavement, patio or swimming pool;

(b) Footing, foundation, bulkhead, wall, or any other structure or device that supports all or part of a building, or other structure;

(c) Retaining wall or bulkhead that does not support all or part of a building or other structure; or

(d) Pier, wharf or dock;

(3) Theft in or to a dwelling under construction, or of materials and supplies for use in the construction until the dwelling is finished and occupied;

(4) Vandalism and malicious mischief, and any ensuing loss caused by any intentional and wrongful act committed in the course of the vandalism or malicious mischief, if the dwelling has been vacant for more than 60 consecutive days immediately before the loss. A dwelling being constructed is not considered vacant;

(5) Mold, fungus or wet rot. However, we do insure for loss caused by mold, fungus or wet rot that is hidden within the walls or ceilings or beneath the floors or above the ceilings of a structure if such loss results from the accidental discharge or overflow of water or steam from within:

(a) A plumbing, heating, air conditioning or automatic fire protective sprinkler system, or a household appliance, on the "residence premises"; or

(b) A storm drain, or water, steam or sewer pipes, off the "residence premises".

For purposes of this provision, a plumbing system or household appliance does not include a sump, sump pump or related equipment or a roof drain, gutter, downspout or similar fixtures or equipment; or

(6) Any of the following:

(a) Wear and tear, marring, deterioration;

(b) Mechanical breakdown, latent defect, inherent vice, or any quality in property that causes it to damage or destroy itself;

(c) Smog, rust or other corrosion, or dry rot;

(d) Smoke from agricultural smudging or industrial operations;

(e) Discharge, dispersal, seepage, migration, release or escape of pollutants unless the discharge, dispersal, seepage, migration, release or escape is itself caused by a Peril Insured Against named under Coverage **C.**

Pollutants means any solid, liquid, gaseous or thermal irritant or contaminant, including smoke, vapor, soot, fumes, acids, alkalis, chemicals and waste. Waste includes materials to be recycled, reconditioned or reclaimed;

(f) Settling, shrinking, bulging or expansion, including resultant cracking, of bulkheads, pavements, patios, footings, foundations, walls, floors, roofs or ceilings;

(g) Birds, vermin, rodents, or insects; or

(h) Animals owned or kept by an "insured".

Exception To c.(6)

Unless the loss is otherwise excluded, we cover loss to property covered under Coverage **A** or **B** resulting from an accidental discharge or overflow of water or steam from within a:

(i) Storm drain, or water, steam or sewer pipe, off the "residence premises"; or

(ii) Plumbing, heating, air conditioning or automatic fire protective sprinkler system or household appliance on the "residence premises". This includes the cost to tear out and replace any part of a building, or other structure, on the "residence premises", but only when necessary to repair the system or appliance. However, such tear out and replacement coverage only applies to other structures if the water or steam causes actual damage to a building on the "residence premises".

We do not cover loss to the system or appliance from which this water or steam escaped.

For purposes of this provision, a plumbing system or household appliance does not include a sump, sump pump or related equipment or a roof drain, gutter, down spout or similar fixtures or equipment.

Section I – Exclusion **A.3.** Water Damage, Paragraphs **a.** and **c.** that apply to surface water and water below the surface of the ground do not apply to loss by water covered under **c.(5)** and **(6)** above.

Under **2.b.** and **c.** above, any ensuing loss to property described in Coverages **A** and **B** not precluded by any other provision in this policy is covered.

B. Coverage C – Personal Property

We insure for direct physical loss to the property described in Coverage **C** caused by any of the following perils unless the loss is excluded in Section I – Exclusions.

1. Fire Or Lightning

2. Windstorm Or Hail

This peril includes loss to watercraft of all types and their trailers, furnishings, equipment, and outboard engines or motors, only while inside a fully enclosed building.

This peril does not include loss to the property contained in a building caused by rain, snow, sleet, sand or dust unless the direct force of wind or hail damages the building causing an opening in a roof or wall and the rain, snow, sleet, sand or dust enters through this opening.

3. Explosion

4. Riot Or Civil Commotion

5. Aircraft

This peril includes self-propelled missiles and spacecraft.

6. Vehicles

7. Smoke

This peril means sudden and accidental damage from smoke, including the emission or puffback of smoke, soot, fumes or vapors from a boiler, furnace or related equipment.

This peril does not include loss caused by smoke from agricultural smudging or industrial operations.

8. Vandalism Or Malicious Mischief

9. Theft

a. This peril includes attempted theft and loss of property from a known place when it is likely that the property has been stolen.

b. This peril does not include loss caused by theft:

(1) Committed by an "insured";

(2) In or to a dwelling under construction, or of materials and supplies for use in the construction until the dwelling is finished and occupied;

(3) From that part of a "residence premises" rented by an "insured" to someone other than another "insured"; or

(4) That occurs off the "residence premises" of:

(a) Trailers, semitrailers and campers;

(b) Watercraft of all types, and their furnishings, equipment and outboard engines or motors; or

(c) Property while at any other residence owned by, rented to, or occupied by an "insured", except while an "insured" is temporarily living there. Property of an "insured" who is a student is covered while at the residence the student occupies to attend school as long as the student has been there at any time during the 60 days immediately before the loss.

10. Falling Objects

This peril does not include loss to property contained in a building unless the roof or an outside wall of the building is first damaged by a falling object. Damage to the falling object itself is not included.

11. Weight Of Ice, Snow Or Sleet

This peril means weight of ice, snow or sleet which causes damage to property contained in a building.

         HO 00 03 10 00

12. **Accidental Discharge Or Overflow Of Water Or Steam**

   a. This peril means accidental discharge or overflow of water or steam from within a plumbing, heating, air conditioning or automatic fire protective sprinkler system or from within a household appliance.

   b. This peril does not include loss:

      (1) To the system or appliance from which the water or steam escaped;

      (2) Caused by or resulting from freezing except as provided in Peril Insured Against **14.** Freezing;

      (3) On the "residence premises" caused by accidental discharge or overflow which occurs off the "residence premises"; or

      (4) Caused by mold, fungus or wet rot unless hidden within the walls or ceilings or beneath the floors or above the ceilings of a structure.

   c. In this peril, a plumbing system or household appliance does not include a sump, sump pump or related equipment or a roof drain, gutter, downspout or similar fixtures or equipment.

   d. Section I – Exclusion **A.3.** Water Damage, Paragraphs **a.** and **c.** that apply to surface water and water below the surface of the ground do not apply to loss by water covered under this peril.

13. **Sudden And Accidental Tearing Apart, Cracking, Burning Or Bulging**

   This peril means sudden and accidental tearing apart, cracking, burning or bulging of a steam or hot water heating system, an air conditioning or automatic fire protective sprinkler system, or an appliance for heating water.

   We do not cover loss caused by or resulting from freezing under this peril.

14. **Freezing**

   a. This peril means freezing of a plumbing, heating, air conditioning or automatic fire protective sprinkler system or of a household appliance but only if you have used reasonable care to:

      (1) Maintain heat in the building; or

      (2) Shut off the water supply and drain all systems and appliances of water.

   However, if the building is protected by an automatic fire protective sprinkler system, you must use reasonable care to continue the water supply and maintain heat in the building for coverage to apply.

   b. In this peril, a plumbing system or household appliance does not include a sump, sump pump or related equipment or a roof drain, gutter, downspout or similar fixtures or equipment.

15. **Sudden And Accidental Damage From Artificially Generated Electrical Current**

   This peril does not include loss to tubes, transistors, electronic components or circuitry that are a part of appliances, fixtures, computers, home entertainment units or other types of electronic apparatus.

16. **Volcanic Eruption**

   This peril does not include loss caused by earthquake, land shock waves or tremors.

SECTION I – EXCLUSIONS

A. We do not insure for loss caused directly or indirectly by any of the following. Such loss is excluded regardless of any other cause or event contributing concurrently or in any sequence to the loss. These exclusions apply whether or not the loss event results in widespread damage or affects a substantial area.

1. **Ordinance Or Law**

   Ordinance Or Law means any ordinance or law:

   a. Requiring or regulating the construction, demolition, remodeling, renovation or repair of property, including removal of any resulting debris. This Exclusion **A.1.a.** does not apply to the amount of coverage that may be provided for in **E.11.** Ordinance Or Law under Section I – Property Coverages;

   b. The requirements of which result in a loss in value to property; or

   c. Requiring any "insured" or others to test for, monitor, clean up, remove, contain, treat, detoxify or neutralize, or in any way respond to, or assess the effects of, pollutants.

   Pollutants means any solid, liquid, gaseous or thermal irritant or contaminant, including smoke, vapor, soot, fumes, acids, alkalis, chemicals and waste. Waste includes materials to be recycled, reconditioned or reclaimed.

   This Exclusion **A.1.** applies whether or not the property has been physically damaged.

2. **Earth Movement**

   Earth Movement means:

   a. Earthquake, including land shock waves or tremors before, during or after a volcanic eruption;

b. Landslide, mudslide or mudflow;

c. Subsidence or sinkhole; or

d. Any other earth movement including earth sinking, rising or shifting;

caused by or resulting from human or animal forces or any act of nature unless direct loss by fire or explosion ensues and then we will pay only for the ensuing loss.

This Exclusion **A.2.** does not apply to loss by theft.

3. Water Damage

Water Damage means:

a. Flood, surface water, waves, tidal water, overflow of a body of water, or spray from any of these, whether or not driven by wind;

b. Water or water-borne material which backs up through sewers or drains or which overflows or is discharged from a sump, sump pump or related equipment; or

c. Water or water-borne material below the surface of the ground, including water which exerts pressure on or seeps or leaks through a building, sidewalk, driveway, foundation, swimming pool or other structure;

caused by or resulting from human or animal forces or any act of nature.

Direct loss by fire, explosion or theft resulting from water damage is covered.

4. Power Failure

Power Failure means the failure of power or other utility service if the failure takes place off the "residence premises". But if the failure results in a loss, from a Peril Insured Against on the "residence premises", we will pay for the loss caused by that peril.

5. Neglect

Neglect means neglect of an "insured" to use all reasonable means to save and preserve property at and after the time of a loss.

6. War

War includes the following and any consequence of any of the following:

a. Undeclared war, civil war, insurrection, rebellion or revolution;

b. Warlike act by a military force or military personnel; or

c. Destruction, seizure or use for a military purpose.

Discharge of a nuclear weapon will be deemed a warlike act even if accidental.

7. Nuclear Hazard

This Exclusion **A.7.** pertains to Nuclear Hazard to the extent set forth in **M.** Nuclear Hazard Clause under Section **I** – Conditions.

8. Intentional Loss

Intentional Loss means any loss arising out of any act an "insured" commits or conspires to commit with the intent to cause a loss.

In the event of such loss, no "insured" is entitled to coverage, even "insureds" who did not commit or conspire to commit the act causing the loss.

9. Governmental Action

Governmental Action means the destruction, confiscation or seizure of property described in Coverage **A, B** or **C** by order of any governmental or public authority.

This exclusion does not apply to such acts ordered by any governmental or public authority that are taken at the time of a fire to prevent its spread, if the loss caused by fire would be covered under this policy.

B. We do not insure for loss to property described in Coverages **A** and **B** caused by any of the following. However, any ensuing loss to property described in Coverages **A** and **B** not precluded by any other provision in this policy is covered.

1. Weather conditions. However, this exclusion only applies if weather conditions contribute in any way with a cause or event excluded in **A.** above to produce the loss.

2. Acts or decisions, including the failure to act or decide, of any person, group, organization or governmental body.

3. Faulty, inadequate or defective:

a. Planning, zoning, development, surveying, siting;

b. Design, specifications, workmanship, repair, construction, renovation, remodeling, grading, compaction;

c. Materials used in repair, construction, renovation or remodeling; or

d. Maintenance;

of part or all of any property whether on or off the "residence premises".

       HO 00 03 10 00

SECTION I – CONDITIONS

A. Insurable Interest And Limit Of Liability

Even if more than one person has an insurable interest in the property covered, we will not be liable in any one loss:

1. To an "insured" for more than the amount of such "insured's" interest at the time of loss; or

2. For more than the applicable limit of liability.

B. Duties After Loss

In case of a loss to covered property, we have no duty to provide coverage under this policy if the failure to comply with the following duties is prejudicial to us. These duties must be performed either by you, an "insured" seeking coverage, or a representative of either:

1. Give prompt notice to us or our agent;

2. Notify the police in case of loss by theft;

3. Notify the credit card or electronic fund transfer card or access device company in case of loss as provided for in **E.6.** Credit Card, Electronic Fund Transfer Card Or Access Device, Forgery And Counterfeit Money under Section **I** – Property Coverages;

4. Protect the property from further damage. If repairs to the property are required, you must:

   a. Make reasonable and necessary repairs to protect the property; and

   b. Keep an accurate record of repair expenses;

5. Cooperate with us in the investigation of a claim;

6. Prepare an inventory of damaged personal property showing the quantity, description, actual cash value and amount of loss. Attach all bills, receipts and related documents that justify the figures in the inventory;

7. As often as we reasonably require:

   a. Show the damaged property;

   b. Provide us with records and documents we request and permit us to make copies; and

   c. Submit to examination under oath, while not in the presence of another "insured", and sign the same;

8. Send to us, within 60 days after our request, your signed, sworn proof of loss which sets forth, to the best of your knowledge and belief:

   a. The time and cause of loss;

   b. The interests of all "insureds" and all others in the property involved and all liens on the property;

   c. Other insurance which may cover the loss;

d. Changes in title or occupancy of the property during the term of the policy;

e. Specifications of damaged buildings and detailed repair estimates;

f. The inventory of damaged personal property described in **6.** above;

g. Receipts for additional living expenses incurred and records that support the fair rental value loss; and

h. Evidence or affidavit that supports a claim under **E.6.** Credit Card, Electronic Fund Transfer Card Or Access Device, Forgery And Counterfeit Money under Section **I** – Property Coverages, stating the amount and cause of loss.

C. Loss Settlement

In this Condition **C.**, the terms "cost to repair or replace" and "replacement cost" do not include the increased costs incurred to comply with the enforcement of any ordinance or law, except to the extent that coverage for these increased costs is provided in **E.11.** Ordinance Or Law under Section **I** – Property Coverages. Covered property losses are settled as follows:

1. Property of the following types:

   a. Personal property;

   b. Awnings, carpeting, household appliances, outdoor antennas and outdoor equipment, whether or not attached to buildings;

   c. Structures that are not buildings; and

   d. Grave markers, including mausoleums;

   at actual cash value at the time of loss but not more than the amount required to repair or replace.

2. Buildings covered under Coverage **A** or **B** at replacement cost without deduction for depreciation, subject to the following:

   a. If, at the time of loss, the amount of insurance in this policy on the damaged building is 80% or more of the full replacement cost of the building immediately before the loss, we will pay the cost to repair or replace, after application of any deductible and without deduction for depreciation, but not more than the least of the following amounts:

      (1) The limit of liability under this policy that applies to the building;

      (2) The replacement cost of that part of the building damaged with material of like kind and quality and for like use; or

      (3) The necessary amount actually spent to repair or replace the damaged building.

If the building is rebuilt at a new premises, the cost described in **(2)** above is limited to the cost which would have been incurred if the building had been built at the original premises.

b. If, at the time of loss, the amount of insurance in this policy on the damaged building is less than 80% of the full replacement cost of the building immediately before the loss, we will pay the greater of the following amounts, but not more than the limit of liability under this policy that applies to the building:

(1) The actual cash value of that part of the building damaged; or

(2) That proportion of the cost to repair or replace, after application of any deductible and without deduction for depreciation, that part of the building damaged, which the total amount of insurance in this policy on the damaged building bears to 80% of the replacement cost of the building.

c. To determine the amount of insurance required to equal 80% of the full replacement cost of the building immediately before the loss, do not include the value of:

(1) Excavations, footings, foundations, piers, or any other structures or devices that support all or part of the building, which are below the undersurface of the lowest basement floor;

(2) Those supports described in **(1)** above which are below the surface of the ground inside the foundation walls, if there is no basement; and

(3) Underground flues, pipes, wiring and drains.

d. We will pay no more than the actual cash value of the damage until actual repair or replacement is complete. Once actual repair or replacement is complete, we will settle the loss as noted in **2.a.** and **b.** above.

However, if the cost to repair or replace the damage is both:

(1) Less than 5% of the amount of insurance in this policy on the building; and

(2) Less than $2,500;

we will settle the loss as noted in **2.a.** and **b.** above whether or not actual repair or replacement is complete.

e. You may disregard the replacement cost loss settlement provisions and make claim under this policy for loss to buildings on an actual cash value basis. You may then make claim for any additional liability according to the provisions of this Condition **C. Loss Settlement**, provided you notify us of your intent to do so within 180 days after the date of loss.

D. Loss To A Pair Or Set

In case of loss to a pair or set we may elect to:

1. Repair or replace any part to restore the pair or set to its value before the loss; or

2. Pay the difference between actual cash value of the property before and after the loss.

E. Appraisal

If you and we fail to agree on the amount of loss, either may demand an appraisal of the loss. In this event, each party will choose a competent and impartial appraiser within 20 days after receiving a written request from the other. The two appraisers will choose an umpire. If they cannot agree upon an umpire within 15 days, you or we may request that the choice be made by a judge of a court of record in the state where the "residence premises" is located. The appraisers will separately set the amount of loss. If the appraisers submit a written report of an agreement to us, the amount agreed upon will be the amount of loss. If they fail to agree, they will submit their differences to the umpire. A decision agreed to by any two will set the amount of loss.

Each party will:

1. Pay its own appraiser; and

2. Bear the other expenses of the appraisal and umpire equally.

F. Other Insurance And Service Agreement

If a loss covered by this policy is also covered by:

1. Other insurance, we will pay only the proportion of the loss that the limit of liability that applies under this policy bears to the total amount of insurance covering the loss; or

2. A service agreement, this insurance is excess over any amounts payable under any such agreement. Service agreement means a service plan, property restoration plan, home warranty or other similar service warranty agreement, even if it is characterized as insurance.

G. Suit Against Us

No action can be brought against us unless there has been full compliance with all of the terms under Section **I** of this policy and the action is started within two years after the date of loss.

     HO 00 03 10 00

H. Our Option

If we give you written notice within 30 days after we receive your signed, sworn proof of loss, we may repair or replace any part of the damaged property with material or property of like kind and quality.

I. Loss Payment

We will adjust all losses with you. We will pay you unless some other person is named in the policy or is legally entitled to receive payment. Loss will be payable 60 days after we receive your proof of loss and:

1. Reach an agreement with you;

2. There is an entry of a final judgment; or

3. There is a filing of an appraisal award with us.

J. Abandonment Of Property

We need not accept any property abandoned by an "insured".

K. Mortgage Clause

1. If a mortgagee is named in this policy, any loss payable under Coverage **A** or **B** will be paid to the mortgagee and you, as interests appear. If more than one mortgagee is named, the order of payment will be the same as the order of precedence of the mortgages.

2. If we deny your claim, that denial will not apply to a valid claim of the mortgagee, if the mortgagee:

   a. Notifies us of any change in ownership, occupancy or substantial change in risk of which the mortgagee is aware;

   b. Pays any premium due under this policy on demand if you have neglected to pay the premium; and

   c. Submits a signed, sworn statement of loss within 60 days after receiving notice from us of your failure to do so. Paragraphs **E.** Appraisal, **G.** Suit Against Us and **I.** Loss Payment under Section I – Conditions also apply to the mortgagee.

3. If we decide to cancel or not to renew this policy, the mortgagee will be notified at least 10 days before the date cancellation or nonrenewal takes effect.

4. If we pay the mortgagee for any loss and deny payment to you:

   a. We are subrogated to all the rights of the mortgagee granted under the mortgage on the property; or

   b. At our option, we may pay to the mortgagee the whole principal on the mortgage plus any accrued interest. In this event, we will receive a full assignment and transfer of the mortgage and all securities held as collateral to the mortgage debt.

5. Subrogation will not impair the right of the mortgagee to recover the full amount of the mortgagee's claim.

L. No Benefit To Bailee

We will not recognize any assignment or grant any coverage that benefits a person or organization holding, storing or moving property for a fee regardless of any other provision of this policy.

M. Nuclear Hazard Clause

1. "Nuclear Hazard" means any nuclear reaction, radiation, or radioactive contamination, all whether controlled or uncontrolled or however caused, or any consequence of any of these.

2. Loss caused by the nuclear hazard will not be considered loss caused by fire, explosion, or smoke, whether these perils are specifically named in or otherwise included within the Perils Insured Against.

3. This policy does not apply under Section I to loss caused directly or indirectly by nuclear hazard, except that direct loss by fire resulting from the nuclear hazard is covered.

N. Recovered Property

If you or we recover any property for which we have made payment under this policy, you or we will notify the other of the recovery. At your option, the property will be returned to or retained by you or it will become our property. If the recovered property is returned to or retained by you, the loss payment will be adjusted based on the amount you received for the recovered property.

O. Volcanic Eruption Period

One or more volcanic eruptions that occur within a 72 hour period will be considered as one volcanic eruption.

P. Policy Period

This policy applies only to loss which occurs during the policy period.

Q. Concealment Or Fraud

We provide coverage to no "insureds" under this policy if, whether before or after a loss, an "insured" has:

1. Intentionally concealed or misrepresented any material fact or circumstance;

2. Engaged in fraudulent conduct; or

3. Made false statements;

relating to this insurance.

R. Loss Payable Clause

If the Declarations show a loss payee for certain listed insured personal property, the definition of "insured" is changed to include that loss payee with respect to that property.

If we decide to cancel or not renew this policy, that loss payee will be notified in writing.

SECTION II – LIABILITY COVERAGES

A. Coverage E – Personal Liability

If a claim is made or a suit is brought against an "insured" for damages because of "bodily injury" or "property damage" caused by an "occurrence" to which this coverage applies, we will:

1. Pay up to our limit of liability for the damages for which an "insured" is legally liable. Damages include prejudgment interest awarded against an "insured"; and

2. Provide a defense at our expense by counsel of our choice, even if the suit is groundless, false or fraudulent. We may investigate and settle any claim or suit that we decide is appropriate. Our duty to settle or defend ends when our limit of liability for the "occurrence" has been exhausted by payment of a judgment or settlement.

B. Coverage F – Medical Payments To Others

We will pay the necessary medical expenses that are incurred or medically ascertained within three years from the date of an accident causing "bodily injury". Medical expenses means reasonable charges for medical, surgical, x-ray, dental, ambulance, hospital, professional nursing, prosthetic devices and funeral services. This coverage does not apply to you or regular residents of your household except "residence employees". As to others, this coverage applies only:

1. To a person on the "insured location" with the permission of an "insured"; or

2. To a person off the "insured location", if the "bodily injury":

  a. Arises out of a condition on the "insured location" or the ways immediately adjoining;

  b. Is caused by the activities of an "insured";

  c. Is caused by a "residence employee" in the course of the "residence employee's" employment by an "insured"; or

  d. Is caused by an animal owned by or in the care of an "insured".

SECTION II – EXCLUSIONS

A. "Motor Vehicle Liability"

1. Coverages **E** and **F** do not apply to any "motor vehicle liability" if, at the time and place of an "occurrence", the involved "motor vehicle":

  a. Is registered for use on public roads or property;

  b. Is not registered for use on public roads or property, but such registration is required by a law, or regulation issued by a government agency, for it to be used at the place of the "occurrence"; or

  c. Is being:

    (1) Operated in, or practicing for, any pre-arranged or organized race, speed contest or other competition;

    (2) Rented to others;

    (3) Used to carry persons or cargo for a charge; or

    (4) Used for any "business" purpose except for a motorized golf cart while on a golfing facility.

2. If Exclusion **A.1.** does not apply, there is still no coverage for "motor vehicle liability" unless the "motor vehicle" is:

  a. In dead storage on an "insured location";

  b. Used solely to service an "insured's" residence;

  c. Designed to assist the handicapped and, at the time of an "occurrence", it is:

    (1) Being used to assist a handicapped person; or

    (2) Parked on an "insured location";

  d. Designed for recreational use off public roads and:

    (1) Not owned by an "insured"; or

    (2) Owned by an "insured" provided the "occurrence" takes place on an "insured location" as defined in Definitions **B. 6.a., b., d., e.** or **h.**; or

  e. A motorized golf cart that is owned by an "insured", designed to carry up to 4 persons, not built or modified after manufacture to exceed a speed of 25 miles per hour on level ground and, at the time of an "occurrence", is within the legal boundaries of:

    (1) A golfing facility and is parked or stored there, or being used by an "insured" to:

      (a) Play the game of golf or for other recreational or leisure activity allowed by the facility;

       HO 00 03 10 00

(b) Travel to or from an area where "motor vehicles" or golf carts are parked or stored; or

(c) Cross public roads at designated points to access other parts of the golfing facility; or

(2) A private residential community, including its public roads upon which a motorized golf cart can legally travel, which is subject to the authority of a property owners association and contains an "insured's" residence.

B. "Watercraft Liability"

1. Coverages **E** and **F** do not apply to any "watercraft liability" if, at the time of an "occurrence", the involved watercraft is being:

a. Operated in, or practicing for, any prearranged or organized race, speed contest or other competition. This exclusion does not apply to a sailing vessel or a predicted log cruise;

b. Rented to others;

c. Used to carry persons or cargo for a charge; or

d. Used for any "business" purpose.

2. If Exclusion **B.1.** does not apply, there is still no coverage for "watercraft liability" unless, at the time of the "occurrence", the watercraft:

a. Is stored;

b. Is a sailing vessel, with or without auxiliary power, that is:

(1) Less than 26 feet in overall length; or

(2) 26 feet or more in overall length and not owned by or rented to an "insured"; or

c. Is not a sailing vessel and is powered by:

(1) An inboard or inboard-outdrive engine or motor, including those that power a water jet pump, of:

(a) 50 horsepower or less and not owned by an "insured"; or

(b) More than 50 horsepower and not owned by or rented to an "insured"; or

(2) One or more outboard engines or motors with:

(a) 25 total horsepower or less;

(b) More than 25 horsepower if the outboard engine or motor is not owned by an "insured";

(c) More than 25 horsepower if the outboard engine or motor is owned by an "insured" who acquired it during the policy period; or

(d) More than 25 horsepower if the outboard engine or motor is owned by an "insured" who acquired it before the policy period, but only if:

(i) You declare them at policy inception; or

(ii) Your intent to insure them is reported to us in writing within 45 days after you acquire them.

The coverages in **(c)** and **(d)** above apply for the policy period.

Horsepower means the maximum power rating assigned to the engine or motor by the manufacturer.

C. "Aircraft Liability"

This policy does not cover "aircraft liability".

D. "Hovercraft Liability"

This policy does not cover "hovercraft liability".

E. Coverage E – Personal Liability And Coverage F – Medical Payments To Others

Coverages **E** and **F** do not apply to the following:

1. Expected Or Intended Injury

"Bodily injury" or "property damage" which is expected or intended by an "insured" even if the resulting "bodily injury" or "property damage":

a. Is of a different kind, quality or degree than initially expected or intended; or

b. Is sustained by a different person, entity, real or personal property, than initially expected or intended.

However, this Exclusion **E.1.** does not apply to "bodily injury" resulting from the use of reasonable force by an "insured" to protect persons or property;

2. "Business"

a. "Bodily injury" or "property damage" arising out of or in connection with a "business" conducted from an "insured location" or engaged in by an "insured", whether or not the "business" is owned or operated by an "insured" or employs an "insured".

This Exclusion **E.2.** applies but is not limited to an act or omission, regardless of its nature or circumstance, involving a service or duty rendered, promised, owed, or implied to be provided because of the nature of the "business".

b. This Exclusion **E.2.** does not apply to:

(1) The rental or holding for rental of an "insured location";

(a) On an occasional basis if used only as a residence;

(b) In part for use only as a residence, unless a single family unit is intended for use by the occupying family to lodge more than two roomers or boarders; or

(c) In part, as an office, school, studio or private garage; and

(2) An "insured" under the age of 21 years involved in a part-time or occasional, self-employed "business" with no employees;

3. Professional Services

"Bodily injury" or "property damage" arising out of the rendering of or failure to render professional services;

4. "Insured's" Premises Not An "Insured Location"

"Bodily injury" or "property damage" arising out of a premises:

a. Owned by an "insured";

b. Rented to an "insured"; or

c. Rented to others by an "insured";

that is not an "insured location";

5. War

"Bodily injury" or "property damage" caused directly or indirectly by war, including the following and any consequence of any of the following:

a. Undeclared war, civil war, insurrection, rebellion or revolution;

b. Warlike act by a military force or military personnel; or

c. Destruction, seizure or use for a military purpose.

Discharge of a nuclear weapon will be deemed a warlike act even if accidental;

6. Communicable Disease

"Bodily injury" or "property damage" which arises out of the transmission of a communicable disease by an "insured";

7. Sexual Molestation, Corporal Punishment Or Physical Or Mental Abuse

"Bodily injury" or "property damage" arising out of sexual molestation, corporal punishment or physical or mental abuse; or

8. Controlled Substance

"Bodily injury" or "property damage" arising out of the use, sale, manufacture, delivery, transfer or possession by any person of a Controlled Substance as defined by the Federal Food and Drug Law at 21 U.S.C.A. Sections 811 and 812. Controlled Substances include but are not limited to cocaine, LSD, marijuana and all narcotic drugs. However, this exclusion does not apply to the legitimate use of prescription drugs by a person following the orders of a licensed physician.

Exclusions **A.** "Motor Vehicle Liability", **B.** "Watercraft Liability", **C.** "Aircraft Liability", **D.** "Hovercraft Liability" and **E.4.** "Insured's" Premises Not An "Insured Location" do not apply to "bodily injury" to a "residence employee" arising out of and in the course of the "residence employee's" employment by an "insured".

F. Coverage E – Personal Liability

Coverage **E** does not apply to:

1. Liability:

a. For any loss assessment charged against you as a member of an association, corporation or community of property owners, except as provided in **D.** Loss Assessment under Section **II** – Additional Coverages;

b. Under any contract or agreement entered into by an "insured". However, this exclusion does not apply to written contracts:

(1) That directly relate to the ownership, maintenance or use of an "insured location"; or

(2) Where the liability of others is assumed by you prior to an "occurrence";

unless excluded in **a.** above or elsewhere in this policy;

2. "Property damage" to property owned by an "insured". This includes costs or expenses incurred by an "insured" or others to repair, replace, enhance, restore or maintain such property to prevent injury to a person or damage to property of others, whether on or away from an "insured location";

3. "Property damage" to property rented to, occupied or used by or in the care of an "insured". This exclusion does not apply to "property damage" caused by fire, smoke or explosion;

4. "Bodily injury" to any person eligible to receive any benefits voluntarily provided or required to be provided by an "insured" under any:

a. Workers' compensation law;

b. Non-occupational disability law; or

c. Occupational disease law;

5. "Bodily injury" or "property damage" for which an "insured" under this policy:

a. Is also an insured under a nuclear energy liability policy issued by the:

(1) Nuclear Energy Liability Insurance Association;

(2) Mutual Atomic Energy Liability Underwriters;

(3) Nuclear Insurance Association of Canada;

or any of their successors; or

b. Would be an insured under such a policy but for the exhaustion of its limit of liability; or

6. "Bodily injury" to you or an "insured" as defined under Definitions **5.a.** or **b.**

This exclusion also applies to any claim made or suit brought against you or an "insured":

a. To repay; or

b. Share damages with;

another person who may be obligated to pay damages because of "bodily injury" to an "insured".

G. Coverage F – Medical Payments To Others

Coverage **F** does not apply to "bodily injury":

1. To a "residence employee" if the "bodily injury":

a. Occurs off the "insured location"; and

b. Does not arise out of or in the course of the "residence employee's" employment by an "insured";

2. To any person eligible to receive benefits voluntarily provided or required to be provided under any:

a. Workers' compensation law;

b. Non-occupational disability law; or

c. Occupational disease law;

3. From any:

a. Nuclear reaction;

b. Nuclear radiation; or

c. Radioactive contamination;

all whether controlled or uncontrolled or however caused; or

d. Any consequence of any of these; or

4. To any person, other than a "residence employee" of an "insured", regularly residing on any part of the "insured location".

SECTION II – ADDITIONAL COVERAGES

We cover the following in addition to the limits of liability:

A. Claim Expenses

We pay:

1. Expenses we incur and costs taxed against an "insured" in any suit we defend;

2. Premiums on bonds required in a suit we defend, but not for bond amounts more than the Coverage **E** limit of liability. We need not apply for or furnish any bond;

3. Reasonable expenses incurred by an "insured" at our request, including actual loss of earnings (but not loss of other income) up to $250 per day, for assisting us in the investigation or defense of a claim or suit; and

4. Interest on the entire judgment which accrues after entry of the judgment and before we pay or tender, or deposit in court that part of the judgment which does not exceed the limit of liability that applies.

B. First Aid Expenses

We will pay expenses for first aid to others incurred by an "insured" for "bodily injury" covered under this policy. We will not pay for first aid to an "insured".

C. Damage To Property Of Others

1. We will pay, at replacement cost, up to $1,000 per "occurrence" for "property damage" to property of others caused by an "insured".

2. We will not pay for "property damage":

a. To the extent of any amount recoverable under Section **I**;

b. Caused intentionally by an "insured" who is 13 years of age or older;

c. To property owned by an "insured";

d. To property owned by or rented to a tenant of an "insured" or a resident in your household; or

e. Arising out of:

(1) A "business" engaged in by an "insured";

(2) Any act or omission in connection with a premises owned, rented or controlled by an "insured", other than the "insured location"; or

(3) The ownership, maintenance, occupancy, operation, use, loading or unloading of aircraft, hovercraft, watercraft or "motor vehicles".

This exclusion **e.(3)** does not apply to a "motor vehicle" that:

(a) Is designed for recreational use off public roads;

(b) Is not owned by an "insured"; and

(c) At the time of the "occurrence", is not required by law, or regulation issued by a government agency, to have been registered for it to be used on public roads or property.

D. Loss Assessment

1. We will pay up to $1,000 for your share of loss assessment charged against you, as owner or tenant of the "residence premises", during the policy period by a corporation or association of property owners, when the assessment is made as a result of:

   a. "Bodily injury" or "property damage" not excluded from coverage under Section II – Exclusions; or

   b. Liability for an act of a director, officer or trustee in the capacity as a director, officer or trustee, provided such person:

      (1) Is elected by the members of a corporation or association of property owners; and

      (2) Serves without deriving any income from the exercise of duties which are solely on behalf of a corporation or association of property owners.

2. Paragraph I. Policy Period under Section II – Conditions does not apply to this Loss Assessment Coverage.

3. Regardless of the number of assessments, the limit of $1,000 is the most we will pay for loss arising out of:

   a. One accident, including continuous or repeated exposure to substantially the same general harmful condition; or

   b. A covered act of a director, officer or trustee. An act involving more than one director, officer or trustee is considered to be a single act.

4. We do not cover assessments charged against you or a corporation or association of property owners by any governmental body.

SECTION II – CONDITIONS

A. Limit Of Liability

Our total liability under Coverage **E** for all damages resulting from any one "occurrence" will not be more than the Coverage **E** limit of liability shown in the Declarations. This limit is the same regardless of the number of "insureds", claims made or persons injured. All "bodily injury" and "property damage" resulting from any one accident or from continuous or repeated exposure to substantially the same general harmful conditions shall be considered to be the result of one "occurrence".

Our total liability under Coverage **F** for all medical expense payable for "bodily injury" to one person as the result of one accident will not be more than the Coverage **F** limit of liability shown in the Declarations.

B. Severability Of Insurance

This insurance applies separately to each "insured". This condition will not increase our limit of liability for any one "occurrence".

C. Duties After "Occurrence"

In case of an "occurrence", you or another "insured" will perform the following duties that apply. We have no duty to provide coverage under this policy if your failure to comply with the following duties is prejudicial to us. You will help us by seeing that these duties are performed:

1. Give written notice to us or our agent as soon as is practical, which sets forth:

   a. The identity of the policy and the "named insured" shown in the Declarations;

   b. Reasonably available information on the time, place and circumstances of the "occurrence"; and

   c. Names and addresses of any claimants and witnesses;

2. Cooperate with us in the investigation, settlement or defense of any claim or suit;

3. Promptly forward to us every notice, demand, summons or other process relating to the "occurrence";

4. At our request, help us:

   a. To make settlement;

   b. To enforce any right of contribution or indemnity against any person or organization who may be liable to an "insured";

       HO 00 03 10 00

c. With the conduct of suits and attend hearings and trials; and

d. To secure and give evidence and obtain the attendance of witnesses;

5. With respect to **C.** Damage To Property Of Others under Section **II** – Additional Coverages, submit to us within 60 days after the loss, a sworn statement of loss and show the damaged property, if in an "insured's" control;

6. No "insured" shall, except at such "insured's" own cost, voluntarily make payment, assume obligation or incur expense other than for first aid to others at the time of the "bodily injury".

D. Duties Of An Injured Person – Coverage F – Medical Payments To Others

1. The injured person or someone acting for the injured person will:

a. Give us written proof of claim, under oath if required, as soon as is practical; and

b. Authorize us to obtain copies of medical reports and records.

2. The injured person will submit to a physical exam by a doctor of our choice when and as often as we reasonably require.

E. Payment Of Claim – Coverage F – Medical Payments To Others

Payment under this coverage is not an admission of liability by an "insured" or us.

F. Suit Against Us

1. No action can be brought against us unless there has been full compliance with all of the terms under this Section **II**.

2. No one will have the right to join us as a party to any action against an "insured".

3. Also, no action with respect to Coverage **E** can be brought against us until the obligation of such "insured" has been determined by final judgment or agreement signed by us.

G. Bankruptcy Of An "Insured"

Bankruptcy or insolvency of an "insured" will not relieve us of our obligations under this policy.

H. Other Insurance

This insurance is excess over other valid and collectible insurance except insurance written specifically to cover as excess over the limits of liability that apply in this policy.

I. Policy Period

This policy applies only to "bodily injury" or "property damage" which occurs during the policy period.

J. Concealment Or Fraud

We do not provide coverage to an "insured" who, whether before or after a loss, has:

1. Intentionally concealed or misrepresented any material fact or circumstance;

2. Engaged in fraudulent conduct; or

3. Made false statements;

relating to this insurance.

SECTIONS I AND II – CONDITIONS

A. Liberalization Clause

If we make a change which broadens coverage under this edition of our policy without additional premium charge, that change will automatically apply to your insurance as of the date we implement the change in your state, provided that this implementation date falls within 60 days prior to or during the policy period stated in the Declarations.

This Liberalization Clause does not apply to changes implemented with a general program revision that includes both broadenings and restrictions in coverage, whether that general program revision is implemented through introduction of:

1. A subsequent edition of this policy; or

2. An amendatory endorsement.

B. Waiver Or Change Of Policy Provisions

A waiver or change of a provision of this policy must be in writing by us to be valid. Our request for an appraisal or examination will not waive any of our rights.

C. Cancellation

1. You may cancel this policy at any time by returning it to us or by letting us know in writing of the date cancellation is to take effect.

2. We may cancel this policy only for the reasons stated below by letting you know in writing of the date cancellation takes effect. This cancellation notice may be delivered to you, or mailed to you at your mailing address shown in the Declarations. Proof of mailing will be sufficient proof of notice.

a. When you have not paid the premium, we may cancel at any time by letting you know at least 10 days before the date cancellation takes effect.

b. When this policy has been in effect for less than 60 days and is not a renewal with us, we may cancel for any reason by letting you know at least 10 days before the date cancellation takes effect.

c. When this policy has been in effect for 60 days or more, or at any time if it is a renewal with us, we may cancel:

    (1) If there has been a material misrepresentation of fact which if known to us would have caused us not to issue the policy; or

    (2) If the risk has changed substantially since the policy was issued.

    This can be done by letting you know at least 30 days before the date cancellation takes effect.

d. When this policy is written for a period of more than one year, we may cancel for any reason at anniversary by letting you know at least 30 days before the date cancellation takes effect.

3. When this policy is canceled, the premium for the period from the date of cancellation to the expiration date will be refunded pro rata.

4. If the return premium is not refunded with the notice of cancellation or when this policy is returned to us, we will refund it within a reasonable time after the date cancellation takes effect.

D. Nonrenewal

We may elect not to renew this policy. We may do so by delivering to you, or mailing to you at your mailing address shown in the Declarations, written notice at least 30 days before the expiration date of this policy. Proof of mailing will be sufficient proof of notice.

E. Assignment

Assignment of this policy will not be valid unless we give our written consent.

F. Subrogation

An "insured" may waive in writing before a loss all rights of recovery against any person. If not waived, we may require an assignment of rights of recovery for a loss to the extent that payment is made by us.

If an assignment is sought, an "insured" must sign and deliver all related papers and cooperate with us.

Subrogation does not apply to Coverage **F** or Paragraph **C.** Damage To Property Of Others under Section **II** – Additional Coverages.

G. Death

If any person named in the Declarations or the spouse, if a resident of the same household, dies, the following apply:

1. We insure the legal representative of the deceased but only with respect to the premises and property of the deceased covered under the policy at the time of death; and

2. "Insured" includes:

    a. An "insured" who is a member of your household at the time of your death, but only while a resident of the "residence premises"; and

    b. With respect to your property, the person having proper temporary custody of the property until appointment and qualification of a legal representative.

HO 00 03 10 00

COMMERCIAL GENERAL LIABILITY COVERAGE FORM

Various provisions in this policy restrict coverage. Read the entire policy carefully to determine rights, duties and what is and is not covered.

Throughout this policy the words "you" and "your" refer to the Named Insured shown in the Declarations, and any other person or organization qualifying as a Named Insured under this policy. The words "we", "us" and "our" refer to the company providing this insurance.

The word "insured" means any person or organization qualifying as such under Section **II** – Who Is An Insured.

Other words and phrases that appear in quotation marks have special meaning. Refer to Section **V** – Definitions.

SECTION I – COVERAGES

COVERAGE A BODILY INJURY AND PROPERTY DAMAGE LIABILITY

1. Insuring Agreement

   a. We will pay those sums that the insured becomes legally obligated to pay as damages because of "bodily injury" or "property damage" to which this insurance applies. We will have the right and duty to defend the insured against any "suit" seeking those damages. However, we will have no duty to defend the insured against any "suit" seeking damages for "bodily injury" or "property damage" to which this insurance does not apply. We may, at our discretion, investigate any "occurrence" and settle any claim or "suit" that may result. But:

   (1) The amount we will pay for damages is limited as described in Section **III** – Limits Of Insurance; and

   (2) Our right and duty to defend end when we have used up the applicable limit of insurance in the payment of judgments or settlements under Coverages **A** or **B** or medical expenses under Coverage **C**.

   No other obligation or liability to pay sums or perform acts or services is covered unless explicitly provided for under Supplementary Payments – Coverages **A** and **B**.

   b. This insurance applies to "bodily injury" and "property damage" only if:

   (1) The "bodily injury" or "property damage" is caused by an "occurrence" that takes place in the "coverage territory"; and

   (2) The "bodily injury" or "property damage" occurs during the policy period.

   c. Damages because of "bodily injury" include damages claimed by any person or organization for care, loss of services or death resulting at any time from the "bodily injury".

2. Exclusions

This insurance does not apply to:

a. Expected Or Intended Injury

   "Bodily injury" or "property damage" expected or intended from the standpoint of the insured. This exclusion does not apply to "bodily injury" resulting from the use of reasonable force to protect persons or property.

b. Contractual Liability

   "Bodily injury" or "property damage" for which the insured is obligated to pay damages by reason of the assumption of liability in a contract or agreement. This exclusion does not apply to liability for damages:

   (1) That the insured would have in the absence of the contract or agreement; or

   (2) Assumed in a contract or agreement that is an "insured contract", provided the "bodily injury" or "property damage" occurs subsequent to the execution of the contract or agreement. Solely for the purposes of liability assumed in an "insured contract", reasonable attorney fees and necessary litigation expenses incurred by or for a party other than an insured are deemed to be damages because of "bodily injury" or "property damage", provided:

   (a) Liability to such party for, or for the cost of, that party's defense has also been assumed in the same "insured contract"; and

(b) Such attorney fees and litigation expenses are for defense of that party against a civil or alternative dispute resolution proceeding in which damages to which this insurance applies are alleged.

c. Liquor Liability

"Bodily injury" or "property damage" for which any insured may be held liable by reason of:

(1) Causing or contributing to the intoxication of any person;

(2) The furnishing of alcoholic beverages to a person under the legal drinking age or under the influence of alcohol; or

(3) Any statute, ordinance or regulation relating to the sale, gift, distribution or use of alcoholic beverages.

This exclusion applies only if you are in the business of manufacturing, distributing, selling, serving or furnishing alcoholic beverages.

d. Workers' Compensation And Similar Laws

Any obligation of the insured under a workers' compensation, disability benefits or unemployment compensation law or any similar law.

e. Employer's Liability

"Bodily injury" to:

(1) An "employee" of the insured arising out of and in the course of:

(a) Employment by the insured; or

(b) Performing duties related to the conduct of the insured's business; or

(2) The spouse, child, parent, brother or sister of that "employee" as a consequence of Paragraph **(1)** above.

This exclusion applies:

(1) Whether the insured may be liable as an employer or in any other capacity; and

(2) To any obligation to share damages with or repay someone else who must pay damages because of the injury.

This exclusion does not apply to liability assumed by the insured under an "insured contract".

f. Pollution

(1) "Bodily injury" or "property damage" arising out of the actual, alleged or threatened discharge, dispersal, seepage, migration, release or escape of "pollutants":

(a) At or from any premises, site or location which is or was at any time owned or occupied by, or rented or loaned to, any insured. However, this subparagraph does not apply to:

(i) "Bodily injury" if sustained within a building and caused by smoke, fumes, vapor or soot from equipment used to heat that building;

(ii) "Bodily injury" or "property damage" for which you may be held liable, if you are a contractor and the owner or lessee of such premises, site or location has been added to your policy as an additional insured with respect to your ongoing operations performed for that additional insured at that premises, site or location and such premises, site or location is not and never was owned or occupied by, or rented or loaned to, any insured, other than that additional insured; or

(iii) "Bodily injury" or "property damage" arising out of heat, smoke or fumes from a "hostile fire";

(b) At or from any premises, site or location which is or was at any time used by or for any insured or others for the handling, storage, disposal, processing or treatment of waste;

(c) Which are or were at any time transported, handled, stored, treated, disposed of, or processed as waste by or for any insured or any person or organization for whom you may be legally responsible; or

(d) At or from any premises, site or location on which any insured or any contractors or subcontractors working directly or indirectly on any insured's behalf are performing operations if the "pollutants" are brought on or to the premises, site or location in connection with such operations by such insured, contractor or subcontractor. However, this subparagraph does not apply to:

(i) "Bodily injury" or "property damage" arising out of the escape of fuels, lubricants or other operating fluids which are needed to perform the normal electrical, hydraulic or mechanical functions necessary for the operation of "mobile equipment" or its parts, if such fuels, lubricants or other operating fluids escape from a vehicle part designed to hold, store or receive them. This exception does not apply if the "bodily injury" or "property damage" arises out of the intentional discharge, dispersal or release of the fuels, lubricants or other operating fluids, or if such fuels, lubricants or other operating fluids are brought on or to the premises, site or location with the intent that they be discharged, dispersed or released as part of the operations being performed by such insured, contractor or subcontractor;

(ii) "Bodily injury" or "property damage" sustained within a building and caused by the release of gases, fumes or vapors from materials brought into that building in connection with operations being performed by you or on your behalf by a contractor or subcontractor; or

(iii) "Bodily injury" or "property damage" arising out of heat, smoke or fumes from a "hostile fire".

(e) At or from any premises, site or location on which any insured or any contractors or subcontractors working directly or indirectly on any insured's behalf are performing operations if the operations are to test for, monitor, clean up, remove, contain, treat, detoxify or neutralize, or in any way respond to, or assess the effects of, "pollutants".

(2) Any loss, cost or expense arising out of any:

(a) Request, demand, order or statutory or regulatory requirement that any insured or others test for, monitor, clean up, remove, contain, treat, detoxify or neutralize, or in any way respond to, or assess the effects of, "pollutants"; or

(b) Claim or suit by or on behalf of a governmental authority for damages because of testing for, monitoring, cleaning up, removing, containing, treating, detoxifying or neutralizing, or in any way responding to, or assessing the effects of, "pollutants".

However, this paragraph does not apply to liability for damages because of "property damage" that the insured would have in the absence of such request, demand, order or statutory or regulatory requirement, or such claim or "suit" by or on behalf of a governmental authority.

g. Aircraft, Auto Or Watercraft

"Bodily injury" or "property damage" arising out of the ownership, maintenance, use or entrustment to others of any aircraft, "auto" or watercraft owned or operated by or rented or loaned to any insured. Use includes operation and "loading or unloading".

This exclusion does not apply to:

(1) A watercraft while ashore on premises you own or rent;

(2) A watercraft you do not own that is:

(a) Less than 26 feet long; and

(b) Not being used to carry persons or property for a charge;

(3) Parking an "auto" on, or on the ways next to, premises you own or rent, provided the "auto" is not owned by or rented or loaned to you or the insured;

(4) Liability assumed under any "insured contract" for the ownership, maintenance or use of aircraft or watercraft; or

(5) "Bodily injury" or "property damage" arising out of the operation of any of the equipment listed in Paragraph **f.(2)** or **f.(3)** of the definition of "mobile equipment".

h. Mobile Equipment

"Bodily injury" or "property damage" arising out of:

(1) The transportation of "mobile equipment" by an "auto" owned or operated by or rented or loaned to any insured; or

(2) The use of "mobile equipment" in, or while in practice for, or while being prepared for, any prearranged racing, speed, demolition, or stunting activity.

i. War

"Bodily injury" or "property damage" due to war, whether or not declared, or any act or condition incident to war. War includes civil war, insurrection, rebellion or revolution. This exclusion applies only to liability assumed under a contract or agreement.

j. Damage To Property

"Property damage" to:

(1) Property you own, rent, or occupy;

(2) Premises you sell, give away or abandon, if the "property damage" arises out of any part of those premises;

(3) Property loaned to you;

(4) Personal property in the care, custody or control of the insured;

(5) That particular part of real property on which you or any contractors or subcontractors working directly or indirectly on your behalf are performing operations, if the "property damage" arises out of those operations; or

(6) That particular part of any property that must be restored, repaired or replaced because "your work" was incorrectly performed on it.

Paragraphs (1), (3) and (4) of this exclusion do not apply to "property damage" (other than damage by fire) to premises, including the contents of such premises, rented to you for a period of 7 or fewer consecutive days. A separate limit of insurance applies to Damage To Premises Rented To You as described in Section III – Limits Of Insurance.

Paragraph (2) of this exclusion does not apply if the premises are "your work" and were never occupied, rented or held for rental by you.

Paragraphs (3), (4), (5) and (6) of this exclusion do not apply to liability assumed under a sidetrack agreement.

Paragraph (6) of this exclusion does not apply to "property damage" included in the "products-completed operations hazard".

k. Damage To Your Product

"Property damage" to "your product" arising out of it or any part of it.

l. Damage To Your Work

"Property damage" to "your work" arising out of it or any part of it and included in the "products-completed operations hazard".

This exclusion does not apply if the damaged work or the work out of which the damage arises was performed on your behalf by a subcontractor.

m. Damage To Impaired Property Or Property Not Physically Injured

"Property damage" to "impaired property" or property that has not been physically injured, arising out of:

(1) A defect, deficiency, inadequacy or dangerous condition in "your product" or "your work"; or

(2) A delay or failure by you or anyone acting on your behalf to perform a contract or agreement in accordance with its terms.

This exclusion does not apply to the loss of use of other property arising out of sudden and accidental physical injury to "your product" or "your work" after it has been put to its intended use.

n. Recall Of Products, Work Or Impaired Property

Damages claimed for any loss, cost or expense incurred by you or others for the loss of use, withdrawal, recall, inspection, repair, replacement, adjustment, removal or disposal of:

(1) "Your product";

(2) "Your work"; or

(3) "Impaired property";

if such product, work, or property is withdrawn or recalled from the market or from use by any person or organization because of a known or suspected defect, deficiency, inadequacy or dangerous condition in it.

o. Personal And Advertising Injury

"Bodily injury" arising out of "personal and advertising injury".

Exclusions c. through n. do not apply to damage by fire to premises while rented to you or temporarily occupied by you with permission of the owner. A separate limit of insurance applies to this coverage as described in Section III – Limits Of Insurance.

COVERAGE B PERSONAL AND ADVERTISING INJURY LIABILITY

1. Insuring Agreement

a. We will pay those sums that the insured becomes legally obligated to pay as damages because of "personal and advertising injury" to which this insurance applies. We will have the right and duty to defend the insured against any "suit" seeking those damages. However, we will have no duty to defend the insured against any "suit" seeking damages for "personal and advertising injury" to which this insurance does not apply. We may, at our discretion, investigate any offense and settle any claim or "suit" that may result. But:

  (1) The amount we will pay for damages is limited as described in Section **III** – Limits Of Insurance ; and

  (2) Our right and duty to defend end when we have used up the applicable limit of insurance in the payment of judgments or settlements under Coverages **A** or **B** or medical expenses under Coverage **C**.

No other obligation or liability to pay sums or perform acts or services is covered unless explicitly provided for under Supplementary Payments – Coverages **A** and **B**.

b. This insurance applies to "personal and advertising injury" caused by an offense arising out of your business but only if the offense was committed in the "coverage territory" during the policy period.

2. Exclusions

This insurance does not apply to:

a. "Personal and advertising injury":

  (1) Caused by or at the direction of the insured with the knowledge that the act would violate the rights of another and would inflict "personal and advertising injury";

  (2) Arising out of oral or written publication of material, if done by or at the direction of the insured with knowledge of its falsity;

  (3) Arising out of oral or written publication of material whose first publication took place before the beginning of the policy period;

  (4) Arising out of a criminal act committed by or at the direction of any insured;

  (5) For which the insured has assumed liability in a contract or agreement. This exclusion does not apply to liability for damages that the insured would have in the absence of the contract or agreement;

  (6) Arising out of a breach of contract, except an implied contract to use another's advertising idea in your "advertisement";

  (7) Arising out of the failure of goods, products or services to conform with any statement of quality or performance made in your "advertisement";

  (8) Arising out of the wrong description of the price of goods, products or services stated in your "advertisement";

  (9) Committed by an insured whose business is advertising, broadcasting, publishing or telecasting. However, this exclusion does not apply to Paragraphs **14.a., b.** and **c.** of "personal and advertising injury" under the Definitions Section; or

  (10) Arising out of the actual, alleged or threatened discharge, dispersal, seepage, migration, release or escape of "pollutants" at any time.

b. Any loss, cost or expense arising out of any:

  (1) Request, demand or order that any insured or others test for, monitor, clean up, remove, contain, treat, detoxify or neutralize, or in any way respond to, or assess the effects of, "pollutants"; or

  (2) Claim or suit by or on behalf of a governmental authority for damages because of testing for, monitoring, cleaning up, removing, containing, treating, detoxifying or neutralizing, or in any way responding to, or assessing the effects of, "pollutants".

COVERAGE C MEDICAL PAYMENTS

1. Insuring Agreement

a. We will pay medical expenses as described below for "bodily injury" caused by an accident:

  (1) On premises you own or rent;

  (2) On ways next to premises you own or rent; or

  (3) Because of your operations;

  provided that:

  (1) The accident takes place in the "coverage territory" and during the policy period;

  (2) The expenses are incurred and reported to us within one year of the date of the accident; and

  (3) The injured person submits to examination, at our expense, by physicians of our choice as often as we reasonably require.

b. We will make these payments regardless of fault. These payments will not exceed the applicable limit of insurance. We will pay reasonable expenses for:

   (1) First aid administered at the time of an accident;

   (2) Necessary medical, surgical, x-ray and dental services, including prosthetic devices; and

   (3) Necessary ambulance, hospital, professional nursing and funeral services.

2. Exclusions

We will not pay expenses for "bodily injury":

   a. To any insured.

   b. To a person hired to do work for or on behalf of any insured or a tenant of any insured.

   c. To a person injured on that part of premises you own or rent that the person normally occupies.

   d. To a person, whether or not an "employee" of any insured, if benefits for the "bodily injury" are payable or must be provided under a workers' compensation or disability benefits law or a similar law.

   e. To a person injured while taking part in athletics.

   f. Included within the "products-completed operations hazard".

   g. Excluded under Coverage **A**.

   h. Due to war, whether or not declared, or any act or condition incident to war. War includes civil war, insurrection, rebellion or revolution.

SUPPLEMENTARY PAYMENTS – COVERAGES A AND B

1. We will pay, with respect to any claim we investigate or settle, or any "suit" against an insured we defend:

   a. All expenses we incur.

   b. Up to $250 for cost of bail bonds required because of accidents or traffic law violations arising out of the use of any vehicle to which the Bodily Injury Liability Coverage applies. We do not have to furnish these bonds.

   c. The cost of bonds to release attachments, but only for bond amounts within the applicable limit of insurance. We do not have to furnish these bonds.

   d. All reasonable expenses incurred by the insured at our request to assist us in the investigation or defense of the claim or "suit", including actual loss of earnings up to $250 a day because of time off from work.

   e. All costs taxed against the insured in the "suit".

   f. Prejudgment interest awarded against the insured on that part of the judgment we pay. If we make an offer to pay the applicable limit of insurance, we will not pay any prejudgment interest based on that period of time after the offer.

   g. All interest on the full amount of any judgment that accrues after entry of the judgment and before we have paid, offered to pay, or deposited in court the part of the judgment that is within the applicable limit of insurance.

These payments will not reduce the limits of insurance.

2. If we defend an insured against a "suit" and an indemnitee of the insured is also named as a party to the "suit", we will defend that indemnitee if all of the following conditions are met:

   a. The "suit" against the indemnitee seeks damages for which the insured has assumed the liability of the indemnitee in a contract or agreement that is an "insured contract";

   b. This insurance applies to such liability assumed by the insured;

   c. The obligation to defend, or the cost of the defense of, that indemnitee, has also been assumed by the insured in the same "insured contract";

   d. The allegations in the "suit" and the information we know about the "occurrence" are such that no conflict appears to exist between the interests of the insured and the interests of the indemnitee;

   e. The indemnitee and the insured ask us to conduct and control the defense of that indemnitee against such "suit" and agree that we can assign the same counsel to defend the insured and the indemnitee; and

   f. The indemnitee:

      (1) Agrees in writing to:

         (a) Cooperate with us in the investigation, settlement or defense of the "suit";

         (b) Immediately send us copies of any demands, notices, summonses or legal papers received in connection with the "suit";

         (c) Notify any other insurer whose coverage is available to the indemnitee; and

         (d) Cooperate with us with respect to coordinating other applicable insurance available to the indemnitee; and

CG 00 01 07 98

(2) Provides us with written authorization to:

    (a) Obtain records and other information related to the "suit"; and

    (b) Conduct and control the defense of the indemnitee in such "suit".

So long as the above conditions are met, attorneys' fees incurred by us in the defense of that indemnitee, necessary litigation expenses incurred by us and necessary litigation expenses incurred by the indemnitee at our request will be paid as Supplementary Payments. Notwithstanding the provisions of Paragraph **2.b.(2)** of Section **I** – Coverage **A** – Bodily Injury And Property Damage Liability, such payments will not be deemed to be damages for "bodily injury" and "property damage" and will not reduce the limits of insurance.

Our obligation to defend an insured's indemnitee and to pay for attorneys' fees and necessary litigation expenses as Supplementary Payments ends when:

a. We have used up the applicable limit of insurance in the payment of judgments or settlements; or

b. The conditions set forth above, or the terms of the agreement described in Paragraph **f.** above, are no longer met.

SECTION II – WHO IS AN INSURED

1. If you are designated in the Declarations as:

a. An individual, you and your spouse are insureds, but only with respect to the conduct of a business of which you are the sole owner.

b. A partnership or joint venture, you are an insured. Your members, your partners, and their spouses are also insureds, but only with respect to the conduct of your business.

c. A limited liability company, you are an insured. Your members are also insureds, but only with respect to the conduct of your business. Your managers are insureds, but only with respect to their duties as your managers.

d. An organization other than a partnership, joint venture or limited liability company, you are an insured. Your "executive officers" and directors are insureds, but only with respect to their duties as your officers or directors. Your stockholders are also insureds, but only with respect to their liability as stockholders.

2. Each of the following is also an insured:

a. Your "employees", other than either your "executive officers" (if you are an organization other than a partnership, joint venture or limited liability company) or your managers (if you are a limited liability company), but only for acts within the scope of their employment by you or while performing duties related to the conduct of your business. However, none of these "employees" is an insured for:

    (1) "Bodily injury" or "personal and advertising injury":

        (a) To you, to your partners or members (if you are a partnership or joint venture), to your members (if you are a limited liability company), or to a co-"employee" while that co-"employee" is either in the course of his or her employment or performing duties related to the conduct of your business;

        (b) To the spouse, child, parent, brother or sister of that co-"employee" as a consequence of Paragraph **(1)(a)** above;

        (c) For which there is any obligation to share damages with or repay someone else who must pay damages because of the injury described in Paragraphs **(1)(a)** or **(b)** above; or

        (d) Arising out of his or her providing or failing to provide professional health care services.

    (2) "Property damage" to property:

        (a) Owned, occupied or used by,

        (b) Rented to, in the care, custody or control of, or over which physical control is being exercised for any purpose by

    you, any of your "employees", any partner or member (if you are a partnership or joint venture), or any member (if you are a limited liability company).

b. Any person (other than your "employee"), or any organization while acting as your real estate manager.

c. Any person or organization having proper temporary custody of your property if you die, but only:

    (1) With respect to liability arising out of the maintenance or use of that property; and

    (2) Until your legal representative has been appointed.

d. Your legal representative if you die, but only with respect to duties as such. That representative will have all your rights and duties under this Coverage Part.

3. With respect to "mobile equipment" registered in your name under any motor vehicle registration law, any person is an insured while driving such equipment along a public highway with your permission. Any other person or organization responsible for the conduct of such person is also an insured, but only with respect to liability arising out of the operation of the equipment, and only if no other insurance of any kind is available to that person or organization for this liability. However, no person or organization is an insured with respect to:

a. "Bodily injury" to a co-"employee" of the person driving the equipment; or

b. "Property damage" to property owned by, rented to, in the charge of or occupied by you or the employer of any person who is an insured under this provision.

4. Any organization you newly acquire or form, other than a partnership, joint venture or limited liability company, and over which you maintain ownership or majority interest, will qualify as a Named Insured if there is no other similar insurance available to that organization. However:

a. Coverage under this provision is afforded only until the 90th day after you acquire or form the organization or the end of the policy period, whichever is earlier;

b. Coverage **A** does not apply to "bodily injury" or "property damage" that occurred before you acquired or formed the organization; and

c. Coverage **B** does not apply to "personal and advertising injury" arising out of an offense committed before you acquired or formed the organization.

No person or organization is an insured with respect to the conduct of any current or past partnership, joint venture or limited liability company that is not shown as a Named Insured in the Declarations.

SECTION III – LIMITS OF INSURANCE

1. The Limits of Insurance shown in the Declarations and the rules below fix the most we will pay regardless of the number of:

a. Insureds;

b. Claims made or "suits" brought; or

c. Persons or organizations making claims or bringing "suits".

2. The General Aggregate Limit is the most we will pay for the sum of:

a. Medical expenses under Coverage **C**;

b. Damages under Coverage **A**, except damages because of "bodily injury" or "property damage" included in the "products-completed operations hazard"; and

c. Damages under Coverage **B**.

3. The Products-Completed Operations Aggregate Limit is the most we will pay under Coverage **A** for damages because of "bodily injury" and "property damage" included in the "products-completed operations hazard".

4. Subject to **2.** above, the Personal and Advertising Injury Limit is the most we will pay under Coverage **B** for the sum of all damages because of all "personal and advertising injury" sustained by any one person or organization.

5. Subject to **2.** or **3.** above, whichever applies, the Each Occurrence Limit is the most we will pay for the sum of:

a. Damages under Coverage **A**; and

b. Medical expenses under Coverage **C**

because of all "bodily injury" and "property damage" arising out of any one "occurrence".

6. Subject to **5.** above, the Damage To Premises Rented To You Limit is the most we will pay under Coverage **A** for damages because of "property damage" to any one premises, while rented to you, or in the case of damage by fire, while rented to you or temporarily occupied by you with permission of the owner.

7. Subject to **5.** above, the Medical Expense Limit is the most we will pay under Coverage **C** for all medical expenses because of "bodily injury" sustained by any one person.

The Limits of Insurance of this Coverage Part apply separately to each consecutive annual period and to any remaining period of less than 12 months, starting with the beginning of the policy period shown in the Declarations, unless the policy period is extended after issuance for an additional period of less than 12 months. In that case, the additional period will be deemed part of the last preceding period for purposes of determining the Limits of Insurance.

SECTION IV – COMMERCIAL GENERAL LIABILITY CONDITIONS

1. Bankruptcy

Bankruptcy or insolvency of the insured or of the insured's estate will not relieve us of our obligations under this Coverage Part.

2. Duties In The Event Of Occurrence, Offense, Claim Or Suit

a. You must see to it that we are notified as soon as practicable of an "occurrence" or an offense which may result in a claim. To the extent possible, notice should include:

(1) How, when and where the "occurrence" or offense took place;

(2) The names and addresses of any injured persons and witnesses; and

(3) The nature and location of any injury or damage arising out of the "occurrence" or offense.

b. If a claim is made or "suit" is brought against any insured, you must:

(1) Immediately record the specifics of the claim or "suit" and the date received; and

(2) Notify us as soon as practicable.

You must see to it that we receive written notice of the claim or "suit" as soon as practicable.

c. You and any other involved insured must:

(1) Immediately send us copies of any demands, notices, summonses or legal papers received in connection with the claim or "suit";

(2) Authorize us to obtain records and other information;

(3) Cooperate with us in the investigation or settlement of the claim or defense against the "suit"; and

(4) Assist us, upon our request, in the enforcement of any right against any person or organization which may be liable to the insured because of injury or damage to which this insurance may also apply.

d. No insured will, except at that insured's own cost, voluntarily make a payment, assume any obligation, or incur any expense, other than for first aid, without our consent.

3. Legal Action Against Us

No person or organization has a right under this Coverage Part:

a. To join us as a party or otherwise bring us into a "suit" asking for damages from an insured; or

b. To sue us on this Coverage Part unless all of its terms have been fully complied with.

A person or organization may sue us to recover on an agreed settlement or on a final judgment against an insured obtained after an actual trial; but we will not be liable for damages that are not payable under the terms of this Coverage Part or that are in excess of the applicable limit of insurance. An agreed settlement means a settlement and release of liability signed by us, the insured and the claimant or the claimant's legal representative.

4. Other Insurance

If other valid and collectible insurance is available to the insured for a loss we cover under Coverages **A** or **B** of this Coverage Part, our obligations are limited as follows:

a. Primary Insurance

This insurance is primary except when **b.** below applies. If this insurance is primary, our obligations are not affected unless any of the other insurance is also primary. Then, we will share with all that other insurance by the method described in **c.** below.

b. Excess Insurance

This insurance is excess over:

(1) Any of the other insurance, whether primary, excess, contingent or on any other basis:

(a) That is Fire, Extended Coverage, Builder's Risk, Installation Risk or similar coverage for "your work";

(b) That is Fire insurance for premises rented to you or temporarily occupied by you with permission of the owner;

(c) That is insurance purchased by you to cover your liability as a tenant for "property damage" to premises rented to you or temporarily occupied by you with permission of the owner; or

(d) If the loss arises out of the maintenance or use of aircraft, "autos" or watercraft to the extent not subject to Exclusion **g.** of Section **I** – Coverage **A** – Bodily Injury And Property Damage Liability.

(2) Any other primary insurance available to you covering liability for damages arising out of the premises or operations for which you have been added as an additional insured by attachment of an endorsement.

When this insurance is excess, we will have no duty under Coverages **A** or **B** to defend the insured against any "suit" if any other insurer has a duty to defend the insured against that "suit". If no other insurer defends, we will undertake to do so, but we will be entitled to the insured's rights against all those other insurers.

When this insurance is excess over other insurance, we will pay only our share of the amount of the loss, if any, that exceeds the sum of:

(1) The total amount that all such other insurance would pay for the loss in the absence of this insurance; and

(2) The total of all deductible and self-insured amounts under all that other insurance.

We will share the remaining loss, if any, with any other insurance that is not described in this Excess Insurance provision and was not bought specifically to apply in excess of the Limits of Insurance shown in the Declarations of this Coverage Part.

c. Method Of Sharing

If all of the other insurance permits contribution by equal shares, we will follow this method also. Under this approach each insurer contributes equal amounts until it has paid its applicable limit of insurance or none of the loss remains, whichever comes first.

If any of the other insurance does not permit contribution by equal shares, we will contribute by limits. Under this method, each insurer's share is based on the ratio of its applicable limit of insurance to the total applicable limits of insurance of all insurers.

5. Premium Audit

a. We will compute all premiums for this Coverage Part in accordance with our rules and rates.

b. Premium shown in this Coverage Part as advance premium is a deposit premium only. At the close of each audit period we will compute the earned premium for that period. Audit premiums are due and payable on notice to the first Named Insured. If the sum of the advance and audit premiums paid for the policy period is greater than the earned premium, we will return the excess to the first Named Insured.

c. The first Named Insured must keep records of the information we need for premium computation, and send us copies at such times as we may request.

6. Representations

By accepting this policy, you agree:

a. The statements in the Declarations are accurate and complete;

b. Those statements are based upon representations you made to us; and

c. We have issued this policy in reliance upon your representations.

7. Separation Of Insureds

Except with respect to the Limits of Insurance, and any rights or duties specifically assigned in this Coverage Part to the first Named Insured, this insurance applies:

a. As if each Named Insured were the only Named Insured; and

b. Separately to each insured against whom claim is made or "suit" is brought.

8. Transfer Of Rights Of Recovery Against Others To Us

If the insured has rights to recover all or part of any payment we have made under this Coverage Part, those rights are transferred to us. The insured must do nothing after loss to impair them. At our request, the insured will bring "suit" or transfer those rights to us and help us enforce them.

9. When We Do Not Renew

If we decide not to renew this Coverage Part, we will mail or deliver to the first Named Insured shown in the Declarations written notice of the nonrenewal not less than 30 days before the expiration date.

If notice is mailed, proof of mailing will be sufficient proof of notice.

SECTION V – DEFINITIONS

1. "Advertisement" means a notice that is broadcast or published to the general public or specific market segments about your goods, products or services for the purpose of attracting customers or supporters.

2. "Auto" means a land motor vehicle, trailer or semitrailer designed for travel on public roads, including any attached machinery or equipment. But "auto" does not include "mobile equipment".

3. "Bodily injury" means bodily injury, sickness or disease sustained by a person, including death resulting from any of these at any time.

4. "Coverage territory" means:

a. The United States of America (including its territories and possessions), Puerto Rico and Canada;

b. International waters or airspace, provided the injury or damage does not occur in the course of travel or transportation to or from any place not included in **a.** above; or

c. All parts of the world if:

(1) The injury or damage arises out of:

(a) Goods or products made or sold by you in the territory described in **a.** above; or

(b) The activities of a person whose home is in the territory described in **a.** above, but is away for a short time on your business; and

(2) The insured's responsibility to pay damages is determined in a "suit" on the merits, in the territory described in **a.** above or in a settlement we agree to.

5. "Employee" includes a "leased worker". "Employee" does not include a "temporary worker".

6. "Executive officer" means a person holding any of the officer positions created by your charter, constitution, by-laws or any other similar governing document.

7. "Hostile fire" means one which becomes uncontrollable or breaks out from where it was intended to be.

8. "Impaired property" means tangible property, other than "your product" or "your work", that cannot be used or is less useful because:

a. It incorporates "your product" or "your work" that is known or thought to be defective, deficient, inadequate or dangerous; or

b. You have failed to fulfill the terms of a contract or agreement;

if such property can be restored to use by:

a. The repair, replacement, adjustment or removal of "your product" or "your work"; or

b. Your fulfilling the terms of the contract or agreement.

9. "Insured contract" means:

a. A contract for a lease of premises. However, that portion of the contract for a lease of premises that indemnifies any person or organization for damage by fire to premises while rented to you or temporarily occupied by you with permission of the owner is not an "insured contract";

b. A sidetrack agreement;

c. Any easement or license agreement, except in connection with construction or demolition operations on or within 50 feet of a railroad;

d. An obligation, as required by ordinance, to indemnify a municipality, except in connection with work for a municipality;

e. An elevator maintenance agreement;

f. That part of any other contract or agreement pertaining to your business (including an indemnification of a municipality in connection with work performed for a municipality) under which you assume the tort liability of another party to pay for "bodily injury" or "property damage" to a third person or organization. Tort liability means a liability that would be imposed by law in the absence of any contract or agreement.

Paragraph **f.** does not include that part of any contract or agreement:

(1) That indemnifies a railroad for "bodily injury" or "property damage" arising out of construction or demolition operations, within 50 feet of any railroad property and affecting any railroad bridge or trestle, tracks, road-beds, tunnel, underpass or crossing;

(2) That indemnifies an architect, engineer or surveyor for injury or damage arising out of:

(a) Preparing, approving, or failing to prepare or approve, maps, shop drawings, opinions, reports, surveys, field orders, change orders or drawings and specifications; or

(b) Giving directions or instructions, or failing to give them, if that is the primary cause of the injury or damage; or

(3) Under which the insured, if an architect, engineer or surveyor, assumes liability for an injury or damage arising out of the insured's rendering or failure to render professional services, including those listed in (2) above and supervisory, inspection, architectural or engineering activities.

10. "Leased worker" means a person leased to you by a labor leasing firm under an agreement between you and the labor leasing firm, to perform duties related to the conduct of your business. "Leased worker" does not include a "temporary worker".

11. "Loading or unloading" means the handling of property:

a. After it is moved from the place where it is accepted for movement into or onto an aircraft, watercraft or "auto";

b. While it is in or on an aircraft, watercraft or "auto"; or

c. While it is being moved from an aircraft, watercraft or "auto" to the place where it is finally delivered;

but "loading or unloading" does not include the movement of property by means of a mechanical device, other than a hand truck, that is not attached to the aircraft, watercraft or "auto".

12. "Mobile equipment" means any of the following types of land vehicles, including any attached machinery or equipment:

a. Bulldozers, farm machinery, forklifts and other vehicles designed for use principally off public roads;

b. Vehicles maintained for use solely on or next to premises you own or rent;

c. Vehicles that travel on crawler treads;

d. Vehicles, whether self-propelled or not, maintained primarily to provide mobility to permanently mounted:

   (1) Power cranes, shovels, loaders, diggers or drills; or

   (2) Road construction or resurfacing equipment such as graders, scrapers or rollers;

e. Vehicles not described in **a.**, **b.**, **c.** or **d.** above that are not self-propelled and are maintained primarily to provide mobility to permanently attached equipment of the following types:

   (1) Air compressors, pumps and generators, including spraying, welding, building cleaning, geophysical exploration, lighting and well servicing equipment; or

   (2) Cherry pickers and similar devices used to raise or lower workers;

f. Vehicles not described in **a.**, **b.**, **c.** or **d.** above maintained primarily for purposes other than the transportation of persons or cargo.

   However, self-propelled vehicles with the following types of permanently attached equipment are not "mobile equipment" but will be considered "autos":

   (1) Equipment designed primarily for:

      (a) Snow removal;

      (b) Road maintenance, but not construction or resurfacing; or

      (c) Street cleaning;

   (2) Cherry pickers and similar devices mounted on automobile or truck chassis and used to raise or lower workers; and

   (3) Air compressors, pumps and generators, including spraying, welding, building cleaning, geophysical exploration, lighting and well servicing equipment.

13. "Occurrence" means an accident, including continuous or repeated exposure to substantially the same general harmful conditions.

14. "Personal and advertising injury" means injury, including consequential "bodily injury", arising out of one or more of the following offenses:

a. False arrest, detention or imprisonment;

b. Malicious prosecution;

c. The wrongful eviction from, wrongful entry into, or invasion of the right of private occupancy of a room, dwelling or premises that a person occupies, committed by or on behalf of its owner, landlord or lessor;

d. Oral or written publication of material that slanders or libels a person or organization or disparages a person's or organization's goods, products or services;

e. Oral or written publication of material that violates a person's right of privacy;

f. The use of another's advertising idea in your "advertisement"; or

g. Infringing upon another's copyright, trade dress or slogan in your "advertisement".

15. "Pollutants" mean any solid, liquid, gaseous or thermal irritant or contaminant, including smoke, vapor, soot, fumes, acids, alkalis, chemicals and waste. Waste includes materials to be recycled, reconditioned or reclaimed.

16. "Products-completed operations hazard":

a. Includes all "bodily injury" and "property damage" occurring away from premises you own or rent and arising out of "your product" or "your work" except:

   (1) Products that are still in your physical possession; or

   (2) Work that has not yet been completed or abandoned. However, "your work" will be deemed completed at the earliest of the following times:

      (a) When all of the work called for in your contract has been completed.

      (b) When all of the work to be done at the job site has been completed if your contract calls for work at more than one job site.

      (c) When that part of the work done at a job site has been put to its intended use by any person or organization other than another contractor or subcontractor working on the same project.

   Work that may need service, maintenance, correction, repair or replacement, but which is otherwise complete, will be treated as completed.

Copyright, Insurance Services Office, Inc., 1997   CG 00 01 07 98

b. Does not include "bodily injury" or "property damage" arising out of:

    (1) The transportation of property, unless the injury or damage arises out of a condition in or on a vehicle not owned or operated by you, and that condition was created by the "loading or unloading" of that vehicle by any insured;

    (2) The existence of tools, uninstalled equipment or abandoned or unused materials; or

    (3) Products or operations for which the classification, listed in the Declarations or in a policy schedule, states that products-completed operations are subject to the General Aggregate Limit.

17. "Property damage" means:

    a. Physical injury to tangible property, including all resulting loss of use of that property. All such loss of use shall be deemed to occur at the time of the physical injury that caused it; or

    b. Loss of use of tangible property that is not physically injured. All such loss of use shall be deemed to occur at the time of the "occurrence" that caused it.

18. "Suit" means a civil proceeding in which damages because of "bodily injury", "property damage" or "personal and advertising injury" to which this insurance applies are alleged. "Suit" includes:

    a. An arbitration proceeding in which such damages are claimed and to which the insured must submit or does submit with our consent; or

    b. Any other alternative dispute resolution proceeding in which such damages are claimed and to which the insured submits with our consent.

19. "Temporary worker" means a person who is furnished to you to substitute for a permanent "employee" on leave or to meet seasonal or short-term workload conditions.

20. "Your product" means:

    a. Any goods or products, other than real property, manufactured, sold, handled, distributed or disposed of by:

        (1) You;

        (2) Others trading under your name; or

        (3) A person or organization whose business or assets you have acquired; and

    b. Containers (other than vehicles), materials, parts or equipment furnished in connection with such goods or products.

"Your product" includes:

    a. Warranties or representations made at any time with respect to the fitness, quality, durability, performance or use of "your product"; and

    b. The providing of or failure to provide warnings or instructions.

"Your product" does not include vending machines or other property rented to or located for the use of others but not sold.

21. "Your work" means:

    a. Work or operations performed by you or on your behalf; and

    b. Materials, parts or equipment furnished in connection with such work or operations.

"Your work" includes:

    a. Warranties or representations made at any time with respect to the fitness, quality, durability, performance or use of "your work"; and

    b. The providing of or failure to provide warnings or instructions.

Key Words and Phrases

Define or describe each of the words and phrases listed below.

Occurrence (p. 3.3)

Exposure rule (p. 3.6)

Manifestation rule (p. 3.6)

Coverage trigger (p. 3.6)

Property damage (p. 3.8)

Punitive damages (pp. 3.9–3.10)

Motor vehicle (p. 3.13)

Expected results (p. 3.15)

Unintended consequences (p. 3.16)

Parental liability (p. 3.18)

Business activity (p. 3.20)

Insured location (p. 3.22)

Communicable disease (p. 3.23)

Controlled substance (p. 3.25)

Additional Coverages in Section II (p. 3.28)

Damage to Property of Others (p. 3.29)

Severability of interest (p. 3.31)

Insured contract (p. 3.39)

Mobile equipment (p. 3.45)

Negligent entrustment (with auto liability) (p. 3.46)

Loading and unloading (p. 3.47)

Your product (p. 3.51)

Your work (p. 3.51)

Each-occurrence limit (p. 3.53)

General aggregate limit (p. 3.54)

Products-completed operations aggregate limit (p. 3.54)

Products-completed operations hazard (p. 3.54)

Personal and advertising injury (p. 3.57)

Review Questions

1. Identify three controversial issues related to the determination of the term "occurrence." (pp. 3.3–3.7)

2. Coverage for punitive damages under insurance policies is controversial. Give one reason punitive damages should not be covered by insurance and two reasons courts have permitted coverage for punitive damages. (pp. 3.9–3.10)

3. Describe four requirements that a claim must meet in order to fall within the insuring agreement provisions of homeowners and commercial general liability (CGL) policies. (pp. 3.11–3.12)

4. Explain how the medical payments coverage under the homeowners policy (pp. 3.12–3.13)

   a.   Differs from the medical payments coverage found in auto policies.

   b. Is similar to the medical payments coverage found in auto policies.

5. Describe one exception to the motor vehicle exclusion in the homeowners policy. (p. 3.13)

6. Give an example of an unintended consequence of a deliberate act. Explain how coverage interpretation under the homeowners 2000 edition would likely apply to your example. (pp. 3.16–3.17)

7. Explain how an insured's deliberate injury of another, while the insured is intoxicated, might be covered in some states. (p. 3.17)

8. Describe three activities that claim representatives should perform in assessing coverage for intentional injuries. (p. 3.18)

9. Give an example of a business activity that does not make a profit that would likely be excluded under the homeowners 2000 policy. Give two examples of business activities that generate income that would not be excluded under the homeowners 2000 policy. (pp. 3.20–3.22)

10. Which of the following would be considered a communicable disease based on the *Dictionary of Epidemiology* and therefore excluded under the homeowners policy? (pp. 3.22–3.24)
    a. AIDS
    b. Flu
    c. Malaria
    d. Measles

11. Both the homeowners and CGL policies have exclusions for contractual liability. Identify two exceptions to this exclusion under the homeowners policy and two under the CGL. (p. 3.26 and pp. 3.39–3.41)

12. Give an example of a situation in which the homeowners Section II—Additional Coverages might apply. (pp. 3.28–3.30)

13. Give three examples of situations covered under the premises and operations coverage provided by Coverage A of the CGL. (pp. 3.35–3.36)

14. An insured has a CGL policy. Explain how a claim by an insured's leased employee under the dual capacity doctrine would be handled by the CGL. (p. 3.42)

15. What are three questions a claim representative should ask regarding coverage of a pollution claim under a CGL policy? (p. 3.44)

16. Give three examples of vehicles that would fall within the CGL definition of "mobile equipment." (p. 3.45)

17. Explain whether the following deliberate acts would be covered under a CGL policy: (pp. 3.57–3.58)

    a. Slander or libel of an employee who is wrongfully terminated.

    b. The insured is accused of copyright infringement by a competitor.

    c. The insured is accused of false arrest, wrongful detention, or assault and battery of a customer stopped by a security guard for suspicion of shoplifting.

Application Questions

1. An insured's twelve-year-old son vandalizes a neighbor's house with spray paint. The cost to remove the spray paint and repaint the house is $1,500. The state where this occurs has a statute making parents liable for property damage caused by their children who are minors. Explain how an insurer with the ISO homeowners 2000 edition policy should respond to this claim.

2. In the fall of 1999, Faye sprayed a powerful herbicide on weeds growing near her fence. At that time, she was insured under a homeowners policy with Americanwide Insurance. Four months later, in the spring of 2000, Faye's and her neighbor's lawn remained brown. A test determined that the herbicide killed large portions of both lawns. At the time this was discovered, Faye had switched to Goodhands Insurance Company. Which insurer would be responsible for the neighbor's lawn under the following rules?

   a. Exposure rule

   b. Manifestation rule

3. Bob has a homeowners policy. Without his knowledge, Bob's two boys and two neighbor boys went into the nearby woods to have a BB gun fight. The boys range from eight to eleven years in age. The boys established a rule that all shots must be aimed below the knees. As the fighting became intense, Bob's eleven-year-old son shot at a neighbor boy without taking much time to aim. The shots blinded the neighbor boy in one eye. His parents sued Bob and his son. Explain whether this injury is covered.

4. An insured's son and a neighbor overdose from huffing aerosol cleaners in the insured's garage. The neighbor's son suffers brain damage, and the parents sue the insured. Is this covered under the homeowners policy or excluded because it involves a controlled substance?

5. Verbotten's Jewelers is insured under a CGL. A security guard for Verbotten's interrupts a holdup of the store. One of the robbers exits the store with a bag of jewelry. The security guard requests that the robber stop. He does not, and the security guard shoots him. The robber was not threatening any person. The security guard tells the police that he intended to shoot the robber. Is the injury to the robber covered under Verbotten's CGL?

6. Charlie's Glass Company delivers a large plate glass to First Bank after a hail storm damaged one of First Bank's picture windows. Charlie delivers the plate glass and leaves it leaning against the building next to the broken window. While Charlie is completing the paper work with the bank manager, a gust of wind blows the glass onto a customer's minivan. Which carrier would cover this loss, Charlie's business auto insurance carrier, Charlie's CGL carrier, or First's CGL carrier?

7. Aggregate and Each Occurrence Limits

Conglomerate Corporation has a CGL policy with these limits:

General aggregate	$2,000,000
Each occurrence	$1,000,000
Products-completed operations aggregate	$2,000,000
Personal and advertising injury	$500,000
Medical payments	$5,000

Conglomerate had the following damages for ten different occurrences or offenses during this policy period.

	Damages	Type of Occurrence or Offense
1.	$50,000	Premises/operations
2.	$350,000	Premises/operations
3.	$1,500,000	Premises/operations
4.	$400,000	Premises/operations
5.	$900,000	Products
6.	$1,200,000	Completed operation of Conglomerate's work
7.	$400,000	Products
8.	$600,000	Personal and advertising injury
9.	$300,000	Personal and advertising injury
10.	$8,000	Medical payments

Question: How much would Conglomerate's CGL insurer pay for each occurrence or offense listed above? Assume that the claims were paid in the order listed above and that no other claims were received during the same policy period.

Answers to Assignment 3 Questions

NOTE: These answers are provided to give students a basic understanding of acceptable types of responses. They often are not the only valid answers and are not intended to provide an exhaustive response to the questions.

Review Questions

1. What constitutes an occurrence?

   How are the number of occurrences determined?

   When does an occurrence take place?

2. Should not: It is against public policy for insurers to pay because the purpose of punitive damages is to punish the wrongdoer, not the insurer.

   Should:

   - The policy wording is ambiguous and does not support NOT paying them.
   - The reasonable expectation of insureds might be to pay all of these types of damages.
   - It would be worse to bankrupt the insured by making the insured pay rather than having the insurer pay.

3. - Whether the insured has a legal obligation to pay
   - Whether the claim is for some damage covered in the insuring agreement, such as "bodily injury" or "property damage"
   - Whether damages were caused by an "occurrence"
   - Whether the occurrence took place in a covered territory

4. a. The homeowners coverage does not pay for medical expenses of an insured—only for the medical expenses of others.

   b. It is similar to the auto medical payments coverage in that it is a no-fault coverage. The insured does not have to be liable for medical payments to be owed.

5. Exceptions include nonlicensed vehicles used to serve the residence premises, vehicles used to serve handicapped people, or golf carts.

6. This policy specifically excludes the unintended consequences of deliberate acts. Before this wording was in place, courts were divided on the issue of coverage for unintended consequences.

7. According to some courts, intoxication can affect a person's ability to form intent. An intoxicated person doesn't always know what he or she is doing. This means that the deliberate act of an intoxicated person may be covered in some states.

8. - Read the policy wording.
   - Reserve the company's rights.
   - Take a detailed statement from the insured, claimant, and witness. (Determine the subjective and objective intent of the insured based on these statements.)
   - Assess whether injury or damage worsened because of some intervening act following the insured's deliberate act.
   - Determine whether the state considers intentional injuries "occurrences."

9. An example of an excluded business activity is an unprofitable telemarketing operation at the named insured's home (profit motive). Dog-sitting and dog-walking by the insured's teenage children would be covered (as occasional activities of children under twenty-one). Successful fundraising drives for Girl Scouts operated out of the named insured's home would be covered (no profit motive).

10. a. Yes
    b. Yes
    c. Yes
    d. Yes

    All of these are examples of communicable diseases and are excluded under the homeowners policy.

11. Homeowners policy permits coverage for *written* contracts if the liability is assumed *before* the occurrence for situations relating to the ownership, maintenance, or use of the insured's residence.

    The CGL covers "insured contracts" such as lease agreements made before the accident occurred.

12. First-aid expenses are somewhat common, but perhaps the most common are for borrowed property damaged by an insured. For instance, the insured borrows his friend's video camera to take on vacation. Unfortunately, the insured drops the video camera. The cost to repair or replace up to the limit (usually $500) is covered under Section II—Additional Coverages.

13. Examples include:
    - Slip-and-fall accidents
    - Use of mobile equipment
    - Negligent work performed by an insured's employee that causes harm to others

14. "Leased employees" are employees, and their injuries are not covered under the CGL. Instead, they are covered under employer's liability coverages sold with workers compensation insurance.

15. In addition to issuing a reservation of rights letter, claim representatives should determine:
    - What theory of occurrence (manifestation or exposure) is used?
    - Do older policies have exclusions that may cover the incident? (Compare wording of current coverage to older version and determine how it affects coverage.)
    - Is the claim presented as a PRP letter, and how do the courts recognize this?

16. - Vehicles that travel on crawler treads like bulldozers and backhoes
    - Vehicles maintained for use solely on the premises
    - Cherry pickers and other equipment attached and used with trucks and autos.

17. a. The acts of slander and libel are covered under Coverage B of the CGL unless the insured knew of the falsity of the statements and still published them, or unless slander or libel is a criminal offense in the given state (another exclusion) and the insured is found guilty under the criminal statute. The other coverage issue here is whether an employee can make a claim against the employer's CGL insurance carrier. The CGL Coverage A and Coverage C parts specifically excluded injuries to employees of the insured. Coverage B of personal and advertising injury has no similar exclusion. These acts could be covered under the CGL Coverage B.

    b.   Copyright infringement is a specifically covered offense in Coverage B of the CGL.

    c.   The false arrest and wrongful detention are specifically covered offenses under Coverage B. The assault and battery claims could be covered under Coverage A as long as the security guard was protecting persons or property. All of these are most likely covered under the CGL.

Application Questions

1. Under the homeowners 2000 edition, the policy excludes coverage for intentional damage done by an insured. The son would not be covered. At twelve, he was old enough to form intent. Under this edition of the homeowners, the parents would probably not be covered either. Vicarious liability is also excluded under this new wording (assuming the severability of insurance clause is not applied by a court to provide coverage). Fortunately, the Section II—Additional Coverages of the homeowners policy provides up to $1,000 coverage for damage to the property of others (even if this was intentional damage, because the boy is younger than thirteen). The parents are then left to pay $1,000 to the neighbors out of pocket (which doesn't bode well for junior's future allowances). Another reason not to cover this is that it doesn't meet the definition of an "occurrence" because the damage was not fortuitous. Some states would permit this as a viable defense.

2. Americanwide would have the policy in effect using the exposure rule, while Goodhands would be the insurer with the policy in effect at the time the loss manifested itself.

3. This would most likely be covered. The intent was not to shoot out the eye of the neighbor, and the injury was probably not reasonably foreseeable despite any warning given by parents on the subject of BB guns.

4. The aerosol cleaners are not controlled substances. The insured might not be negligent, but coverage would be provided unless a court felt that it was against public policy to provide insurance coverage for such an incident. However, that would be a somewhat unlikely conclusion for a court to make in today's legal environment.

5. The CGL permits coverage for intentional injuries if the purpose of the act was to *protect people or property*.

6. If the plate glass had been accepted by the bank, then the bank's CGL would apply. It appears that the bank was in the process of completing the paperwork (and accepting delivery) when the event occurred. Charlie's business auto coverage would appropriately cover this.

7. Claim 1: CGL insurer would pay the $50,000. This reduces the general aggregate to $1,950,000.

    Claim 2: CGL insurer would pay $350,000, and this would reduce the general aggregate limit to $1,600,000.

    Claim 3: CGL insurer would pay $1,000,000. This is the limit for any one occurrence. This reduces the general aggregate limit to $600,000.

    Claim 4: CGL insurer would pay $400,000. This reduces the general aggregate limit to $200,000.

    Claim 5: CGL insurer would pay $900,000. This is within the products-completed operations coverage limit. It reduces the aggregate products-completed operations limit to $1,100,000.

    Claim 6: CGL insurer would pay the $1,000,000 occurrence limit. This would reduce the aggregate for products-completed operations to $100,000.

Claim 7: CGL insurer would pay $100,000. This is the remaining amount under the aggregate for products-completed operations.

Claim 8: The CGL insurer would pay only $200,000 because the general aggregate has now been exhausted. Coverage B personal and advertising injury claims fall under the general aggregate limit along with the premises/operations claims.

Claim 9: CGL insurer would pay nothing. Limits exhausted.

Claim 10: CGL would pay nothing. Limits exhausted.

Actively capture information by using the open space in the SMART Review Notes to write out key concepts. Putting information into your own words is an effective way to push that information into your memory.

Direct Your Learning

Avoiding and Handling Coverage Disputes

Educational Objectives

After learning the content of this assignment, you should be able to:

1. Avoid common mistakes that claim representatives sometimes make that can lead to coverage disputes.

2. Investigate coverage issues while protecting the insurer's rights.

3. Write an effective reservation of rights letter.

4. Understand the issues involving the insurer's duty to defend the insured when coverage questions exist. In support of this educational objective, you should be able to:

   • Determine what events trigger the duty to defend.

   • Write a reservation of rights letter when defending a lawsuit.

   • Explain the need for separate legal counsel.

5. Explain the advantages and disadvantages of using negotiation or arbitration to resolve coverage disputes.

6. Write an appropriate denial letter.

7. Explain when and how to use declaratory judgment actions to resolve coverage disputes.

8. Define or describe each of the Key Words and Phrases for this assignment.

Study Materials

Required Reading:
▶ Liability Claim Practices
  • Chapter 4

Study Aids:
▶ SMART Online Practice Exams
▶ SMART Study Aids
  • Review Notes and Flash Cards—Assignment 4

Outline

▶ **Mistakes in Coverage Decisions**
  A. Failing To Read and/or Understand Policy Provisions
  B. Making a Decision Without All of the Facts
  C. Failing To Consider Jurisdictional Differences
  D. Assuming Clear and Unambiguous Policy Wording
  E. Basing a Coverage Decision on Emotional Reactions
  F. Improperly or Inadequately Explaining Coverage
  G. Overcommitting to a Coverage Position

▶ **Investigation Under a Reservation of Rights**
  A. Reservation of Rights Letters and Nonwaiver Agreements
  B. The Content of Reservation of Rights Letters

▶ **The Duty To Defend and Coverage Disputes**
  A. The Duty To Defend and the Insurance Policy
    1. Events That Trigger the Duty To Defend
    2. The Duty To Defend and the Allegations of the Lawsuit
  B. Defense Under a Reservation of Rights
  C. Requirement of Separate Legal Counsel

▶ **Negotiation of Coverage Issues**

▶ **Arbitration of Coverage Issues**
  A. Binding Arbitration as Valid and Enforceable
  B. Binding Arbitration as Void and Unenforceable

▶ **Coverage Denials**
  A. Denials and Unfair Claim Practices Acts
  B. Policy Violations

▶ **Declaratory Judgment Actions**

▶ **Summary**

 **Use the SMART Online Practice Exams to test your understanding of the course material. You can review questions over a single assignment or multiple assignments, or you can take an exam over the entire course. The questions are scored, and you are shown your results. (You score essay exams yourself.)**

Key Words and Phrases

Define or describe each of the words and phrases listed below.

Waiver (p. 4.8)

Estoppel (p. 4.8)

Detrimental reliance (p. 4.8)

Reservation of rights letter (p. 4.8)

Nonwaiver agreement (p. 4.8)

Pleading into coverage (p. 4.13)

Looking beyond the four corners of the complaint (p. 4.14)

Policy buy-back (p. 4.17)

Prejudiced (due to late notice) (p. 4.22)

Declaratory judgment action (p. 4.22)

Review Questions

1. Give an example of a mistake that could occur in making a coverage decision. (pp. 4.1–4.7)

2. List four factors claim representatives should keep in mind to help avoid coverage disputes. (p. 4.7)

3. When should a reservation of rights letter be sent to an insured? (pp. 4.8–4.9)

4. Identify five elements included in a reservation of rights letter. (p. 4.9)

5. What issues should claim representatives consider with respect to the "duty to defend" issue? (p. 4.12)

▶▶

6. What event(s) triggers the "duty to defend" for an insurer?
   (pp. 4.12–4.13)

7. Normally, an insurance carrier must base its decision on whether to defend a lawsuit on the facts pleaded in the lawsuit. However, insurers are permitted to bring in facts outside of those stated in the lawsuit in three circumstances. Name them. (p. 4.14)

8. Describe the role of arbitration in resolving coverage issues.
   (pp. 4.18–4.20)

9. Explain the two different forms coverage denials can take.
   (pp. 4.20–4.21)

10. What is the purpose of a notice provision in an insurance policy?
    (p. 4.21)

11. What factors should claim representatives consider in determining whether late notice prejudiced the insurer? (p. 4.22)

12. Explain how a declaratory judgment action differs from a lawsuit filed by an insured against an insurer seeking monetary damages. (p. 4.23)

13. List some common coverage questions that can be resolved by declaratory judgment actions. (p. 4.23)

14. List some common "rights and duties" questions that can be resolved by declaratory judgment actions. (p. 4.23)

Application Questions

1. John White is a claim representative with Earthfriends Insurance. One of Earthfriends' insureds, Truck Hauling Company (TH), sent John a potential responsible party (PRP) letter that TH received from the Environmental Protection Agency advising it that it was a potentially responsible party for cleaning up hazardous waste. TH was asking Earthfriends for a legal defense and coverage for pollution cleanup costs resulting from an accident in which TH's truck, carrying hazardous material, ran into a ditch and subsequently polluted a nearby river.

   John White, a staunch environmentalist, immediately called TH and, without checking the policy or asking for details of the accident, advised the company that its policy absolutely excluded all pollution claims and defense for such claims. Furthermore, he advised that the company was not competent to be hauling hazardous materials.

   a. What mistakes did John make in his coverage decision?

   b. How else could John have handled the lawsuit?

2. The Smiths gave their car to their son, Mike, to use while he was at college. There, a roommate of Mike's used the car without Mike's knowledge and had an accident. The Smiths filed a claim, stating that the only person who had permission to use the car was their son. The agent called Mike's roommate to get his side of the story, and he claimed that Mike told him he could use the car if he needed it. What would be the potential implications if the claim representative:

   a. Tried to negotiate coverage with the insureds?

b. Settled with the policyholder although he did not believe that coverage should apply to the claim?

c. Decided to use an arbitrator to resolve the dispute?

d. Filed a declaratory judgment action instead of a coverage denial?

Answers to Assignment 4 Questions

NOTE: These answers are provided to give students a basic understanding of acceptable types of responses. They often are not the only valid answers and are not intended to provide an exhaustive response to the questions.

Review Questions

1. Mistakes that could occur in determining coverage include:
   - Failing to read and/or understand applicable policy provisions
   - Making a coverage decision without knowing all of the facts of the claim
   - Failing to take into account state-by-state differences in coverage interpretation
   - Assuming that policy wording is clear and unambiguous
   - Basing coverage decisions on emotional reactions
   - Improperly or inadequately explaining coverage
   - Overcommitting to a coverage position

2. Claim representatives should consider the following to avoid coverage disputes:
   - Reading the exact coverage wording and not relying on memory
   - Obtaining all necessary facts of the claim before applying coverage
   - Being aware that different states and jurisdictions may have varying coverage interpretations
   - Keeping an open mind on how others might interpret policy wording
   - Properly and adequately explaining coverages
   - Holding judgment and statements about a coverage decision until all pertinent issues have been resolved
   - Separating personal beliefs and emotions from the coverage decisions, which should stand on their own merits

3. A reservation of rights letter is a written notice advising the insured that the insurance company is investigating coverage issues surrounding a claim and that the insurer is reserving the right to deny coverage if such a denial could be supported by the facts gathered in an investigation.

4. The elements contained in a reservation of rights letter include:
   - Acknowledgment of receipt of the loss notice or lawsuit
   - Description of the claim
   - Identification of the named insured(s), policy period, policy number, and limits
   - A statement advising the insured to inform the carrier of any other policies that might apply to the claim
   - A reference to each policy provision that might preclude coverage, with an explanation of why such a provision may result in a coverage denial
   - A description of information needed from the insured
   - A statement that the reservation of rights letter is not a denial of coverage and that the insurer is still investigating

- A statement that any actions the insurer takes will not constitute a waiver of rights or an admission of coverage
- A reservation of the right to add or modify its coverage position later based on additional coverage issues discovered during the investigation

5. With respect to the duty to defend, claim representatives should consider the following:
- Whether the claimed event triggered the duty to defend
- How to defend a lawsuit without losing the right to deny coverage later
- The need to appoint separate legal counsel to the insured

6. In general, the duty to defend is triggered by a civil action (a lawsuit) against the insured. The duty to defend is also normally triggered if the civil action is based on allegations of negligence or some other covered offenses. The Commercial General Liability (CGL) coverage form defines the word "suit" to include informal civil proceedings and arbitration proceedings as well as formal lawsuits. In addition to civil lawsuits, other actions such as administrative proceedings may, in some states, also be considered "suits."

7. The following factors allow an insurer to deny a claim:
- The insured had not paid premiums to keep the policy in force.
- The policy was not in effect at the time of the loss.
- The location of the loss was not covered.

8. Arbitration, which requires a third party to resolve the dispute, is an option for insurers to combat the increasing costs of coverage issues. Arbitration can be either binding, which cannot be appealed in court, or nonbinding, which permits either party to appeal the decision to courts.

9. Coverage denials can take one of two forms: (1) a general denial reserving all policy defenses or (2) a denial based on specific coverage defenses. A general denial invites litigation and is at risk of rejection by the court because it does not adequately explain the coverage decision. For this reason, insurers favor citing all applicable coverage provisions when making a denial.

10. Notice provisions allow the insurance company to
- Determine its rights and liabilities.
- Investigate the claim.
- Protect against fraudulent claims.
- Secure early settlements.

11. Claim representatives should consider the following in determining whether late notice prejudiced the insurer:
- Was information lost because of the late notice?
- Was evidence lost, altered, missing, or destroyed because of the late notice?
- Did damages increase because of the late notice?
- Was the opportunity to settle lost because of the late notice?
- Was the ability to defend an insured lost?

12. A declaratory judgment action is a lawsuit seeking a judicial determination of whether policy coverage applies to a claim. Insurers usually file declaratory judgment actions to determine whether a claim falls within the insuring agreement.

13. Some common coverage questions resolved by declaratory judgment actions include:
    - Does a particular exclusion apply?
    - Do the damages claimed fall within the definition of "bodily injury" or "property damage"?
    - Do other insurance policies apply?
    - Is a vehicle an "uninsured motor vehicle"?
    - When did the event take place?
    - What are the limits of liability?
    - Does a policy violation preclude coverage?

14. Some common rights and duty questions resolved by declaratory judgment actions include:
    - Has the insured violated any policy conditions?
    - Is the insured required to provide additional financial information to meet the policy requirements?
    - Is the insured required to submit to more than one examination under oath?
    - Is a second named insured (for example, a spouse) required to give a separate examination under oath?
    - Is the insured required to permit the insurer to reinvestigate the premises?

Application Questions

1. a. John made several mistakes in his coverage decision:
        - He failed to read the policy to see the extent of the pollution exclusion he cited. He failed to consider that the pollution exclusion might not be absolute, excluding any and all pollution claims.
        - He did not obtain the facts of the accident or the nature of the material involved to determine whether the policy exclusion applied.
        - He allowed his personal beliefs about environmental protection to interfere with his judgment about coverage.
        - He failed to consider any laws that might affect pollution coverage or an insurer's duty to defend.

    b. In addition to avoiding the mistakes mentioned in (a), Bob should also have sought separate legal counsel to help determine whether the EPA letter triggered a duty to defend and whether pollution cleanup costs were somehow covered. Bob should have issued a reservation of rights letter to the insured explaining that the company would have to defer a coverage decision while the facts were being gathered. He would also need to address the issue of what the company would pay for independent legal counsel to defend TH while the investigation was pending.

2. a. It would be premature to make a coverage decision before talking with the Smiths' son to determine whether he had given his roommate permission. If a dispute existed over whether Mike had given permission, then a coverage decision, one way or the other, would need to be made. Typically, negotiations work best when an insured has a longstanding relationship with the insurance company (or an agent of the company) and both parties would like to maintain that relationship. In this case, neither the insured's son nor the person seeking coverage has a relationship that he wants to preserve.

Another obstacle is that trying to negotiate coverage in this claim would likely result in the insurer admitting coverage and paying the entire claim. If, after coverage negotiation, the claim was not settled and was eventually denied, then the insured would likely sue for bad-faith damages, alleging that the insurer failed to provide coverage even though the claim representative knew that it was questionable to issue a denial (based on the claim representative's actions in trying to negotiate coverage rather than issuing an outright denial).

b. Settling this claim would have avoided litigation, but it could potentially set a bad internal precedent and cause a conflict with the named insureds, the Smiths, whose rates might increase as a result the claim. To the Smiths, a settlement might give the impression that the company did not believe their version of the story. Settlements with insureds are also complex legal matters and would require the claim representative and Mike to obtain legal assistance because a standard release form would not be appropriate.

c. Historically, this claim would have been litigated in court. Currently, the trend is to seek alternative ways to resolve disputes, and that might make arbitration an attractive alternative. The claim representative should read the policy arbitration provision wording and check with management or legal counsel to determine whether this claim is appropriate for arbitration. The seriousness of the damages should also be considered.

d. A declaratory judgment action might be used if the loss potential is large. It would be more expensive than arbitration, but it could prevent Mike from filing a bad faith lawsuit for wrongfully denying the claim.

SEGMENT B

Assignments

Segment B is the second of three segments in the AIC 36 course.
These segments are designed to help structure your study.

Direct Your Learning

Determining Legal Liability

Educational Objectives

After learning the content of this assignment, you should be able to:

1. Explain how negligence is determined in tort law by
   - Describing the elements of negligence and related concepts such as foreseeability and proximate cause, and
   - Assessing the elements of negligence given a claim scenario.
2. Explain how the principle of joint and several liability applies in claims involving multiple parties.
3. Describe tort defenses such as:
   - Unforeseeability
   - Intervening cause
   - Acts of God
   - Contributory negligence
   - Comparative negligence
   - Immunity
   - Assumption of risk
   - Statute of limitation, and

   Given a claim scenario, identify all applicable, relevant defenses.
4. Describe and define various intentional torts, such as:
   - False arrest, imprisonment, or detention
   - Malicious prosecution
   - Wrongful eviction
   - Defamation or disparagement
   - Invasion of privacy or breach of confidentiality
   - Copyright or trademark infringement
   - Interference with a business relationship
   - Assault and battery
   - Intentional infliction of emotional distress
   - Conversion
   - Trespass and nuisance
5. Explain situations in which strict liability may apply, other than with product liability claims.
6. Define or describe each of the Key Words and Phrases for this assignment.

Study Materials

Required Reading:
- ▶ Liability Claim Practices
  - Chapter 5

Study Aids:
- ▶ SMART Online Practice Exams
- ▶ SMART Study Aids
  - Review Notes and Flash Cards— Assignment 5

Outline

▶ **Torts**

  A. Negligence

    1. Determination of the Duty Owed and to Whom It Is Owed

    2. Determination of the Breach of Duty Owed

    3. Determination of Causation (Proximate Cause)

    4. Determination That Damages Resulted

  B. Negligent Entrustment

  C. Negligence Per Se

▶ **Other Laws and Legal Principles Affecting Negligence**

  A. Rescue Doctrine

  B. Joint and Several Liability

    1. Concurrent Joint Tortfeasors

    2. Successive Joint Tortfeasors

  C. *Res Ipsa Loquitur* ("The Thing Speaks for Itself")

▶ **Negligence and Other Tort Defenses**

  A. Unforeseeability

  B. Intervening Cause

  C. Act of God

  D. Contributory Negligence

  E. Comparative Negligence

    1. "Pure" Form of Comparative Negligence

    2. "Modified" Form of Comparative Negligence

    3. "Slight" Form of Comparative Negligence

  F. Immunity

    1. Governmental (Sovereign) Immunity

    2. Official Immunity

    3. Charitable Immunity

    4. Family Member Immunity

  G. Assumption of Risk

  H. Statute of Limitation

▶ **Intentional Torts**

  A. False Arrest, Imprisonment, or Detention

  B. Malicious Prosecution

  C. Case Example—Malicious Prosecution

  D. Wrongful Eviction

  E. Defamation and Disparagement

  F. Invasion of Privacy and Breach of Confidentiality

  G. Copyright or Trademark Infringement

  H. Interference With a Business Relationship

  I. Assault and Battery

  J. Intentional Infliction of Emotional Distress

  K. Conversion

  L. Trespass/Nuisance

    1. Nuisance

▶ **Strict Liability in Other Than Product Liability Claims**

  A. Dangerous Instrumentalities

  B. Abnormally Dangerous Activities

  C. Wild Animals

  D. Aircraft

▶ **Summary**

The SMART Online Practice Exams product contains a final practice exam. You should take this exam only when you have completed your study of the entire course. Take this exam under simulated exam conditions. It will be your best indicator of how well prepared you are.

Key Words and Phrases

Define or describe each of the words and phrases listed below.

Common law (p. 5.1)

Stare decisis ("to stand by things decided") (p. 5.1)

Tort (p. 5.2)

Tortfeasor (p. 5.2)

Proximate cause (p. 5.3)

Foreseeable (p. 5.3)

Negligence per se (p. 5.5)

Negligent entrustment (p. 5.5)

Gross negligence (p. 5.6)

Rescue doctrine (p. 5.7)

Joint tortfeasors (p. 5.7)

Successive joint tortfeasors (p. 5.8)

Res ipsa loquitur ("the thing speaks for itself") (p. 5.9)

Intervening cause (p. 5.10)

Comparative negligence (p. 5.11)

Modified comparative negligence (p. 5.12)

Pure comparative negligence (p. 5.12)

Governmental immunity (p. 5.13)

Sovereign immunity (p. 5.13)

Proprietary function (p. 5.14)

Discretionary acts (p. 5.14)

Ministerial acts (p. 5.14)

Statute of limitation (p. 5.18)

Discovery doctrine (p. 5.18)

Defamation (p. 5.21)

Disparagement (of reputation) (p. 5.21)

Libel (p. 5.21)

Slander (p. 5.21)

Breach of confidentiality (p. 5.22)

Invasion of privacy (p. 5.22)

Infringement of copyright (p. 5.23)

Infringement of trademark or service mark (p. 5.23)

Business torts (p. 5.24)

Infringement of trade dress (p. 5.24)

Interference with business relations (p. 5.24)

Patent infringement (p. 5.24)

Assault (p. 5.25)

Battery (p. 5.25)

Intentional infliction of emotional distress (p. 5.25)

Conversion (p. 5.26)

Trespass (p. 5.26)

Nuisance (p. 5.27)

Private nuisance (p. 5.27)

Public nuisance (p. 5.27)

Review Questions

1. What elements are required for establishing negligence?
(pp. 5.2–5.3)

2. ☐ True   ☐ False   The standard used to determine a general duty
owed requires acts that an ordinary, reasonable person would do under
similar circumstances. (p. 5.3)

3. To be deemed negligent, a person must first have what duty?
(p. 5.3)

4. ☐ True   ☐ False   Proof of negligence requires that the conduct of the claimant fall below the standard of care owed, constituting a breach of duty. (p. 5.3)

5. A requirement for proving negligence is that the breach of duty resulted in what? (p. 5.4)

6. Calvin, a grocery store employee, left an empty, wheeled pallet near the end of a grocery aisle when he went to the stockroom. Veronica, a customer, did not see the pallet and tripped over it. The pallet rolled into the path of her fall, and she suffered a broken leg and a dislocated shoulder. Identify the elements of negligence in this case. (pp. 5.2–5.5)

7. Because joint tortfeasors can be held individually responsible for the entire amount of a claimant's damages, what term could be substituted for the term "several" in the doctrine of joint and several liability? (p. 5.8)

8. Explain how a claimant might use the doctrine of joint and several liability to his or her advantage if one of the joint tortfeasors does not have insurance. (p. 5.8)

9. Identify the tort defenses described. (pp. 5.10–5.18)

a. A doctrine that bars recovery by the claimant when the claimant's own negligence, even if slight, contributes to the accident and the resulting injury or damage.

b. A law that protects persons from having to defend against lawsuits when significant time has passed and evidence has become "stale." It prevents lawsuits after a specified time.

c. A new and independent force that breaks the chain of connection between the original act of negligence by the defendant and the ultimate injury or damage to the claimant.

d. The principle that a governmental entity cannot be responsible for a tort for its employees' wrongful acts and omissions.

e. A reasonably prudent person fails to predict a danger so cannot be required to take action to avoid it.

f.   A doctrine in which a court weighs the defendant's negligence against that of the claimant and attributes a percentage of negligence to each for damages caused by the parties.

g.   A force of nature, such as a tornado, flood, or earthquake, that either directly or indirectly causes an accident.

10. Name the type of negligence described in the following: (pp. 5.12–5.13)

a.   The claimant can recover if his or her fault was only slight and recovery is reduced by the claimant's percentage of negligence.

b.   Damages are apportioned according to the degree of negligence that each of the parties has in the accident, as long as the claimant's negligence is not 100 percent.

c.   Recovery by the claimant is excluded when the claimant's negligence was the major cause of the accident.

▶▶

11. What are two conditions under which waivers of state immunity occur? (p. 5.13)

12. Local municipalities that might enjoy partial immunity include: (p. 5.13)

13. Give examples of proprietary functions. (p. 5.14)

14. For each of the following acts, indicate whether it is discretionary or ministerial. (pp. 5.14–5.15)

    a. Negligence by low-level production workers in bagging, labeling, and transporting fertilizer

    b. Intermingling of patients and employees in a state-run mental health hospital

c. Negligence in establishing procedures for handling chemicals

d. Maintaining a swimming area in a public park

e. Negligence of a police officer who did not complete an accident report at the scene

15. ☐ True ☐ False The public duty doctrine holds that a public official may be held liable for the breach of a duty owed to the general public. (p. 5.16)

16. Identify the type of immunity that might apply in each of the following cases. (pp. 5.16–5.17)

a. A mother is negligent in the supervision of her three-year-old child, who wanders into the street and is injured when struck by a passing motorist.

b. A church had to divert funds from a trust fund to pay a judgment that resulted from a tort claim.

c. A wife wishes to sue her husband for her share of the damage he caused to their jointly owned automobile after he struck another vehicle from behind.

17. What are two essential elements for proving assumption of risk? (p. 5.17)

18. When does the statute of limitation begin running? (p. 5.18)

19. ☐ True ☐ False The discovery doctrine provides that the statute does not begin to run until the injury is discovered. (p. 5.18)

20. Eugene, age twenty-three, suffered a heart attack after experimenting with a mind-altering drug. One of his friends immediately called 911, and Western Ambulance dispatched an ambulance. The driver of a pickup failed to yield the right-of-way to the ambulance, resulting in an accident. The ambulance driver reported the accident to Western and it dispatched a second ambulance, but when that ambulance arrived, Eugene had stopped breathing. Despite their efforts, medical personnel could not revive him. Eugene's parents filed a negligence suit against Western Ambulance for wrongful death. What defenses might Western Ambulance use in this case? (pp. 5.10–5.18)

21. What are the four components that must be met to prove malicious prosecution? (p. 5.20)

22. ☐ True   ☐ False   A property owner who evicted a tenant when he learned that the tenant had a Hispanic background could be held liable for wrongful eviction. (p. 5.21)

23. List the three elements needed to prove defamation, including libel and slander. (p. 5.21)

24. ☐ True   ☐ False   Truth is the defense for defamation and relieves insurers from the duty to defend in a lawsuit. (p. 5.21)

25. List four specific examples of invasion of privacy. (p. 5.22)

26. Identify the type of infringement described in the following: (pp. 5.23–5.24)

    a.   The use of a specific color and package design for a product

b. The use or sale of any product, process, or apparatus of a legally protected item without the owner's consent

27. ☐ True   ☐ False   Interference with the performance of a contract is an example of wrongful interference with business relations. (p. 5.24)

28. Identify each offense described in the following: (p. 5.25)
a. Following through on a threat to cause injury or death, including any unwanted, physical touching of another person

b. A physical, verbal, or implied threat to cause injury or death

29. Elements required to prove intentional infliction of emotional distress include: (pp. 5.25–5.26)

30. ☐ True   ☐ False   A person who throws a brick though an office window can be charged with trespass. (p. 5.26)

31. Indicate whether the type of nuisance described is public or private. (p. 5.27)

    a. A young boy works on his car every evening. He often revs the motor after midnight. The car has no exhaust system, so the noise disturbs the neighbors.

    b. An industrial plant releases toxic waste into a nearby river.

    c. A nuclear power plant has smoke stacks that pump radioactive chemicals into the atmosphere, resulting in acid rain.

    d. A pet food manufacturer opens a plant next to a residential subdivision. Odor from the plant affects the neighborhood throughout the plant's hours of operation.

32. Strict liability, other than product liability, can be invoked in claims involving what four areas? (p. 5.27)

33. In addition to using them, what other kinds of handling of dangerous instrumentalities require the highest degree of care? (p. 5.27)

34. Indicate which of the following items are examples of dangerous instrumentalities and require the highest degree of care. (p. 5.27–5.28)

   a.   Crop-dusting chemicals being spread from an airplane

   b.   Flammable gas stored in populated areas

   c.   A wild tiger kept fenced in a residential neighborhood

   d.   A fireworks display near multi-story office buildings

35. Factors to consider in determining whether an activity is abnormally dangerous include: (p. 5.28)

36. ☐ True   ☐ False   Some examples of dangerous activities to which strict liability applies are erecting dams, drilling oil wells, and blasting operations. (p. 5.28)

37. ☐ True   ☐ False   Owners and lessees of aircraft are never held strictly responsible for damage that results from accidents involving the aircraft. (p. 5.28)

Application Questions

1. Danielle slips on a puddle of water in front of a refrigerated case in her local supermarket. There are no warning signs or cones to alert customers to the water on the floor. Bill sees Danielle fall and goes to assist her. Bill tells Danielle that he regularly shops at this market and has reported similar puddles to the store manager on three prior visits. Danielle cannot stand and fears her ankle is broken. Bill gets the store manager and Emergency Medical Services take Danielle to the hospital for treatment.

   a.   Identify the elements of negligence in this case. (pp. 5.2–5.3)

b. The supermarket tries to avoid responsibility for Danielle's injuries by asserting the defenses of contributory negligence and assumption of risk.

Explain how these defenses may or may not be successfully used by the supermarket. (pp. 5.9–5.18)

2. An uninsured driver strikes and kills a young child at a school crossing, despite a stop sign and a crossing guard. Investigation shows that the car had faulty brakes. The plaintiff argues that the accident might have been avoided if the car had been properly maintained and the crossing guard had attempted to get the child out of harm's way.

The jury finds the owner/driver of the car to be 98 percent at fault for the accident and the city, who employed the crossing guard, to be 2 percent at fault.

Explain how the doctrine of joint and several liability will affect the plaintiff's recovery in this case. (pp. 5.7–5.8)

3. Jake has been put on probation at his job because of customer complaints. Jake feels this action is unjustified and decides to retaliate against his boss. Jake knows his boss has a teenage son attending an out-of-state college. Jake calls his boss when he knows he is in a meeting and leaves a message that his son has been killed in a car accident. The boss gets the message and is distraught for several hours until he is able to reach his son by phone. An internal investigation reveals that Jake is the person who placed the call. As a result of this incident, Jake's boss has sought treatment with a psychiatrist. Jake's boss sues Jake for intentional infliction of emotional distress.

Will Jake's boss be successful in his suit? Explain your answer. (pp. 5.25–5.26)

Answers to Assignment 5 Questions

NOTE: These answers are provided to give students a basic understanding of acceptable types of responses. They often are not the only valid answers and are not intended to provide an exhaustive response to the questions.

Review Questions

1. Elements required for establishing negligence:
   - Duty owed to others
   - Breach of the duty owed
   - Proximate causation
   - Damages

2. True

3. To exercise a level of care to protect others from harm

4. False—The conduct of the insured must fall below the standard of care owed.

5. Compensable damages

6. Elements of negligence:
   - Calvin, representing the grocery store, owed a duty of care to the customers.
   - Calvin breached the duty by leaving the pallet in the aisle.
   - The pallet left in the aisle was the proximate cause of Veronica's injury.
   - Veronica was injured in the accident.

7. Separate

8. The claimant could choose to pursue damages only from the joint tortfeasor who has insurance coverage available to pay the claim, avoiding any problems of recovery against the party who has no insurance.

9. a. Contributory negligence
   b. Statute of limitation
   c. Intervening cause
   d. Governmental immunity
   e. Unforeseeability
   f. Comparative negligence
   g. Act of God

10. a. Slight comparative
    b. Pure comparative
    c. Modified comparative

11. Conditions for waivers of state immunity:
    - When damages are caused by auto accidents
    - When a condition has been reported to the government, but the government has failed to take measures to correct the problem

▶▶

12. Police and fire departments, school districts, and public hospitals

13. Operating gas and water utilities, casinos, maintaining public streets, and snow removal operations

14. a. Ministerial
    b. Discretionary
    c. Discretionary
    d. Discretionary
    e. Ministerial

15. False

16. a. Parental immunity
    b. Charitable immunity
    c. Interspousal immunity

17. The two elements for proving assumption of risk:
    (1) Knowledge and understanding of the risk involved
    (2) Voluntary assumption of the risk

18. When the cause of action "accrues" or when the accident took place

19. False—The statute also begins to run when the injury should have been discovered.

20. The following defenses might apply, depending on state laws:
    Intervening cause, contributory negligence, comparative negligence, immunity, assumption of risk

21. The four malicious prosecution components:
    (1) The defendant files charges for a criminal prosecution against the claimant.
    (2) The case is resolved in favor of the claimant.
    (3) The defendant was motivated by malice in filing charges against the claimant.
    (4) The defendant filed charges without probable cause.

22. True

23. The three elements needed to prove defamation:
    (1) A false statement tending to hold the person up to public disgrace
    (2) Publication of the statement
    (3) Damages

24. False—The insurer has a duty to defend in a lawsuit regardless of the truth.

25. Some examples of invasions of privacy (answers may vary):
    • Sharing private medical records indicating that a person suffers from an illness, without that person's permission
    • Publicizing that a person, who is not a public figure, has a sexually transmitted disease
    • Interference with personal mail or telephone conversations
    • Trespassing into a person's home

26. a. Trade dress

b. Patent

27. True

28. a. Battery

b. Assault

29. Elements required to prove intentional infliction of emotional distress:

- The misconduct is intentional or reckless.
- The misconduct is extreme or outrageous.
- The misconduct leads to emotional distress (and damages).
- The emotional distress must be severe.

30. True

31. a. Private

b. Public

c. Public

d. Private

32. Strict liability claims:

(1) Dangerous instrumentalities

(2) Dangerous activities

(3) Wild animals

(4) Aircraft

33. Storing or transporting them

34. a, b, and d—Keeping a tiger (c) would evoke strict liability, but the tiger is not a dangerous instrumentality.

35. Factors to determine abnormally dangerous activities:

- The activity involves a high degree of risk of harm to the person, land, or chattels of others.
- The gravity of the harm that may result from it is likely to be great.
- The risk cannot be eliminated by the exercise of reasonable care.
- The activity is not a matter of common usage.
- The activity is inappropriate to the place where it is carried on.
- The value of the activity to the community.

36. True

37. False

Application Questions

1. a. The supermarket has a duty of care to its customers to protect them from harm. The supermarket breached that duty by knowingly continuing to use a leaky refrigerator and not warning customers of the potential for a leak in the area. The puddle on the floor was the proximate cause of Danielle's injuries.

   Danielle received treatment at the hospital, so the expenses incurred resulted from the fall.

   b. Under a contributory negligence defense, the supermarket would have to show that Danielle was partly responsible for her injuries. There is nothing in the case to suggest that Danielle contributed to her own injuries.

   The supermarket would also be unsuccessful in asserting an assumption of risk defense because Danielle would not assume that shopping at the supermarket was an unusual risk.

2. Joint and several liability allows a plaintiff to recover all damages from anyone or any combination of defendants. In this case, the plaintiff would elect to recover all of the damages from the city because the city is insured and has assets to pay the judgment, even though the city is only 2 percent at fault. The uninsured driver, although 98 percent at fault, has no insurance, and so recovery from the driver is unlikely.

3. Jake's boss will be successful in his lawsuit. The tort of intentional infliction of emotional distress requires the following:

   - The misconduct is intentional or reckless—Jake intended to hurt his boss and intentionally placed the call.

   - The misconduct is extreme or outrageous—outrageous conduct is more than mere insults or petty oppressions. Jake's conduct in this case would be characterized as extreme.

   - The misconduct leads to emotional distress (and damages). Because he is under treatment from a psychiatrist, Jake's boss can establish damages.

   - The emotional distress must be severe—in this case, it would be easy to believe the loss of a child would cause severe distress.

Direct Your Learning

Other Bases of Legal Liability

Educational Objectives

After learning the content of this assignment, you should be able to:

1. Describe relationships and situations in which vicarious liability applies, including:

   - Agency

   - Partnerships and joint enterprises

   - Independent contractors (and exceptions to rule)

   - Parental liability

2. Explain how liquor liability laws apply.

3. Describe various ways in which environmental impairment liability may apply.

4. Identify the factors courts use in determining when claims may become class-action lawsuits and mass tort litigation.

5. Describe the basic concepts of bailment law.

6. Explain when a party becomes contractually liable by describing the elements of a contract and the rules of enforcing contracts.

7. Define or describe each of the Key Words and Phrases for this assignment.

Study Materials

Required Reading:
- ▶ Liability Claim Practices
  - Chapter 6

Study Aids:
- ▶ SMART Online Practice Exams
- ▶ SMART Study Aids
  - Review Notes and Flash Cards— Assignment 6

Outline

▶ **Vicarious Liability**
  A. Agency
      1. Sub-Agency
      2. Temporary or Special Employee
      3. Deviation From Agent's Duties
  B. Partnerships and Joint Enterprises
  C. Independent Contractors
  D. Parental Liability
      1. Liability of Minor Children
      2. Negligent Entrustment and Negligent Parental Supervision

▶ **Liquor Liability Laws**
  A. Dram Shop and Liquor Control Statutes
  B. Employer Hosts/Company Parties
  C. Social Hosts and Manufacturers
  D. Common-Law Defenses to Liquor Liability
  E. Non-Auto Cases

▶ **Environmental Impairment Liability**
  A. Air Pollution
  B. Water Pollution
  C. Ground Contamination
  D. Pollution Liability—Legal Bases of Recovery
      1. Negligence
      2. Statutory Enactments
      3. Nuisance
      4. Trespass
  E. Defenses to Pollution Liability Claims

▶ **Class Actions and Mass Tort Litigation**
  A. Legal Basis for Filing Class Actions in Tort Claims

▶ **Bailments**
  A. Kinds of Bailments
      1. License Versus Bailment
      2. Acts of Employees
  B. Defenses and Limitations on Bailee Liability
      1. Contributory and Comparative Negligence
      2. Laws of Particular Bailments
      3. Disclaimers

▶ **Contracts**
  A. Contractual Liability and the Nature of Contracts
  B. Parol Evidence Rule
  C. Validity and Enforceability of Contracts
  D. Contractual Concepts Applying to Insurance Policies
  E. Hold Harmless Agreements
  F. Exculpatory Agreements

▶ **Summary**

When you take the randomized full practice exams in the SMART Online Practice Exams product, you are using the same software you will use when you take the actual exam. Take advantage of your time and learn the features of the software now.

Key Words and Phrases

Define or describe each of the words and phrases listed below.

Vicarious liability (p. 6.1)

Agent (p. 6.2)

Principal (p. 6.2)

Sub-agency (p. 6.2)

Partnership (p. 6.3)

Dram shop acts (p. 6.6)

Noninnocent participant (p. 6.9)

Multiple chemical sensitivity (MCS) (p. 6.10)

Sick building syndrome (SBS) (p. 6.10)

Comprehensive Environmental Response, Compensation, and Liability Act (CERCLA) or Superfund law (p. 6.11)

Leaking underground storage tank (LUST) (p. 6.11)

Continuing trespass (p. 6.13)

Innocent landowner defense (p. 6.13)

Brownfields (p. 6.14)

Mass tort litigation (p. 6.15)

Class action (p. 6.15)

Bailee (p. 6.16)

Bailment (p. 6.16)

Bailor (p. 6.16)

Breach of a contract (p. 6.20)

Acceptance (p. 6.21)

Express contracts (p. 6.21)

Implied contracts (p. 6.21)

Offer (p. 6.21)

Offeree (p. 6.21)

Offeror (p. 6.21)

Parol evidence (p. 6.22)

Unenforceable contracts (p. 6.22)

Valid contract (p. 6.22)

Void contract (p. 6.22)

Voidable contracts (p. 6.22)

Contracts of adhesion (p. 6.23)

Hold harmless agreement (p. 6.23)

Statutes of Fraud (p. 6.23)

Exculpatory agreements (p. 6.24)

Review Questions

1. Vicarious liability exists when the superior party has liability for the conduct of another party because of some relationship between the two parties. The responsible party is not personally negligent. Of the following relationships, indicate those in which vicarious liability often exists. (p. 6.1)

   a. Employer/employee

   b. Business partner/associate

   c. Teacher/student

   d. Automobile owner/driver who borrows vehicle

   e. Person/friend running an errand for the person

   f. Principal/agent

   g. Parent/child

   h. Principal/independent contractor

   i. Temporary employer/special employee

   j. Organization president/members

   k. Partnership/employees

2. A principal is vicariously liable for the actions of an agent tortfeasor when he or she is acting within the scope of the work requested by the principal. Factors that determine whether the work is within the scope include: (p. 6.2)

3. When is a principal's liability for the acts of an agent limited? (p. 6.2)

4. When can agency duties be delegated to a sub-agent? (p. 6.2)

5. What type of liability applies to partnerships and allows an injured party to choose to sue just one partner or all the partners? (p. 6.3)

6. In deciding a person's status as an employee or an independent contractor, what is the determining factor? (p. 6.3)

7. List four ways that a property owner or person who hires an independent contractor can be held responsible for the contractor's acts. (p. 6.4)

8. In determining negligence in the acts of a child, what standard of care is usually required? (p. 6.5)

9. Identify each of the following as either negligent entrustment or negligent supervision. (pp. 6.5–6.6)

   a.   A man leaves his hunting knife lying on the dining room table. A three-year-old child finds the knife and plays with it, injuring one of his playmates.

   b.   A mother asks her fourteen-year-old daughter to hop in the car, drive to the corner grocery, and bring back a quart of milk.

   c.   A parent sits by while her child cuts down all of the seedlings in the neighbor's yard.

10. Dram shop acts are statutes that hold establishments that serve alcoholic beverages responsible for harm resulting from serving patrons alcohol in violation of statutes. In most states, such a violation occurs when two types of patrons are served. What are the two types of patrons? (p. 6.6)

11. Who is protected by dram shop acts? (p. 6.7)

12. Most states' dram shop laws do not apply to employers serving alcohol to employees as employer-hosts, because they do not make any immediate short-term profit from serving liquor. What benefit to the employer-host creates an argument to make the employer vicariously liable for injuries caused by and to intoxicated employees? (p. 6.7)

13. Of the following circumstances, indicate those under which courts have commonly found the party to be liable under dram shop laws. (pp. 6.6–6.9)

    a. A social host served alcohol to an obviously intoxicated guest, knowing that the guest would be driving soon. Innocent parties were injured in an ensuing accident.

    b. A social host served alcohol at a high-school graduation party and was sued when an intoxicated student injured others in an automobile accident.

    c. The manufacturer of beer consumed by a high-school student was sued when the intoxicated student injured others in an automobile accident.

    d. The claimant purchased rounds of drinks and was later injured as a passenger of a car driven by one of the drinking participants.

    e. The distiller of tequila consumed by a college student who died of alcohol poisoning provided no warning label of the danger of drinking too much alcohol.

    f. A tavern served alcohol to a minor who consumed several alcoholic drinks. The minor left the tavern, then started to cook dinner on the stove. He left the stove unattended, went into the next room, and fell asleep, inadvertently starting a damaging fire.

14. Environmental impairment liability can stem from three types of pollution. Give an example of each type of pollution. (pp. 6.9–6.11)

   a. Air pollution

   b. Water pollution

   c. Ground pollution

15. Pollution liability arises out of statutory enactment and what three common-law theories? (p. 6.11)

16. For pollution liability negligence cases, what must the claimant prove? (p. 6.11)

17. Of the following parties, identify those who are designated as potentially responsible parties (PRPs) and who must eliminate contaminants and clean up sites under CERCLA or the Superfund law. (p. 6.12)

    a. The current property owner

    b. All previous property owners from the time when the hazardous waste was deposited

    c. The owner of the facility when the hazardous waste was deposited

    d. The leasee of the facility when the hazardous waste was deposited

    e. The owner of the property when the hazardous waste was deposited

    f. Any person who accepted the hazardous waste for transportation or disposal

    g. Any person who contracted or arranged for disposal of the hazardous waste

18. ☐ True   ☐ False   CERCLA law creates an advantage for plaintiffs for environmental pollution liability cases because the EPA can initiate enforcement any time there is a release or threatened release of a hazardous substance and will do the expensive testing required to prove contamination. (p. 6.12)

19. ☐ True   ☐ False   Cleanup costs cannot be imposed retroactively against those who deposited hazardous waste before the CERCLA statute became law on December 11, 1980. (p. 6.12)

20. Why would a plaintiff prefer to file a nuisance claim for hazardous waste as opposed to filing under the Superfund law? (p. 6.13)

21. ☐ True   ☐ False   Trespass, as it relates to pollution liability, involves intentional invasion of one's interest in property, or the property itself, and intentional harm that results. (p. 6.13)

22. From the following list, identify the defenses that might be available in pollution liability cases. (pp. 6.13–6.14)

    a. Acts of war

    b. Innocent landowner who purchased property after appropriate investigation

    c. Zoning ordinances

    d. Landowner's ignorance of the contamination

    e. Acts of God

    f. Rights of trade over a victim's right to use and enjoy land when no health issues arise

    g. Innocent landowner who was unaware of contamination by a leasee

    h. Parties who remediate "brownfields"

23. Cite commonalities that help a case qualify as a class-action lawsuit. (pp. 6.14–6.15)

24. Describe the four rules that must be met to certify a class action under the Federal Rule of Civil Procedure 23. (p. 6.16)

    a. Numerosity

    b. Commonality

    c. Typicality

d. Adequacy of representation

25. Indicate which of the following additional factors are considered before a class-action lawsuit is permitted. (p. 6.16)

a. The decisions of parties to exclude themselves from membership in a class for purposes of the suit

b. The extent and nature of any litigation already commenced

c. The extent to which individual class members would have interests in controlling the prosecution in a separate action

d. The difficulties to be encountered in the management of a class proceeding

e. The ramifications of a class-action penalty in similar litigation

f. The desirability of concentrating the litigation in one forum

26. Give an example of each of the following types of bailment. (p. 6.17)

a. Bailments for the sole benefit of the bailor

b. Bailments for the sole benefit of the bailee

c. Bailments for the mutual benefit of the bailor and bailee

27. Identify the duty of care owed in each type of bailment. (p. 6.17)
    a. Bailment for the sole benefit of the bailor

    b. Bailment for the mutual benefit of both parties

    c. Bailment for the sole benefit of the bailee

28. Bert asked to borrow Aaron's motor boat for a trip to the lake the
    following day. For each of the following actions, indicate whether
    Bert exercised an ordinary degree of care or the greatest degree of
    care, as required. (p. 6.17)
    a. Bert parked the boat in the street by his neighbors' house.
        The boat was damaged by a passing motorist who swerved to
        miss a dog.
    b. Bert moved the boat into his garage when he heard of a
        pending hail storm before the trip to the lake. The boat was
        damaged when heavy winds blew in the garage door.
    c. Bert parked the boat in his driveway. The neighborhood
        children caused damage to the boat when their softball hit it.
    d. Bert parked the boat in his garage. His children found the key
        and played with the boat, causing damage to the propeller.

29. From the following list, identify each situation that would likely be interpreted as a bailment rather than a license. (p. 6.18)

    a.   Paula parks her car in her designated space in the Security Park parking lot and walks to her place of employment.

    b.   Sam parks his car in a space in the Security Park parking lot. He leaves his keys with the attendant so that his car can be moved during snow removal.

    c.   Jane parks her minivan in her designated space in the Empire parking garage. The attendant issues her a printed ticket limiting Empire's liability to $1,000 per incident.

    d.   Marvin drives his car into the Heath Regency parking garage, then turns the keys and car over to the parking lot attendant to park the car.

30. The Heath Regency hired Adam as an attendant to park its guests' cars in its parking garage. It did not check Adam's references or his legal record before hiring him. Mills, a customer of the Heath, left his Jaguar for Adam to park. Adam, who was on probation for automobile theft, took the Jaguar for a joy ride. He returned to the garage and parked the car after one of his friends damaged the upholstery. Regarding liability for damage to the Jaguar, the Heath would (p. 6.18)

    a.   Not be held liable for Adam's acts because they extended beyond the scope of his authority.

    b.   Not be held liable for Adam's acts because he did eventually park the car.

    c.   Be held liable for Adam's acts whether or not they were within the scope of his authority.

    d.   Be held liable for Adam's acts even though they extended beyond the scope of his authority because of negligent hiring.

31. Refer to the case in Review Question 30. Assume that Mills was a lawyer and had represented the plaintiff in Adam's automobile theft case. Suppose that Mills warned Adam not to "mess with" his car when he gave possession to Adam. If the Heath management learned of this interaction between Adam and Mills, what defenses might they be able to assert? (pp. 6.18–6.19)

32. Laws specifically address certain types of bailments. For each of the following bailments, indicate how laws affect liability. (p. 6.19)

    a. Innkeepers (hotels and motels)/guests' property in rented rooms

    b. Storekeepers/personal clothing of customers removed to try on new clothes

    c. Restaurateurs/overcoats (when hooks are provided near the customer's seat)

    d. Restaurateurs/overcoats left in a cloak closet at the front of the restaurant

    e. Common carriers/damage to goods left in their care

33. From the following list, identify each disclaimer that would be likely to exempt the bailee from liability. (pp. 6.19–6.20)

   a. Printed disclaimer on the back of a cloak-closet claim token the size of a nickel.

   b. Large, clearly written disclaimer posted on the wall and counter of a dry cleaner.

   c. Small print disclaimer on the back of a receipt that is given to a customer for each roll of film to be developed. Customer service representatives are trained to alert each customer to the disclaimer on the back.

   d. Small, clearly written disclaimer posted inside a cloak closet. The sign is covered when the closet is filled near capacity.

34. Briefly describe each requirement for a contract to be enforceable. (p. 6.21)

   a. Agreement

   b. Consideration

   c. Competent parties

   d. Legality of purpose

35. What are the two contract elements necessary to establish agreement? (p. 6.21)

36. Identify the contract concepts for each description. (p. 6.21)
    a. A proposal in which one party promises to give something in return for a promise or an act by the other party

    b. Formed when the intentions and terms of a contract are indicated by the actions of the parties and the surrounding circumstances

    c. The offeree's agreement to the terms of the offer, which must mirror the original offer

    d. The party to a contract who promises to give something in return for a promise or an act by another party

e.   Contracts that explicitly state the terms and intentions of the agreement

f.   The party to a contract who makes a promise or acts in return for something offered by another party

37. State two basic legal principles regarding the contract law. (p. 6.21)

38. Which type of contract avoids controversy in the interpretation and enforcement, implied or express? (p. 6.21)

39. Under what circumstances might parol evidence be allowed to alter a written contract? (p. 6.22)

40. Identify each of the following contracts as a voidable contract or an unenforceable contract. (p. 6.22)

    a. A contract that a minor entered into to purchase an automobile

    b. A sales contract in which one party lies to the other about a latent defect in the property

    c. A real estate sales contract that is not stated in writing

    d. An insurance policy on the life of a pet, represented by the policyholder to have been a person

    e. After a loss, an insured makes a claim for reimbursement of additional expenses that the policy did not provide for

41. Identify each of the following contractual concepts that apply to most insurance policies. (pp. 6.23–6.24)

    a. A contract of adhesion, thus ambiguities are construed against the writer

    b. Assignable at will

    c. A personal contract

    d. Interpretation is subject to the law of the jurisdiction where the contract was written

    e. Interpretation is subject to the law of the jurisdiction where a contractual event occurs

    f. A hold harmless agreement

42. Identify the contract agreement in each of the following descriptions. (pp. 6.23–6.25)

    a. A contractual provision that enables one party to avoid liability for negligence by including a "release of liability" for activities specified in the contract.

    b. A contractual provision by which one party agrees to indemnify another party in the event of a specified loss.

43. Courts will usually uphold an exculpatory agreement in a contract under what circumstances? (p. 6.24)

44. ☐ True   ☐ False   Exculpatory agreements excuse or limit liability for willful or wanton misconduct. (p. 6.24)

Answers to Assignment 6 Questions

NOTE: These answers are provided to give students a basic understanding of acceptable types of responses. They often are not the only valid answers and are not intended to provide an exhaustive response to the questions.

Review Questions

1. a, b, d, f, g, i, and k

2. Factors that determine whether the agent is acting within the scope of the work requested by the principal:
   - Whether the conduct was of the type the agent was hired to perform
   - Whether it occurred within the time and space limitations of the agency relationship
   - Whether it was motivated, even in part, by an intent or a purpose of serving the principal

3. When the agent deviates from the assigned authority or directives

4. Agency duties can be delegated to a sub-agent:
   - When the principal specifically authorizes the delegation
   - When the act is unlawful for the agent but not the sub-agent
   - When the act to be performed is purely mechanical
   - When it is common custom in the industry to delegate the act

5. Joint and several liability

6. Control of the operation

7. Property owners may be held responsible for a contractor's acts (answers may vary):
   - If the work the independent contractor is required to do is unlawful
   - If the work constitutes a public nuisance
   - If by statute the owner must make certain repairs
   - If the property owner has agreed to become legally liable for damages caused by the independent contractor

8. That which is ordinarily shown by the average child of similar age and mentality, under similar circumstances

9. a. Negligent entrustment
   b. Negligent entrustment
   c. Negligent supervision

10. Patrons served in violation of dram shop acts:
    - Anyone who is visibly intoxicated
    - Any minor

11. Dram shop acts protect innocent parties from the actions of intoxicated persons

12. Establishing or keeping good employer-employee relations

13. a, d, e, and f

14. Answers will vary:
    a. Smoke emitted from a stack that causes damage to others' property
    b. Spillage from an overturned truck that contaminates the water supply
    c. Rupture of a pipeline transporting fuel that contaminates the soil

15. Common-law theories applicable to pollution liability:
    - Negligence
    - Nuisance
    - Trespass

16. That the defendant owed a duty to use care to avoid injury or damage, but did not act like an ordinary prudent person under similar circumstances

17. a, c, e, f, and g

18. True

19. False

20. Because they can recover more in damages through higher jury awards

21. False—The resultant harm need not be intentional for liability to apply.

22. a, b, c, e, f, and h

23. Commonalities to qualify as a class-action lawsuit:
    - All of the injured parties have nearly identical injuries and the same cause of action against the wrongdoer.
    - There are common questions of law or fact.
    - The amount of damages in each claim is so small as not to warrant individual suits.

24. a. People constituting a class must be so numerous that it would be impractical to bring all of them separately into court.
    b. There must be an ascertainable class with a well-defined common interest in the questions of law and fact affecting the parties.
    c. The claims or defenses of the representative parties must be typical of all the class members.
    d. The named parties must fairly and adequately protect the interests of unnamed class members.

25. b, c, d, and f

26. a. A person's request of a neighbor to store his own meat in the neighbor's freezer rather than the refrigerator
    b. Borrowing a lawn mower from a neighbor with no compensation
    c. Renting a lawn mower and paying the rental fee

27. a. Slight care
    b. Ordinary care
    c. Greatest degree of care

28. a. Ordinary degree of care
    b. Greatest degree of care—Even though the boat was damaged, Bert did exercise the greatest degree of care to avoid it.
    c. Ordinary degree of care
    d. Ordinary degree of care—Parking the boat in the garage would indicate the greatest degree of care, but Bert is responsible for seeing that nothing within his control damages the boat.

29. b and d

30. d

31. Contributory or comparative negligence

32. a. Held strictly liable for guests' property
    b. Responsible for the personal clothing of customers
    c. Not liable for overcoats
    d. Responsible for overcoats
    e. Liable for loss or damage of the goods

33. b and c

34. a. Parties must have a "meeting of minds."
    b. Each party must give up something of value.
    c. Parties must have the legal ability to enter into contracts.
    d. The objective of the contract must be legal and not opposed to public policy.

35. Necessary contract elements:
    - An offer
    - Acceptance

36. a. Offer
    b. Implied contracts
    c. Acceptance
    d. Offeror
    e. Express contracts
    f. Offeree

37. Two basic legal principles regarding contract law:
    (1) The law of the jurisdiction specified in the contract would be applicable, all else being equal.
    (2) If the contract is silent on the applicable law, the governing law is ordinarily that of the place where the contract was made.

38. Express contracts

39. Parol evidence allowed:
    - When the meaning of the written terms is ambiguous
    - To provide essential terms to a written contract that is not complete

40. a. Voidable
     b. Voidable
     c. Unenforceable
     d. Voidable
     e. Unenforceable

41. a, c, d, and e

42. a. Exculpatory agreement
     b. Hold harmless agreement

43. Exculpatory agreement upheld:
     • It is not adverse to a public interest or against public policy.
     • The party excused from liability is not under a duty to perform.
     • The parties had equal bargaining power, and the contract was conscionable.

44. False

Direct Your Learning

Investigating Liability Claims

Educational Objectives

After learning the content of this assignment, you should be able to:

1. Describe the various categories of evidence, provide examples of evidence commonly gathered in liability claim investigations, and explain the purpose of taking statements.

2. Describe the legal challenges involved in obtaining statements from

   - People in hospitals,

   - Illiterate people,

   - Non-English speakers, and

   - Minors

3. Describe the admissibility issues of oral testimony by explaining the hearsay evidence rule and identifying exceptions to this rule.

4. Describe the various issues involved in obtaining statements from insureds, claimants, and other witnesses, including the criteria for impeaching a witness's testimony.

5. Describe the uses of various expert witnesses.

6. Identify and describe different types of scientific evidence claim representatives may need to consider.

7. Identify and describe different types of demonstrative, documentary, and real evidence claim representatives may obtain and explain some of the admissibility issues associated with these types of evidence.

8. Explain how claim representatives can make liability investigations more effective by properly setting the scope of investigations.

9. Explain the importance of liability claim reports and identify the important parts of a liability report.

10. Define or describe each of the Key Words and Phrases for this assignment.

Study Materials

Required Reading:
▶ Liability Claim Practices
  • Chapter 7

Study Aids:
▶ SMART Online Practice Exams
▶ SMART Study Aids
  • Review Notes and Flash Cards— Assignment 7

Outline

▶ **Introduction**

A. Coverage Versus Liability Questions

B. Recognizing Coverage Questions

C. Recognizing Liability Questions

D. Evidence and Rules of Evidence

E. Statement Taking

   1. Written Statements

   2. Recorded Statements

F. Special Situations Involving Statements

   1. Statements Taken in a Hospital

   2. Statements of Minors

   3. Statements of Illiterate People

   4. Statements of Non-English Speakers

   5. Negative Statements

G. Admissibility of Statements and Other Oral Testimony

   1. Hearsay

H. Statements of Insureds

I. Claimant Statements

J. Statement Priority Considerations

   1. Obtaining Information From the Claimant's Attorney

K. Witness Statements

   1. Locating Witnesses

   2. Classification of Witnesses

   3. Practical Considerations With Witnesses

L. Impeachment of a Witness's Testimony

   1. Competence of Person Giving Testimony

   2. Character of Witness

M. Expert Testimony

   1. Medical Specialists

   2. Accident Reconstruction Expert

   3. Forensic Chemists and Toxicologists

   4. Construction Engineers

   5. Automotive Engineers

   6. Climatological Experts

   7. Accountants

▶ **Scientific Evidence**

A. Voice Identification

B. Detection of Intoxication and Narcotics

C. Psychological Testimony

▶ **Demonstrative and Documentary Evidence**

A. Police Reports

B. Diagrams

C. Photographs, Videos, and Films

D. Manuals and Instructional Materials

E. Weather Reports

F. Motor Vehicle Reports

G. Traffic or Criminal Court Hearings

H. Claim Database

I. Newspaper Articles

J. Medical Records

K. Autopsy Report and Death Certificate

L. School Records

M. Income Tax Records

N. Other Records

▶ **Physical (Real) Evidence**

A. Spoliation of Evidence

▶ **Admissibility of Other Types of Evidence**

A. Habit and Routine Practice

B. Subsequent Remedial Measures

C. Privilege

▶ **Setting the Scope of the Investigation**

A. Coverage Questions

B. Potential Damage Exposure

C. Accident Complexity

D. Liability Assessment

E. Telephone Investigations

   1. Obtaining Help From the Field

F. Setting Investigation Priorities

G. Investigating the Injury and Damages

H. Reporting on Liability Claims

▶ **Conclusion**

▶ **Appendix A—Recorded Statements**

▶ **Appendix B—Written Statements**

▶ **Appendix C—Liability Claim Report**

▶▶

Key Words and Phrases

Define or describe each of the words and phrases listed below.

Oral evidence (p. 7.4)

Pictorial evidence (p. 7.4)

Real evidence (p. 7.4)

Relevant evidence (p. 7.4)

Documentary evidence (p. 7.4)

Demonstrative evidence (p. 7.4)

Material evidence (consequential evidence) (p. 7.4)

Competent evidence (p. 7.5)

Negative statement (p. 7.8)

Hearsay (p. 7.9)

Hearsay evidence rule (p. 7.9)

Admissions against interest (p. 7.10)

Prior contradictory statements (p. 7.10)

Spontaneous, excited utterances (p. 7.10)

Business or financial records (p. 7.11)

Past recorded recollections (p. 7.11)

Public records (p. 7.11)

Guilty pleas (p. 7.12)

Prior convictions (p. 7.12)

Witness (p. 7.14)

Hostile witness (p. 7.15)

Impeachment (p. 7.17)

Autopsy (p. 7.27)

Death certificate (p. 7.28)

Toxicology reports (p. 7.28)

Spoliation (p. 7.29)

Privilege (p. 7.30)

Review Questions

1. The difference between coverage and liability issues lies in the basis of each. Explain this difference. (p. 7.2)

2. What are the four loosely defined categories of evidence? (p. 7.4)

3. Identify the type of evidence that fits each description. (p. 7.4)

   a.   Written items such as contracts, letters, instruction manuals,
        sales brochures, and other writings that can help establish
        liability or damages.

   b.   Animate or inanimate, physical and tangible items that
        are related to the original litigated occurrence, including
        mechanical parts, weapons, scars on a person's body, and simi-
        lar physical items directly related to the claim.

   c.   Statements made by insureds, claimants, and witnesses,
        including expert witnesses.

   d.   Tangible items that were constructed after the original occur-
        rence to prove the facts presented by the litigants, such as a
        time line of events, a diagram of an accident scene, a map, a
        model of a building, or pictorial exhibits.

4. Name the type of demonstrative evidence that preserves a visual
   image of physical facts, such as photographs, X-rays, and videos.
   (p. 7.4)

5. Describe the three characteristics of evidence required for admissibility in court. (pp. 7.4–7.5)

   a.   Relevant

b.   Material

c.   Competent

6. Why do many jurisdictions have rules that preclude or restrict taking a statement from a hospitalized person? (p. 7.7)

7. ☐ True   ☐ False   Parents must give permission for their child to be interviewed and witness and attest to the statement regardless of the child's age. (p. 7.7)

8. List three concerns that explain why hearsay is inadmissible in court. (p. 7.9)

9. ☐ True   ☐ False   The hearsay evidence rule applies to oral statements, letters, affidavits, declarations, diaries, memos, notes, and e-mails. (p. 7.9)

10. Identify the exception to the hearsay evidence rule that fits each description. (pp. 7.10–7.12)

   a. A witness makes a statement that subjects him to civil or criminal liability.

   b. Documents that account for the spending of a corporation and its corporate objectives.

   c. Admission at trial that the defendant was speeding.

   d. Prison record for time served for fraud and theft used to establish the lack of credibility of a witness.

   e. A statement that the road conditions were good, when later testimony suggests the roads were hazardous.

f. A remark to the emergency room physician that the claimant's left knee had been bothering him for years.

g. A witness writes down her recollection of an accident the day it occurs, and even though she does not recall all the details during later testimony, she does testify that she wrote the description soon after the accident and it was accurate.

h. An investigative officer's report of factual findings at the accident scene, such as the resting position of the vehicles, skid marks, and the physical condition of the vehicle occupants.

11. ☐ True   ☐ False   While an insured is obliged under contract to provide statements to claim representatives as often as needed, third-party claimants have no legal obligation to give any statements to claim representatives of the other party's insurer. (p. 7.12)

12. When is a third-party claimant most likely to cooperate with a claim representative investigating a case? Why? (p. 7.12)

13. From the following list of claim situations, identify those in which the claim representative should contact the claimant before the insured. (p. 7.13)

   a. The liability situation is complicated or unclear.

   b. The insured was clearly liable, and the claimant's injuries are serious.

   c. A question of coverage exists concerning the accident.

   d. The claimant's injuries are minor, and no real question of liability exists.

   e. Rapport with the claimant is the overriding factor in the claim.

14. ☐ True   ☐ False   A formal statement is usually required to obtain information from an attorney about his or her client's injuries and wage loss. (p. 7.13)

15. Witnesses are usually limited to furnishing evidence on facts. From the following list, identify those exceptions to this rule that indicate opinions or conclusions to which a witness may testify. (p. 7.14)

   a. The emotional state of another

   b. The length of time needed for recovery based on injuries

   c. The speed of cars

   d. The identity of a person by his or her appearance or voice

   e. The severity of a claimant's injury

   f. The drunk or sober condition of another

   g. The value of objects or services with which he or she is familiar

16. What does a claim representative risk by not contacting a witness promptly? (p. 7.14)

17. List several sources for identifying witnesses to an accident. (pp. 7.14–7.16)

18. Identify the witness classification that fits each description. (p. 7.15)

  a. One who cooperates willingly with the claim representative in the investigation because of an obligation to tell the truth or because he or she is a friend of the insured or claimant and wants the truth to be known

  b. One whose response to the insured is negative or may display an attitude of bias or prejudice against the insured or claimant

  c. One who does not cooperate in the investigation; he or she might just avoid getting involved, dislike insurance companies, or exhibit basic antisocial behavior

  d. One whose position on the liability does not support the insured

  e. One whose position on the liability is favorable to the insured's interests

19. ☐ True   ☐ False   At trial, a lawyer can only ask leading questions of friendly or cooperative witnesses. (p. 7.16)

20. What pieces of information can a claim representative get from a witness to help ensure that he or she can be located if a trial ensues? (p. 7.17)

21. List three grounds for impeachment of testimony. (p. 7.17)

22. What must a lawyer establish to prove the competency of a witness? (p. 7.17)

23. Identify three ways, besides criminal conviction, that the character of a witness might be impeached described in the following: (pp. 7.17–7.18)

    a. By showing that on a previous occasion the witness made a statement that is inconsistent with a material portion of the present testimony

    b. By presenting evidence that a witness is biased or has an interest in the outcome of the suit or claim

    c. By presenting evidence referring to a witness's reputation for truthfulness or untruthfulness

24. Identify the type of expert who might be used to testify in each of the following scenarios. (pp. 7.18–7.19)

   a. To determine the content of a product that was ingested and determine whether it was the cause of the injury

   b. To assist in evaluating the inventory that was damaged when a large truck crashed through the storefront

   c. To determine whether the wind velocity on a particular day was strong enough to blow a healthy tree over onto a neighbor's garage, causing damage

   d. To determine the extent of healing that could be expected following reconstructive surgery of an injured claimant

   e. To determine whether a defect in a tire caused a fatality

f. To draw scientific and mathematical conclusions about the speed and direction of vehicles involved in an accident based on physical evidence

g. To assess the construction of a building and determine whether some defect in the materials or methods resulted in damages and injuries

25. Scientific opinions can be offered only after the trial judge has decided two things about the opinion. What are they? (p. 7.20)

26. ☐ True   ☐ False   Voice identification devices that produce a graphic impression of a person's voice can help confirm that the person heard on a recorded statement is the person identified in the recording. (p. 7.20)

27. Identify two devices used to detect intoxication and the recent use of narcotics. (pp. 7.20–7.21)

28. ☐ True   ☐ False   Psychological testimony is usually reliable enough to prove a defendant's innocence; thus, admissibility is not an issue. (p. 7.21)

29. Besides the description of the accident, what helpful information can be obtained from a police report of an accident? (pp. 7.21–7.22)

30. Identify all of the following that should be represented in a diagram of an accident. (p. 7.23)

    a. A legend or table showing the date, time, and location of the diagram; the accident date; and any other identifying marks, such as landmarks

    b. Location of traffic control devices

    c. Weather conditions at the time of the accident

    d. Any obstructions such as trees, shrubs, or fences

    e. The distances between items

    f. The point of impact of vehicles or persons

    g. Street names

    h. The names of surrounding businesses

31. How should a diagram be used when interviewing insureds, claimants, or witnesses? (p. 7.23)

32. ☐ True   ☐ False   In moderate to serious claims, it is advisable to have a professional photographer photograph the scene, skid marks, road factors, and damage to property. (pp. 723–7.24)

33. Besides the skill of the professional, what personal factor should a claim representative consider when selecting a professional photographer or an investigator who will provide videos? (p. 7.25)

34. ☐ True   ☐ False   When a traffic court finds an insured defendant guilty of a traffic infraction, even though he or she pled "not guilty," that determination is admissible in a civil court involving a lawsuit against the insured. (p. 7.26)

35. How can a claim representative use the ISO ClaimSearch system to avoid paying fraudulent claims? (p. 7.27)

36. When is an autopsy report, a death certificate, or a toxicology report beneficial to a claim representative investigating an accident? (pp. 7.27–7.28)

37. Identify the type of evidence that fits each description. (pp. 7.25–7.29)

   a. Information on a minor regarding attendance at an educational institution, grades, athletic ability, and time lost because of the accident

   b. Report that must be completed and filed with the state by a motorist involved in an auto accident involving property damage over a specified amount or any bodily injury

c. Records that can help determine whether a claimant continued to exercise during an alleged period of disability

d. Writings that can be used to prove the terms of a contested writing

e. Records that indicate the financial condition of the insured and a possible motive for committing fraud or arson

f. Evidence of the extent and type of precipitation that occurred in an area, helpful in automobile accidents and premises fall-down claims that are reported months or years after the accident occurred

g. Reports from emergency rooms, physicians, hospitals, labs, and X-ray providers that convey vital information about a claimant's injuries and help to establish damages

h. Records that can indicate when a claimant called an insurance agent or a claim representative, useful in coverage disputes involving modified coverage dates or late notice of claims

i. Information to help determine lost wages and provide an overall picture of the person's wages when a disability extends over several months or years

j. Information published periodically that lists names of witnesses who can be consulted in a claim investigation

38. Indicate one admissibility issue that might apply to the type of evidence listed. (pp. 7.25–7.30)

a. Manuals and instructional materials

b. Motor vehicle reports

c. Medical records

d. Wage information

e. Physical evidence removed from an accident scene

f. Crucial physical property destroyed or altered

g. Habits distinguished from character traits

39. ☐ True   ☐ False   Evidence that an insured establishment
    hired security guards to protect its clientele following a stabbing
    in its parking lot can be used to prove its liability. (p. 7.30)

40. List four examples of privilege that make certain evidence inadmissible in court. (pp. 7.30–7.31)

41. List five factors that help determine the necessary scope of a liability investigation. (p. 7.31)

42. Identify the liability assessment that fits each description. (pp. 7.32–7.33)

   a. In all likelihood the insured was not negligent or legally liable for the accident; the scope of the investigation is determined by how hard the plaintiff presses the issue.

   b. There is no real question that the insured was entirely at fault for the accident; minimal investigation is required.

   c. It is unclear which party bears primary responsibility for the accident; a thorough investigation of liability and damages is required.

d. The insured was likely at fault for the accident, but the liability is not clear-cut; the liability investigation might be minimal although the damages might require extensive investigation.

43. What determines the types of claims that should be handled by a telephone unit versus a field claim representative? (p. 7.33)

44. What tool can claim representatives develop in the early stages of a claim to help conduct the investigation in an organized manner and set investigation priorities? (p. 7.34)

45. Of the following pieces of information, identify those that should be obtained from a claimant who previously sustained injuries similar to the current injury. (pp. 7.34–7.35)

    a. Nature of the prior injury

    b. Treatment obtained for the prior injury

    c. Time lost from work because of the prior injury

    d. Amount of insurance settlement received for the prior injury

    e. Any disability resulting from the prior injury

46. Of the following items, indicate those that explain why a claim file must be documented and organized to "speak for itself."
(p. 7.35)

    a. Claim representatives cannot recall all the important details of all their files.

    b. Claim representatives might have little time to review a file before negotiations.

    c. A claim representative might need to review a file quickly when an attorney calls, because missed calls are common with lawyers.

    d. A judge and jury should be able to review the file quickly.

    e. Supervisors, managers, and defense attorneys might need to make a decision in the claim representative's absence.

    f. Claim representatives could resign, get transferred, take vacations, and become ill, so they might not always be available to answer questions.

    g. Any member of a claim unit should be able to answer a call for another team member.

47. List the items that are commonly captioned in an initial report.
(p. 7.35)

 Set aside a specific, realistic amount of time to study every day.

Answers to Assignment 7 Questions

NOTE: These answers are provided to give students a basic understanding of acceptable types of responses. They often are not the only valid answers and are not intended to provide an exhaustive response to the questions.

Review Questions

1. The basis of coverage questions is the insurance policy; the basis of liability issues is the applicable laws.

2. Four categories of evidence:
   (1) Oral evidence
   (2) Real evidence
   (3) Demonstrative evidence
   (4) Documentary evidence

3. a. Documentary evidence
   b. Real evidence
   c. Oral evidence
   d. Demonstrative evidence

4. Pictorial evidence

5. a. Must prove that something is more or less likely to be true
   b. Tends to establish a particular element of a claim that has legal significance
   c. Relates to the source of the evidence and whether it is adequate to justify admission into court

6. The patient may be on medication or may be in pain or under stress from the accident.

7. False—No special handling is usually required for children in their middle or late teens.

8. Reasons hearsay is inadmissible:
   - The potential inaccuracy in secondhand reporting of the witness's statement.
   - The original witness's statement is not made under oath, and the jury could not view the demeanor of the witness making that original statement.
   - The witness making the original statement may not be available to be cross-examined.

9. True

10. a. Admissions against interests
    b. Business and financial records
    c. Guilty pleas
    d. Previous convictions
    e. Prior contradictory statements
    f. Statements made for purposes of making a medical diagnosis
    g. Recorded recollection
    h. Public records

11. True

12. During the prompt, initial contact; helps gain the claimant's confidence and trust and establishes rapport with the claimant

13. b, d, and e

14. False

15. a, c, d, f, and g

16. The witness may forget important aspects of the accident or become indifferent or resistant to helping with the claim.

17. Sources for identifying witnesses (answers may vary):
    - The insured
    - The police report
    - The motor vehicle report filed by the adverse driver
    - Service people who might have been in the vicinity of the accident
    - Tow-truck operators who might have removed the cars from the scene

18. a. Friendly
    b. Hostile
    c. Unfriendly
    d. Adverse
    e. Supporting

19. False—Leading questions can only be asked of hostile witnesses.

20. Information to ensure location of a witness:
    - His or her Social Security number
    - Name and address of his or her employer
    - Identity of relatives or close friends who live nearby

21. Grounds for impeachment of testimony:
    - Subject matter inaccuracies or inconsistencies
    - Lack of competency of the person giving testimony
    - Character problem with the person giving testimony

22. That the witness had an opportunity to see what happened, did see what happened, and still recalls what was seen many months ago

23. a. The witness made prior inconsistent statements
    b. The witness is biased
    c. The witness's truthfulness or untruthfulness

24. a. Forensic chemist, toxicologist
    b. Accountant
    c. Climatological expert
    d. Medical specialist

e. Automotive engineer

f. Accident reconstruction expert

g. Construction engineer

25. Scientific opinion admissibility:
   - They are based on good scientific knowledge.
   - They will assist the court in understanding the issue in question.

26. True

27. Intoxication and narcotics identification:
   - Breathalyzers
   - Nalline

28. False

29. Information from a police report (answers may vary):
   - Names and addresses of witnesses and those involved in the accident
   - Information about claimed injuries
   - Points of impact and vehicle damage
   - Contributing factors
   - Any traffic violations or arrests

30. a, b, d, e, f, and g

31. The interviewee should draw a diagram before the statement is taken and use it as the basis for discussion.

32. True

33. The reliability and witness quality of the professional; would he or she make a good, credible witness?

34. False

35. They can gain information about the person's claim history to avoid duplicate payments for past injuries.

36. When there is a possibility that the claimant's death may have been caused by a factor other than the accident

37. a. School records
   b. Motor vehicle reports
   c. Health club records
   d. Contracts, sales brochures
   e. Liens and bankruptcy records
   f. Weather reports
   g. Medical records
   h. Telephone records
   i. Incomes tax records
   j. Newspaper articles

38. a. Chain of custody.
    b. Confidential in some states and cannot be obtained by insurers.
    c. A signed medical authorization from the claimant is needed.
    d   Signed authorization from the claimant.
    e. Chain of custody.
    f. Spoliation of evidence.
    g. Character traits are not admissible, but habits are.

39. False

40. Privilege (answers may vary):
    - Attorney-client
    - Physician-patient
    - Husband-wife (marital)
    - Clergy-penitent

41. Factors that determine the scope of a liability investigation:
    - The existence of coverage questions
    - The potential damage exposure or the damages alleged
    - The nature and complexity of the accident or loss
    - The likely degree of liability
    - The insurance company's claim philosophy

42. a. Doubtful liability
    b. Clear liability
    c. Questionable liability
    d. Probable liability

43. The company claim philosophy

44. An investigation outline

45. a, b, c, and e

46. a, b, c, e, f, and g

47. Commonly captioned items:
    - Date, time, and place of accident
    - Coverage information and coverage questions
    - Accident description
    - Insured's data
    - Claimant's data
    - Assessment of liability
    - Injury and damages
    - Subrogation possibilities
    - Recommendations for future handling

Direct Your Learning

Evaluating and Valuing Liability Claims

Educational Objectives

After learning the content of this assignment, you should be able to:

1. Explain why liability claims are difficult to evaluate and value.

2. Given the facts of a claim, be able to identify the factors that would affect the value of the claim.

3. Explain how the "choice of law" affects the value of a claim.

4. Explain the nature of punitive damages and the factors courts consider in awarding punitive damages.

5. Identify and describe the various damages that constitute the value of bodily injury claims.

6. Explain how death claims should be evaluated and valued by describing the various damages that states consider in survival actions and wrongful death cases for adults and children.

7. Explain when experts may be needed to help evaluate and value claims.

8. Explain how other non-damage factors influence claim values, such as:

   • Attorney representation

   • Characteristics of insured, claimant, or witnesses

   • Aggravating circumstances

   • The venue of the case

9. Describe how the following valuation methods are used to evaluate and value claims and explain any advantages or disadvantages of each method:

   • Individual case valuation method

   • Roundtable technique

   • Formula method

   • BATNA

   • Expert systems

   • Settlement value templates

10. Define or describe each of the Key Words and Phrases for this assignment.

Study Materials

Required Reading:
▶ Liability Claim Practices
  • Chapter 8

Study Aids:
▶ SMART Online Practice Exams
▶ SMART Study Aids
  • Review Notes and Flash Cards— Assignment 8

Outline

▶ **Nature of Liability Claims Evaluations**

▶ **Trends and Patterns in Liability Awards**

▶ **Factors Affecting Liability Awards**

   A. Evaluating Liability and Legal Factors

      1. Determine the Applicable Choice(s) of Law

      2. General Assessment of Liability

   B. Evaluating Damages in Tort Actions

      1. Punitive Damages

      2. Property Damage Claims

      3. Bodily Injury Claim Valuation Factors

      4. Emotional Distress Claims

      5. Death Cases

      6. Excessive Damages Award

      7. Collateral Source Rule

      8. Mitigation of Damages

   C. Attorney Representation

   D. Expert Witnesses

   E. Other Factors Influencing Jury Awards

      1. Characteristics of Insureds, Claimants, and Witnesses

      2. Aggravating Circumstances

      3. The Venue

▶ **Methods for Calculating Settlement Ranges**

   A. Individual Case Valuation Method

   B. Roundtable Technique

   C. Formula Method

   D. Best Alternative to Negotiated Agreement (BATNA)

   E. Expert Systems

      1. Advantages of Expert Claim Evaluation Systems

      2. Disadvantages of Expert Claim Evaluation Systems

   F. Settlement Value Template

▶ **Valuations and Liability Claim Reserves**

▶ **Conclusion**

Plan to take one week to complete each assignment in your course.

Key Words and Phrases

Define or describe each of the words and phrases listed below.

Substantive law (p. 8.5)

Procedural law (p. 8.5)

Significant contacts rule (p. 8.5)

Forum shopping (or jurisdiction shopping) (p. 8.5)

Diversity of citizenship (p. 8.6)

Compensatory damages (p. 8.7)

Special damages (specials) (p. 8.7)

General damages (p. 8.7)

Punitive damages (exemplary damages) (p. 8.7)

Diminution in value (p. 8.10)

Hedonic damages (loss of enjoyment damages) (p. 8.16)

Diminished earning capacity (p. 8.17)

Eggshell claimant (p. 8.19)

Decedent (p. 8.21)

Estate (p. 8.21)

Survival action (p. 8.22)

Wrongful death actions (p. 8.22)

Pecuniary loss (p. 8.22)

Household services (p. 8.23)

Intrinsic value of children (p. 8.25)

Remittitur (p. 8.25)

Additur (p. 8.25)

Collateral source rule (p. 8.25)

Mitigation of damages rule (p. 8.26)

Aggravating circumstances (p. 8.28)

Best alternative to a negotiated agreement (BATNA) (p. 8.31)

Expert system (p. 8.31)

Review Questions

1. ☐ True   ☐ False   Liability claims are difficult to evaluate because of the underlying complexity and subjectivity of liability and damage assessments. (p. 8.2)

2. Why do increased jury verdicts lead to higher settlement offers from insurers? (p. 8.4)

3. After reviewing the facts of a case, the claim representative should complete what five steps? (pp. 8.4–8.5)

4. Identify the type of law described. (p. 8.5)
   a. Determined by the law of the place where the lawsuit is filed.
   b. Determined by the law of the place where a tort was committed.

5. ☐ True   ☐ False   When the significant contacts rule applies to a business claim, forum shopping enables the plaintiff to choose the jurisdiction that offers the most favorable substantive law. (pp. 8.5–8.6)

6. Explain why the removal of a case from state court to federal district court based on diversity of citizenship could increase or decrease the award. (p. 8.6)

7. Identify the damages in each of the following cases as special, general, or punitive. (pp. 8.7–8.8)
   a. Wages lost by a claimant who was injured in an automobile accident
   b. An award against the manufacturer of a defective automobile, above the pain and suffering award
   c. Cost to repair a vandalized vehicle
   d. Damages charged against a wealthy, drunken driver who struck and killed two children in a crosswalk; intended to deter similar future behavior
   e. An award to a child who suffered facial scarring following an attack by a vicious dog
   f. Payment of medical bills for a woman injured in a slip-and-fall accident in a supermarket
   g. An award for pain and suffering to a claimant who was burned when a tractor engine malfunctioned and spewed boiling water

8. ☐ True   ☐ False   Unlike punitive damages, compensatory damages might be based on the wealth and financial condition of the tortfeasor or the circumstances of the incident. (pp. 8.7–8.8)

9. List four factors courts consider when determining whether punitive damages should be awarded. (p. 8.8)

10. List the bodily injury damage elements that claim representatives must evaluate. (p. 8.10)

11. Identify all of the following that would be compensable medical expenses, provided they are reasonable and necessary. (pp. 8.11–8.12)

    a. Radiologist bills

    b. Transportation to and from healthcare providers

    c. Lost wages during hospitalization and recovery

    d. Treating physician bills

    e. Anesthesiologist bills

    f. Future physical therapy expense

    g. Visiting nurse

    h. Permanent disfigurement

    i. Pain and suffering

    j. Future medical supplies and equipment

    k. Mental health consulting

12. Identify the type of wage/income loss that fits each description. (p. 8.13)

    a.   Based on future estimated losses resulting from a permanent disability

    b.   Loss of earnings from the time of injury until the time of recovery; based on wages from the job the person performed before the loss

13. List some questions claim representatives should answer when valuing general damages for bodily injury claims. (p. 8.14)

14. List the issues a claim representative should consider with permanent injuries. (p. 8.15)

15. Identify all of the following that might be considered loss of enjoyment damages. (pp. 8.15–8.16)

    a.   Inability to participate in softball, as in the past

    b.   Inability to pay medical expenses associated with the accident

    c.   Inability to engage in play with one's children

    d.   Interference with sexual relations

    e.   Inability to work at a job

    f.   Shortened life expectancy

    g.   Inability to voluntarily prepare food at a local soup kitchen

    h.   Inability to dress oneself

16. ☐ True ☐ False Disfigurement damages compensate a claimant for the emotional toll associated with scars or other physical impairments that could cause embarrassment or self-consciousness for the claimant at the current time or in the future. (p. 8.16)

17. In calculating diminished earning capacity, a claim representative should consider what factors? (p. 8.17)

18. What is the most recurrent and effective defense against the calculations and assumptions used for determining awards for diminished earning capacity of minors? (p. 8.18)

19. Name several losses that loss of consortium/companionship claims allege. (p. 8.19)

20. Identify all of the following parties who might have a claim for loss of consortium/companionship if a loved one suffers bodily injury or death. (p. 8.19)
    a. Friend
    b. Spouse
    c. Parents
    d. Grandchildren
    e. Co-workers
    f. Employer

21. ☐ True   ☐ False   Most courts hold that if a claimant's preexisting condition is aggravated by a new injury, the defendant is not responsible for the full damages of a resultant disability. (p. 8.20)

22. Identify the category of death action based on each description. (p. 8.22)

    a. Action that allows for the pecuniary loss to the survivors in a death case to provide them with the same standard of living that would have been provided had the deceased lived; some states permit recovery for mental anguish, loss of consortium, and other subjective damages

    b. Action in which the personal representative for the decedent makes a claim for medical expenses, loss of earnings, and pain and suffering incurred by the decedent from the time of the accident until death

23. List several household services, including skilled work, that might be compensated in a wrongful death claim. (p. 8.23)

24. There are two approaches to valuing claims for the death of children. Briefly describe these opposing views. (pp. 8.24–8.25)

    a. Historic view

    b. Intrinsic view

25. Identify the damage award concept that fits each description. (pp. 8.25–8.26)

    a. Occurs when a judge uses his or her discretion to increase a jury verdict award deemed insufficient

    b. Requires claimants to make efforts to prevent damages that are avoidable

    c. Occurs when a judge uses his or her discretion to reduce an excessive jury verdict award

    d. Bars the introduction of evidence that a claimant has other sources of recovery, such as health insurance

26. In what ways does a claimant's representation by a competent trial attorney increase the damage award? (p. 8.26)

27. Give examples of the use of expert witnesses in injury or death claims. (p. 8.27)

28. List several characteristics of an insured, a claimant, or a witness that could influence a jury award. (pp. 8.27–8.28)

29. Identify the following items that might constitute aggravating circumstances and influence a jury award. (pp. 8.28–8.29)

    a.   Alcohol or drugs contributed to the accident

    b.   Type of vehicle the claimant drives (such as a motorcycle or a Rolls Royce)

    c.   Status of the individual in the community

    d.   Teenager or older driver

    e.   Pedestrian, elderly, or pregnant claimant

    f.   Urban versus rural area

    g.   Small child bitten by a dog

    h.   Party who nearly died from the accident

30. List several venue factors that influence jury awards. (pp. 8.29–8.30)

31. Identify the methods for calculating settlement ranges with their descriptions. (pp. 8.30–8.34)

    a.   The claim representative applies a mathematical calculation to the damages (for example, estimate medical expenses, then multiply by 3 to determine the general damages amount).

    b.   After considering all the facts of the case, the claim representative determines the highest probable award (as from a trial or arbitration), then adds the costs of the action.

    c.   Two or more claim professionals evaluate the claim file, each suggesting a settlement range. The parties discuss their proposed ranges, then reach a consensus.

    d.   A computerized system applies artificial intelligence to emulate human learning, reasoning, communicating, seeing, and hearing. It uses a database and an inference engine to apply procedures and assumptions to claim details that the claim representative enters through a user interface.

    e.   A manual system that a claim representative can apply by determining the value of a "perfect" case, then adjusting the value based on peculiarities of the case (such as venue, quality of counsel and witnesses, and other intangibles).

    f.   The claim representative evaluates the settlement value based on all circumstances (liability, damages, and miscellaneous factors) of the claim.

32. Match the methods for calculating settlement ranges with their advantages or disadvantages. (pp. 8.30–8.31)

    ___ a. Individual case valuation method

             1. Does not reflect the claimant's desire to avoid litigation or the uncertainty but forces insurers to consider the financial consequences of not reaching a settlement; useful in motivating sidetracked parties toward settlement

    ___ b. Roundtable technique

             2. Values can vary widely but most appropriate for serious injuries, especially when combined with other methods

    ___ c. Formula method

             3. Based on faulty assumptions but is simple and uniform; avoids problems with more rational approaches; and can result in early, mutually agreeable settlements

    ___ d. Best alternative to a negotiated agreement (BATNA)

             4. Taps the knowledge and experience of multiple claim professionals but is time-consuming and inappropriate for minor claims

33. Complete the following table of advantages and disadvantages of using expert systems to establish claim values. (pp. 8.32–8.34)

Advantages	Disadvantages
• Provides a learning tool for new claim	• Much work to create and maintain representatives systems, thus expensive
• Flags areas that need further investigation	• Incorrect input of data can cause costly errors
•	•
•	•
•	•
•	•

34. ☐ True   ☐ False   The advantage of using a settlement value template over an expert system is that a systematic process is applied at a reduced cost. The disadvantage is the extensive time needed to arrive at a range of values. (p. 8.34)

Answers to Assignment 8 Questions

NOTE: These answers are provided to give students a basic understanding of acceptable types of responses. They often are not the only valid answers and are not intended to provide an exhaustive response to the questions.

Review Questions

1. True

2. Insurers offer more money for damages to reduce the risk of a high jury verdict.

3. Steps for evaluating liability:
    (1) Review and apply the applicable law.
    (2) Determine the legal obligations and defenses that apply to the facts.
    (3) Determine what choices, if any, the claimant might have in applying the law.
    (4) Determine what category of liability applies (clear, probable, questionable, or doubtful).
    (5) Review the facts and determine whether other potentially liable parties have been overlooked.

4. a. Procedural law
    b. Substantive law

5. True

6. Federal courts have different procedures, and their juries come from a broader geographic area.

7. a. Special
    b. Punitive
    c. Special
    d. Punitive
    e. General
    f. Special
    g. General

8. False—Punitive damages might be based on the wealth and financial condition of the tortfeasor or the circumstances of the incident.

9. Factors that determine award of punitive damages:
    • Nature of the offense
    • Need to punish the wrongdoer
    • Need to deter the wrongdoer from similar conduct in the future
    • Need to deter others from similar conduct

10. Bodily injury damage elements:
    • The amount of medical expenses
    • The type of injury
    • The claimant's wage loss or loss of earning capacity because of the injury
    • The pain and suffering resulting from the injury

- The extent of disability and impairment
- The claimant's loss of enjoyment from an injury
- Any disfigurement resulting from the injury
- Whether preexisting conditions contributed to the injury

11. a, b, d, e, f, g, j, and k

12. a.   Loss of earning capacity
     b.   Wage loss

13. Questions for valuing general damages (answers may vary):
     - What are the specific injuries and what type of pain is associated with those injuries?
     - Are they consistent with the accident?
     - Did symptoms (and pain) preexist?
     - Are other causes contributing to the pain?
     - Is pain acute (and temporary) or chronic (and long-term)?

14. Issues for valuing permanent injuries:
     - Have job/family and recreation been changed for the worse as a result of this permanent injury?
     - Does chronic pain accompany the injury?
     - Does disability or disfigurement accompany the injury?
     - Has the person's personality been affected?

15. a, c, d, f, g, and h

16. True

17. Factors in calculating diminished earning capacity:
     - Occupation and wages of claimant
     - Age of claimant
     - Expected work life of claimant
     - Life expectancy of claimant
     - Education and training of claimant
     - Previous job history of claimant

18. They are too speculative.

19. Loss of consortium/companionship losses:
     - Love
     - Companionship
     - Services
     - Comfort

20. b, c, and d

21. False

22. a. Wrongful death action
    b. Survival action

23. Household services compensated in a wrongful death claim (answers may vary):
    - Painting
    - Carpentry
    - Personal shopping assistance
    - Lawn care and landscaping
    - Cooking
    - Cleaning

24. a. Children have little economic production and, in fact, are a source of significant costs to parents.
    b. Children have future economic value to aging parents, such as long-term care, assisted living facility care, transportation, and financial guidance.

25. a. Additur
    b. Mitigation of damages rule
    c. Remittitur
    d. Collateral source rule

26. Represented claimants are likely to make frequent trips to chiropractors and incur greater expenses for diagnostic evaluations. The attorney's aggressiveness in claim handling, reputation in the legal community, and presentation in front of a jury can increase awards.

27. Expert witness use in injury or death claims (answers may vary):
    - Establish how a given disability may affect future earnings
    - Assess future expenses that a disabled person will likely incur
    - Guide claim representatives in investigating elements of damage to establish accurate reserves

28. Characteristics that influence a jury award (answers may vary):
    - Individual claimant versus a business or government entity
    - Communication skills of plaintiff and defendant
    - Believable, reasonable claimant; gives clear, concise answers
    - Appearance of plaintiff and defendant

29. a, b, d, e, g, and h

30. Venue factors that influence awards (answers may vary):
    - Economic conditions of community
    - Occupations of people in community
    - Average income level of people in community
    - Education level of people in community
    - General cultural values of community
    - Urban versus rural community/area

31. a. Formula method
    b. Best alternative to a negotiated agreement (BATNA)
    c. Roundtable technique
    d. Expert systems
    e. Settlement valuation templates
    f. Individual case valuation method

32. a. 2
    b. 4
    c. 3
    d. 1

33. Use of expert systems (answers may vary):

    Advantages:

    - Helps classify, store, and assemble enormous amounts of information.
    - Provides consistent and objective evaluations.
    - Adds new depth and encourages a comprehensive review of the medical record.
    - Systems are contemporaneous, portable, and updatable.

    Disadvantages:

    - Work, time, and costs to create the system are formidable.
    - Incorrect data input creates erroneous results.
    - Can be manipulated for "better results."
    - Not a substitute for claim representative's judgment.

34. False—The settlement value template takes less time than entering all the data necessary for valid results.

Direct Your Learning

Settling Liability Claims

Educational Objectives

After learning the content of this assignment, you should be able to:

1. Explain the benefits of alternative dispute resolution (ADR) techniques.

2. Identify the claims suitable for mediation, explain the mediation process, and describe criticisms of mediation.

3. Explain arbitration and describe the different variations of arbitration.

4. Describe the other types of ADR, such as:
   - Mini-trials
   - Neutral expert analysis
   - Summary jury trial
   - Pretrial conferences
   - Settlement days
   - Online settlement forums

5. Explain how structured settlements are used and why they may be helpful in resolving liability claims.

6. Explain the legal components of a release agreement and describe the issues related to releases, such as:
   - Enforceability of releases and who must sign the release
   - Which unnamed parties might also be released
   - Death claims
   - Uninsured motorist claims

7. Explain how to appropriately conclude claims involving claimants who are minors.

8. Explain the claim settlement tactics and issues involving:
   - Nuisance settlements
   - First-call settlements
   - Drop draft settlements
   - Advance payments
   - Liens

9. Describe the various ways in which insurers may recover funds after liability settlements have been made.

10. Define or describe each of the Key Words and Phrases for this assignment.

Study Materials

Required Reading:
▶ Liability Claim Practices
  - Chapter 9

Study Aids:
▶ SMART Online Practice Exams
▶ SMART Study Aids
  - Review Notes and Flash Cards— Assignment 9

Outline

▶ **Alternative Methods for Settling Liability Claims**

A. Overview of Alternative Dispute Resolution (ADR)

B. Benefits of ADR

C. ADR Service Providers

D. Mediation Overview

   1. Types of Cases Suitable for Mediation

E. The Mediation Process

   1. Selecting the Mediator

   2. Preparing for Mediation

   3. Making Effective Opening Statements in Mediation

   4. Presenting the Evidence in Mediation

   5. Negotiating in Mediation

   6. Concluding the Mediation

   7. Criticism of Mediation

   8. Telemediation

F. Arbitration Overview

G. Arbitration Variations

   1. High-Low Agreements

   2. Baseball Arbitration

   3. Mediation-Arbitration

   4. Arbitration-Mediation

   5. Inter-Company Arbitration

H. Mini-Trials

I. Neutral Expert Analysis

J. Summary Jury Trials

K. Pretrial Conferences

L. Settlement Days

M. Online Settlement Forums

N. Structured Settlements

▶ **Settlement Agreements**

A. General Release of All Claims

   1. Issues With Releases

B. Special Releases and Settlement Situations

   1. Releases by and on Behalf of Minors

   2. Releases by Partnerships or Corporations

   3. Releases in Death Claims

   4. Uninsured Motorist Release

   5. Policyholder Releases

C. Nuisance Settlements

D. First-Call Settlements

E. "Drop Draft" Settlements

F. Advance Payments

   1. Guidelines for Issuing Advance Payments

G. Liens

▶ **Recovering Liability Claim Payments**

A. Contribution

B. Indemnity

C. Subrogation

   1. Subrogation Process

   2. The Subrogation Notice

   3. The Subrogation Specialist

D. Salvage

E. Coordination of Insurance Benefits

▶ **Summary**

Try to establish a study area away from any distractions, to be used only for studying.

Key Words and Phrases

Define or describe each of the words and phrases listed below.

Alternative dispute resolution (ADR) (p. 9.2)

Mediation (p. 9.5)

Caucus (p. 9.12)

Mediator (p. 9.12)

Telemediation (p. 9.13)

Arbitration (p. 9.14)

Binding arbitration (p. 9.14)

High-low agreements (p. 9.14)

Nonbinding arbitration (p. 9.14)

Arbitration-mediation (p. 9.15)

Baseball arbitration (p. 9.15)

Mediation-arbitration (p. 9.15)

Inter-company arbitration (p. 9.16)

Mini-trials (p. 9.16)

Paper arbitration (p. 9.16)

Neutral expert (p. 9.17)

Pretrial conference (p. 9.17)

Settlement days (p. 9.17)

Summary jury trial (p. 9.17)

Blind bidding (p. 9.18)

Online settlement forums (p. 9.18)

Structured settlement (p. 9.20)

Release (p. 9.21)

Settlement agreement (p. 9.21)

Covenant not to sue (p. 9.23)

Minor (p. 9.23)

Court-approved settlement (p. 9.24)

Parent-guardian release and indemnity agreement (PG release)
(p. 9.24)

Uninsured motorist release (p. 9.26)

Policyholder releases (p. 9.28)

First-call settlement (p. 9.28)

Nuisance settlement (p. 9.28)

Drop draft (p. 9.29)

Advance payment (p. 9.29)

Lien (p. 9.31)

Perfected lien (p. 9.31)

Medicare liens (p. 9.32)

Contribution (p. 9.32)

Indemnity (p. 9.33)

Subrogation (p. 9.34)

Salvage (p. 9.36)

Collateral sources (p. 9.37)

Review Questions

1. What are the four major elements of the negotiation process? (p. 9.2)

2. Identify the advantage of using ADR that fits the description. (pp. 9.3–9.4)

   a. An ADR process can be concluded within three to six months of submission of a case.

   b. Parties select the procedure to be implemented from a wide range of choices, and procedures can be tailored to meet particular needs.

   c. Rules of evidence are relaxed; usually no record is made of the proceedings; provides a better atmosphere for the disputants to express themselves.

   d. Requires fewer extensive depositions, expert witnesses, and procedural motions than litigation; costs are lower.

   e. Claim values are determined by experienced professionals, mutually selected by the parties, unlike jurors, who normally have no experience setting claim values.

   f. Not matters of public record; most disputants can confirm confidentiality through signed agreements.

   g. Mutually selected, neutral party is a former judge or attorney with significant experience in similar cases; commands the respect needed to effect an agreement.

   h. In many cases, parties have unequal resources, influence, and knowledge; ADR facilitates justice because it is more accessible.

   i. Fewer and less formal procedures help quickly identify the critical disputed facts and issues and promote exchange of required information.

3. Identify which of the following cases would be suitable for mediation. (p. 9.6)

   a. Claims involving coverage disputes

   b. Claims involving multiple parties in which extensive discovery will be required

   c. Claims with potential values that exceed the insured's limit of liability

   d. Claims with highly emotional issues

   e. Claims that will incur more legal expenses than the likely settlement value

   f. Claims that involve fraud

   g. Claims involving plaintiffs with unrealistic expectations

4. List the six steps in the mediation process. (p. 9.6)

5. Complete the list of activities to be undertaken when preparing for mediation. (pp. 9.8–9.9)

   a. Review the claim.

   b.

   c.

   d. Take the proceedings seriously.

   e.

   f. Bring all the relevant information.

   g. Learn from the past.

   h.

   i.

6. While inventing options for mediation, what can a claim representative focus on to take the focus off money? (p. 9.9)

7. ☐ True   ☐ False   Statements made by the parties during mediation are admissible in a subsequent trial. (p. 9.9)

8. When making an effective opening statement in mediation, why is it important to maintain eye contact with the opposing side and address the claimant and his or her attorney and not just the mediator? (p. 9.10)

9. List several strategies that should be considered when negotiating in mediation. (p. 9.11)

10. Identify which of the following items are benefits of using caucuses in mediation. (p. 9.12)
    a. Permits a party to vent emotionally to the mediator without alienating the other side
    b. Permits the mediator to speak frankly about a party's behavior and how it might be counterproductive to negotiations
    c. Encourages parties to polarize the issues
    d. Gives each side a chance to do some homework
    e. Permits the mediator to establish a more personal rapport with each side
    f. Permits the parties to experience what they might feel if the case advances to litigation

11. List several ways that a mediator can be a useful resource. (pp. 9.12–9.13)

12. What type of paperwork should be completed at the conclusion of mediation? (p. 9.13)

13. List three criticisms of mediation. (p. 9.13)

14. ☐ True   ☐ False   Telemediation is beneficial for parties who reside many miles apart to resolve their disputes regardless of the nature and number of issues to be resolved. (pp. 9.13–9.14)

15. Distinguish between these ADR techniques by matching them with their descriptions. (p. 9.14)

    ___ a. Mediation   1. Parties to a dispute decide their own case.

    ___ b. Arbitration   2. A neutral third party decides the case for the parties to a dispute.

16. Distinguish between the two types of arbitration by matching them with their descriptions. (p. 9.14)

    ___ a. Nonbinding arbitration   1. Both parties to the dispute are required to accept the arbitrator's decision.

    ___ b. Binding arbitration   2. Neither party to the dispute is forced to accept the arbitrator's decision.

17. Identify the type of arbitration that fits each description. (pp. 9.14–9.16)

  a. Parties agree to attempt to resolve their dispute through mediation but agree that if mediation fails, they will proceed directly to arbitration.

  b. Each party presents its case to the arbitrator along with its final, realistic money offer. The arbitrator must choose one of the offers. Often parties settle before that choice is made.

  c. Parties to the dispute set high and low figures for the dispute before arbitration begins. The parties agree to accept the arbitrator's award if it falls within that range but also to cap the figures at the high or low figure if the arbitrator's award exceeds or reduces the award beyond those limits.

  d. Parties first present their cases to an arbitrator who decides a confidential award. The parties proceed to mediation. If the parties reach an agreement, the arbitrator's award remains undisclosed. If they do not agree, the arbitrator's award sets the amount.

  e. One party (an insurer) settles with or on behalf of the insured. The case is then submitted to an arbitration service to determine what each insurer owes.

18. Identify the ADR method that fits each description.
    (pp. 9.16–9.18)

    a. The judge acts as mediator and encourages the litigants to
        try one last time to resolve their differences before the formal
        trial begins. The judge might express his or her opinion on
        the litigants' positions, indicating the probable trial outcome.

    b. Arbitration and dispute resolution services for claims and
        virtual courts are offered through the Internet. Many apply
        methods and techniques from traditional ADR.

    c. Much like a regular jury trial, except that only a few witnesses
        present the case. "Mock jurors" might hear evidence and
        witnesses' testimony in oral and written formats. Lawyers
        summarize information, and the mock jurors decide the case.

    d. When negotiations reach an impasse over a technical issue,
        parties enlist the assistance of a mutually acceptable expert
        who helps establish a value.

    e. Two parties to a dispute present an abbreviated version of
        their case to a "judge," who renders an opinion on the out-
        come. This enables parties to test the validity of their posi-
        tions in a trial setting and to continue negotiations.

    f. Parties from several smaller, less complicated disputes come
        together on the same day to a conference center. Attorneys
        and claim representatives go from room to room settling
        different claims. This enables attorneys to block out a time
        period and be available to negotiate person-to-person.

19. List several advantages online settlement forums have over
    traditional ADR methods. (pp. 9.18–9.20)

20. In a structured settlement, after the initial payment, how do insurers generally provide periodic payments for a set number of years? (p. 9.20)

21. Why would a structured settlement offer help a claimant overcome an impasse? (p. 9.20)

22. Identify under which of the following circumstances a structured settlement would be useful. (p. 9.20)

    a.   A claimant requires ongoing, regular medical treatments

    b.   Lump-sum needs on an occasional basis

    c.   To meet educational needs for children

    d.   To provide retirement benefits for the claimant's spouse

    e.   For adequate living expenses to replace wages that cannot be earned

    f.   Ongoing expenses for household help

23. ☐ True   ☐ False   A settlement agreement must include an offer, acceptance, and consideration. The parties must have the legal capacity and authority to settle, and the claimants must have the mental capacity to understand the nature and effect of the agreement. (p. 9.21)

24. List the key elements of a general release. (p. 9.21)

25. As long as the elements of a contract are met, courts generally enforce releases. Explain two exceptions to this rule. (p. 9.22)

26. ☐ True ☐ False Only one spouse must sign the release for claims involving injuries to married persons or property owned by a married person. (pp. 9.22–9.23)

27. For each of the following, indicate unnamed parties who are released. (pp. 9.23–9.27)
    a. General release of the principal
    b. Release of an employee
    c. Release of a partner
    d. Release of a corporation
    e. Traditional "release-of-one" rule

28. How might a claimant use a covenant not to sue a joint tortfeasor to his or her benefit in a legal action? (p. 9.23)

29. ☐ True ☐ False A married or an emancipated minor can legally sign a release on his or her own behalf. (pp. 9.23–9.24)

30. Distinguish between the two common ways to conclude claims involving minors. (pp. 9.24–9.26)

     ___ a. Court-approved settlement   1. Used to settle the claims of the parent and the child on claims involving relatively small dollar amounts and little chance of a permanent injury; parents agree to indemnify the insurer for any amounts paid as the result of the minor bringing action once he or she reaches legal age

     ___ b. Parent-guardian release   2. A legal proceeding in which the court reviews all indemnity agreement details of the settlement, then determines whether it is in the best interest of the minor; if the court accepts the settlement, it issues a judgment approving the settlement terms and amount

31. List the four items to consider when determining the appropriate conclusion for a claim involving a minor. (p. 9.26)

32. In wrongful death and survival cases, state laws determine who must sign the release. Name the parties who might be able to sign the release. (p. 9.26)

33. What are the features of a standard uninsured motorist release? (p. 9.26)

34. ☐ True   ☐ False   When an insured is involved in an uninsured motorist claim, he or she can settle with the claimant, then collect for the same elements of loss from his or her uninsured motorist carrier. (p. 9.26)

35. April was injured in a car accident. Josh, the other driver, was uninsured at the time. April recovered for the damages from her automobile insurer, Progressive Auto, and signed an Uninsured Motorist Release and Trust Agreement. April felt sorry for Josh and wrote him a letter stating that he should not reimburse Progressive Auto for her injuries.

☐ True ☐ False   April breached a contract when she mailed her letter to Josh. (p. 9.26)

36. Complete the table with arguments for and against paying nuisance claims. (p. 9.28)

For	Against
• Reduces legal costs of defending the claim	• Encourages future nuisance claims
•	•
•	•
•	•
•	•

37. Indicate whether a first-call settlement or "drop draft" settlement is appropriate for each of the following. (pp. 9.28–9.29)

   a. A relatively minor claim has reached an impasse, but the claimant has stopped pursuing the claim.

   b. Liability is questionable, but the claimant's injuries are minor and the claim representative thinks the claimant might be persuaded to settle with an immediate draft.

   c. Liability is probable, and the claimant sustained minor injuries.

   d. Liability is clear, and the claimant sustained less serious injuries.

38. What must a claim representative develop to recognize when a first-call settlement is appropriate? (pp. 9.28–9.29)

39. List several advantages of issuing advance payments.
    (pp. 9.29–9.30)

40. Complete the list of guidelines for issuing advance payments.
    (p. 9.30)
    - The claimant's injury should be obvious or undisputed and
      unlikely to be resolved within a matter of days.
    - The claimant should be willing to cooperate in obtaining
      medical and wage loss information.
    - Insurers should make clear that all payments are credited
      against any future settlement amount or court award.
    -
    -
    -

41. What should a receipt for advance payment clarify for the
    claimant? (p. 9.30)

42. Identify the following parties who commonly assert liens against
    settlements or awards to claimants. (p. 9.31)
    a. Lawyers
    b. Private investigators
    c. Workers compensation carriers
    d. Doctors
    e. Hospitals

43. ☐ True   ☐ False   A "perfected" lien is one in which the
    lienholder has been paid for the services provided through the
    settlement funds. (pp. 9.31–9.32)

44. The federal statute requires that Medicare be reimbursed for its payments. If the claimant does not reimburse Medicare within sixty days, what must happen? (p. 9.32)

45. If the government is forced to sue for reimbursement of Medicare payments, what is the government entitled to receive for its lien? (p. 9.32)

46. ☐ True   ☐ False   Medicare has primary responsibility for payment of medical benefits for insured individuals. Automobile/liability providers have secondary responsibility. (p. 9.32)

47. Identify the type of liability claim payment recovery that fits the description. (pp. 9.32–9.37)

    a. Damaged property that is turned over to the insurance company after the total value of the property has been paid on a claim; can often be sold to recover part of the claim payment

    b. Provides that after a settlement has been made on an insured's claim, insurers can seek recovery of their payments from parties responsible for their insured's damages

    c. The amount of a settlement for which a tortfeasor's insurer is liable, after another tortfeasor's insurer has settled with the claimant to avoid litigation

    d. Other nonliability insurance sources of recovery that reimburse claimants for all or some of their medical expenses, wage loss, or disability, such as health insurance, no-fault auto insurance, and workers compensation

    e. Based on an agreement whereby one party agrees to secure another against an anticipated loss or damage

48. ☐ True   ☐ False   An insurer exercising the rights of subrogation can institute a lawsuit against the responsible party. (p. 9.34)

49. How might state bankruptcy laws affect subrogation recoveries? (p. 9.34)

50. Place the steps of the subrogation process in the order in which they generally occur. (p. 9.35)

    _____   a.   Collect subrogation payments from legally responsible parties.

    _____   b.   Place potentially responsible parties on notice.

    _____   c.   Identify potentially responsible parties.

    _____   d.   Investigate third-party liability issues.

51. List the advantages of a centralized subrogation unit. (pp. 9.35–9.36)

52. Name the three possibilities for coordination of benefits. (p. 9.37)

53. What rule of evidence could bar the introduction of evidence that a claimant has other sources of recovery? (p. 9.37)

Answers to Assignment 9 Questions

NOTE: These answers are provided to give students a basic understanding of acceptable types of responses. They often are not the only valid answers and are not intended to provide an exhaustive response to the questions.

Review Questions

1. Elements of negotiation process:
    (1) Communication
    (2) Preparation
    (3) Evaluation
    (4) Power

2. a. Timeliness
    b. Flexibility
    c. Informality
    d. Cost-effectiveness
    e. Predictability
    f. Private and confidential
    g. Professionalism
    h. Protects rights
    i. Efficiency

3. b, c, d, e, and g

4. (1) Selecting a mediator
    (2) Preparing for mediation
    (3) Making opening statements
    (4) Presenting evidence
    (5) Negotiating
    (6) Concluding the mediation

5. Preparing for mediation:
    b. Use objective criteria.
    c. Determine BATNAs.
    e. Empathize.
    h. Invent options.
    i. Establish rules.

6. The underlying needs of the claimant

7. False

8. This might be the only opportunity they have to hear the insurer's version of the facts and law.

9. Strategies for negotiating mediation:
    - Obtain a demand from the claimant before entering mediation.
    - Leave room to negotiate in mediation.
    - Communicate in a conciliatory tone and remember the goal to obtain a satisfactory resolution.
    - Evaluate the other side's emotional need to "win."
    - Negotiate global values when an impasse is reached on sub-issues.

10. a, b, d, and e

11. Mediator as a resource (answers will vary):
    - As a negotiating partner to test ways to respond to arguments
    - To test a party's position
    - To break down communication barriers
    - To get parties beyond an impasse by dividing the issues into smaller parts
    - By allowing silence to force parties to communicate
    - By reminding parties of the consequences of not settling

12. A blank settlement agreement should be completed and signed by each party.

13. Criticisms of mediation:
    (1) It may add to the overall costs if the parties are not serious about settlement.
    (2) Parties involved may lack expertise.
    (3) There is no guarantee of concluding the claim.

14. False—Telemediation works well in disputes with few issues, especially when parties have become emotionally entrenched in their positions.

15. a. 1
    b. 2

16. a. 2
    b. 1

17. a. Mediation-arbitration
    b. Baseball arbitration
    c. High-low agreements
    d. Arbitration-mediation
    e. Inter-company arbitration

18. a. Pretrial conference
    b. Online settlement forums
    c. Summary jury trials
    d. Neutral expert analysis
    e. Mini-trials
    f. Settlement days

19. Advantages of online settlement forums:
    - They permit asynchronous negotiations.
    - They are less threatening for the participants, especially for unrepresented claimants.
    - Some parties may be less likely to make outrageous demands or make "low ball" offers to influence the other side's expectations.
    - Most online services offer follow-up human dispute-resolution mediators who try to bring parties together when they don't settle within an allotted number of rounds.
    - Some online services offer a database that disputants can access to help evaluate their claims.

20. They purchase an annuity from a life insurance company and name the claimant as "beneficiary."

21. a, b, c, e, and f

22. Because the claimant receives more money in total than with a lump-sum payment

23. True—These are the requirements of a legally binding contract.

24. Elements of a general release:
    - Names and addresses of parties involved
    - Date of the accident
    - Amount of the settlement
    - Statement that the release applies to all claims of the claimant now and in the future, whether known or unknown
    - Statement that parties understand and agree to the terms of the release
    - Signatures required for written releases

25. Claims settled with indecent haste and releases taken in hospitals from claimants who are still emotionally upset and on medicine

26. False

27. a. Agents or employees involved in the act
    b. Employer (through *respondeat superior*)
    c. Other partners (provided the partner is a working partner with authority to bind the partnership)
    d. Owners of the corporation (provided the signer is an authorized officer)
    e. Other joint tortfeasors—this principle no longer applies

28. The money provided allows them to prepare for litigation against the other tortfeasor.

29. False—A contract signed by a minor can be voided by the minor at will.

30. a. 2
    b. 1

31. Considerations for claims involving minors:
    (1) The duration of the likely disability
    (2) The nature and severity of the injury
    (3) The amount of the special damages involved
    (4) The integrity and condition of the family and minor's relationship with parents

32. The administrator or executor for the decedent's estate or the decedent's legal heirs

33. Uninsured motorist release features:
     - Deduct the UM payment from any liability payment made to the individual
     - Protect the company's subrogation rights against the tortfeasor
     - Require insured to cooperate with the insurer in pursuing subrogation
     - Require insured to hold in trust and give the insurer any funds the insured receives from the responsible parties

34. False

35. True

36. For:
     - Reduces administrative costs of keeping file open
     - Eliminates uncertainty of litigation from aberrant court awards
     - Eliminates uncertainty of insured

     Against:
     - Paying claims that do not have merit is unethical
     - Can cause insureds' premiums to increase without good cause

37. a. "Drop draft" settlement
     b. First-call settlement
     c. First-call settlement
     d. First-call settlement

38. Experience and judgment

39. Advantages of advance payments:
     - Help relieve the claimant's financial anxiety, which helps develop rapport and trust.
     - Help the claimant get better medical attention, reducing the time off from work and the possibility or extent of permanent injury.
     - Because they obtain the medical records, they are better able to determine the loss exposure and set accurate reserves.
     - Social value in keeping the claimant from the need to file for bankruptcy or seek welfare relief.

40. Guidelines for advance payments:
     - The insured's liability should be apparent.
     - Insurers should set a time limit for issuing advance payments.
     - Insurers should have an amount limit and should pay for only reasonable and necessary expenses.

41. It should stipulate the terms of the payment, and it should expressly state that the advance payments are not an admission of liability and that the insurer will get credit for all advance payments made.

42. a, c, d, and e

43. False—It is a lien for which the insurer has been placed on notice.

44. The insurer must reimburse the government, even if it has already paid the claimant.

45. Double the amount of the lien

46. False

47. a. Salvage
    b. Subrogation
    c. Contribution
    d. Collateral sources
    e. Indemnification

48. True

49. The debt can be discharged so that the insurer can no longer pursue recovery.

50. a. 4
    b. 2
    c. 1
    d. 3

51. Advantages of a centralized subrogation unit:
    - Provides for a coordination of outside services
    - Benefits from a closer proximity to the home office or litigation unit
    - Accountability of results
    - Fewer conflicting priorities

52. Coordination of benefits:
    (1) One policy is primary over the other
    (2) The policies share equally in the loss (up to their liability limits)
    (3) The policies share proportionally in the loss based on their liability limits

53. Collateral source rule

SEGMENT

Assignments

Segment C is the third of three segments in the AIC 36 course.
These segments are designed to help structure your study.

Direct Your Learning

Managing Litigation

Educational Objectives

After learning the content of this assignment, you should be able to:

1. Explain the reasons companies need to manage litigation better.

2. Explain the various issues associated with the relationship between liability insurers and defense counsel representing insureds.

3. Explain the general role of the claim representative in litigated cases such as the following:

   - Handling coverage issues and selecting independent counsel
   - Performing a case evaluation
   - Conducting an investigation
   - Choosing legal counsel
   - Making periodic case evaluations
   - Settling the case

4. Explain the tasks that claim representatives should perform in each of the following stages of litigation:

   - The pleadings stage
   - Pretrial motions and discovery
   - Pretrial conferences and trials
   - Post-verdict activity

5. Identify the benefits and principles of good litigation management.

6. Explain how to manage litigation through the following:

   - Setting performance standard
   - Gathering performance data
   - Establishing litigation guidelines
   - Case litigation plan

7. Explain how to establish appropriate billing guidelines and bill auditing practices.

8. Describe some of the alternatives to (and variations in) hourly billing, such as:

   - Yearly retainer
   - Flat fee schedule
   - Modified flat fee (task-based fees)
   - Capped fee arrangement
   - Blended hourly rate
   - Defense contingency fees
   - Volume discounts

9. Explain the ethical issues in litigation management.

10. Explain how the following might help insurers control litigation costs:

    - Tort reform
    - Court reform
    - Technology

11. Define or describe each of the Key Words and Phrases for this assignment.

Study Materials

Required Reading:
▶ Liability Claim Practices
  • Chapter 10

Study Aids:
▶ SMART Online Practice Exams
▶ SMART Study Aids
  • Review Notes and Flash Cards—Assignment 10

Outline

▶ **Costs of Litigation**

▶ **The Role of the Claim Representative in Litigated Cases**

    A. Handling Coverage Issues

        1. Independent Legal Counsel

    B. Performing a Case Evaluation

    C. Assessing Excess and Bad Faith Exposure

    D. Conducting an Investigation

    E. Choosing Legal Counsel

        1. Customer Service Considerations for Legal Counsel

        2. Technological Considerations

        3. Firm Size

    F. The Claim Representative's Relationship With Legal Counsel

    G. The Tripartite Relationship

    H. Periodic Case Evaluations

    I. Settling the Case

▶ **The Claim Representative's Role in Each Stage of Litigation**

    A. The Pleadings—Summons and Complaint, Answer

        1. Transmitting Case Information to Legal Counsel

        2. Making Counterclaims

    B. Pretrial Motions and Discovery

    C. Pretrial Conferences and Trials

    D. Post-Verdict Activity

    E. Court Reform

▶ **Litigation Management Techniques**

    A. Benefits of Good Litigation Management

    B. Ten Principles of Good Litigation Management

        1. Establish Performance Metrics (Quantifiable Measures)

        2. Gather Performance Data on Litigated Cases

        3. Establish Litigation Guidelines

        4. Legal Bill Guidelines and Bill Audits

        5. Develop Alternatives to Hourly Billing

    C. Be Educated and Know Each Other's Needs

    D. Be a Good Client

    E. Ethical Issues in Litigation Management

▶ **Summary**

▶ **Appendix—Summary of Legal System and Legal Terms**

▶ **Appendix Contents**

    A. Court Systems

        1. State Courts

        2. Federal Courts

    B. Rules of Civil Procedure

    C. Statutes of Limitation

        1. Toll

    D. Pleadings

        1. Complaint

        2. Summons

        3. Answer

    E. Discovery

        1. Depositions

        2. Interrogatories

        3. Requests for Production of Documents

        4. Requests for Admissions

    F. Pretrial Motions

        1. Motion to Dismiss

        2. Motion *in Limine*

        3. Motion for Summary Judgment

    G. Pretrial Conference

    H. Trials

        1. Jury and Nonjury Trials

        2. Burden of Proof

        3. Opening Statements

        4. Introduction of Evidence Through Testimony

        5. Motion for a Directed Verdict

        6. Bench Conferences

        7. Closing Arguments

        8. Jury Instructions

        9. Jury Deliberations and Verdict

        10. Proceedings After the Verdict

        11. Appeals

        12. Enforcement of Judgments

Key Words and Phrases

Define or describe each of the words and phrases listed below.

Lawsuit (p. 10.1)

Plaintiff (p. 10.1)

Defendant (p. 10.1)

Litigation management (p. 10.2)

Excess verdict (p. 10.5)

Excess exposure (p. 10.5)

Tripartite relationship (p. 10.11)

Summons (p. 10.13)

Complaint (p. 10.13)

Counterclaim (p. 10.16)

Discovery (p. 10.19)

Depositions (p. 10.19)

Interrogatories (p. 10.19)

Discovery abuse (p. 10.20)

Motion (p. 10.20)

Subpoena (p. 10.20)

Requests for admissions (p. 10.21)

Directed verdict (p. 10.22)

Judgment notwithstanding the verdict (judgment *n.o.v.*) (p. 10.22)

Appeal (p. 10.24)

Court administration reform (court reform) (p. 10.24)

Mandatory settlement conferences (p. 10.25)

Pretrial conferences (p. 10.25)

Performance metrics (p. 10.28)

Litigation guidelines (p. 10.29)

Case budget (p. 10.31)

Third-party auditors (p. 10.33)

Attorney-client privilege (p. 10.35)

Hourly billing (p. 10.35)

Yearly retainer arrangement (p. 10.36)

Flat fee schedules (p. 10.36)

Modified flat fee arrangement (p. 10.36)

Capped fee arrangement (p. 10.36)

Blended hourly rates (p. 10.37)

Defense contingency fees or outcome-modified billing (also reverse contingency fees) (p. 10.37)

Volume discount (p. 10.37)

Review Questions

1. Of the following, identify the reasons companies need to manage litigation better. (pp. 10.2–10.3)

    a. Increasing numbers of lawsuits are being filed.

    b. Liability insurers are spending more on defense lawyers than on claim department staff salaries and independent adjusting expenses combined.

    c. The high inflation rate of the 1990s has contributed to the rise in the number of lawsuits.

    d. Parties to lawsuits endure enormous emotional strain and time demands.

    e. Courts are expensive for society to operate.

    f. Resources used for litigation are unavailable for other social benefits, such as healthcare subsidies and better education.

2. Place the steps that a claim representative must take in litigated cases in the order in which they generally occur. (pp. 10.3–10.13)

    ____   a. Conduct an investigation.

    ____   b. Perform a case evaluation.

    ____   c. Assess excess and bad faith exposure.

    ____   d. Settle the case.

    ____   e. Choose legal counsel.

    ____   f. Handle coverage issues

    ____   g. Make periodic case evaluations.

3. Explain how coverage issues affect selections of legal counsel. (p. 10.4)

4. At what point does the insurer's duty to defend arise? (p. 10.4)

5. How might the claim representative protect the rights of the insurer when the insured initiates a lawsuit before the coverage issues have been determined? (p. 10.4)

6. ☐ True   ☐ False   When the interests of the insured and the insurer conflict, courts might require that the insured retain independent counsel at his or her own expense. (p. 10.4)

7. Why should a claim representative avoid attacks and hardball antics when dealing with a plaintiff's attorney? (p. 10.5)

8. ☐ True   ☐ False   The defense counsel and the claim representative can relate the value of the claim to the limits of the policy as a means of avoiding bad faith allegations. (pp. 10.5–10.6)

9. How can the claim representative protect the insured's interest and avoid bad faith allegations? (p. 10.6)

10. Once a suit has been filed, who should conduct any ongoing investigation, the attorney or the claim representative? (p. 10.6)

11. List several examples of ways that defense counsel must meet an insurer's expectations on service needs. (p. 10.7)

12. List several technological abilities that might set a law firm apart by helping with better litigation management and offering customer service. (p. 10.9)

13. Explain how a computer interface between the defense lawyer's office and the claims office can save time in case evaluation and progress. (p. 10.9)

14. Complete the table to compare the benefits of small law firms with those of large law firms. (pp. 10.9–10.10)

Small Law Firms	Large Law Firms
• Insurer may have more influence and receive company advantage	• May offer "one-stop shopping"
•	•
•	•
•	•
•	•

15. Claim representatives, defense attorneys, and insureds have a tri-partite relationship, share common goals, and must work together and communicate their expectations. List the areas in which these parties may have differing expectations. (p. 10.11)

16. Of the following, identify each of the written, periodic case evaluations that defense counsel should provide for the claim representative. (p. 10.12)

    a. An overall case status evaluation every sixty or ninety days

    b. An annual case status evaluation

    c. A case evaluation update whenever significant developments occur

17. ☐ True   ☐ False
    Often legal counsel is given a settlement range to use in negotiations with the plaintiff's attorney. If the attorney's evaluation exceeds the settlement range, the case proceeds to trial. (p. 10.12)

18. Who has the ultimate responsibility for reevaluating the settlement value of a claim as new facts are learned through depositions and discovery? (p. 10.12)

19. Why do liability policies demand that insureds immediately forward every demand, notice, summons, or other process they receive to the insurer? (p. 10.13)

20. ☐ True   ☐ False   When an insurer receives a summons and complaint, the claim representative's first duty is to ascertain the date and the manner of the service. (p. 10.14)

21. When a claim representative transmits a case to legal counsel, why is it important that the information transmitted in the file excludes any unnecessary characterizations or opinions and that no statements could be seen as derogatory, demeaning, or suggestive of bias or an unwillingness to deal fairly with the client? (pp. 10.15–10.16)

22. ☐ True   ☐ False   Upon transmittal of a case to legal counsel, claim representatives should include an initial case evaluation form for the attorney to complete and return. (p. 10.16)

23. ☐ True   ☐ False   A defense lawyer can seek to prosecute a counterclaim with the informed consent of the insured, but it might create a conflict of interest that could be detrimental to the insured. (p. 10.19)

24. Identify the pretrial concept that fits each description. (pp. 10.19–10.22)

    a. Applications to the court, made by counsel, for a ruling or an order

    b. Documents issued by the clerk of the court or the attorney, acting as an officer of the court, to require the witness to appear and give testimony before a particular court or magistrate at a particular time

    c. Written questions submitted to a witness and returned with answers

    d. Written facts that reduce the scope of a dispute by establishing an agreed-on set of facts

    e. A witness's testimony taken under oath, before a notary or another person authorized to administer oaths; a question-and-answer record is prepared by a court reporter

25. ☐ True   ☐ False   If defense counsel suggests taking depositions, the claim representative should assume they are necessary to the case. (p. 10.19)

26. Of the following activities, identify those that a claim representative should perform in the pretrial motions and discovery phase of litigation. (pp. 10.19–10.21)

    a. Perform additional investigation in response to leads provided in depositions or interrogatories.

    b. Watch for potential discovery abuse by legal counsel and take measures to deter it.

    c. Issue subpoenas to the witnesses identified by legal counsel.

    d. Communicate with legal counsel to help control litigation costs without harming the quality of the insured's defense.

    e. Take statements and identify necessary medical and hospital records.

    f. Make recommendations to legal counsel on deposing examining physicians and the plaintiff's expert witnesses (as opposed to cross-examining them in court).

    g. Attend all depositions.

    h. Review any requests for admissions or other materials forwarded by defense counsel.

27. Complete the following list of considerations that can help a claim representative determine whether to settle a case or try it in court. (p. 10.22)

    • Plaintiff counsel's level of preparation and his or her willingness and ability to try the case to a verdict

28. What are some reasons claim representatives should attend pretrial conferences, jury selection, and their insureds' trials, if possible? (p. 10.22)

29. ☐ True   ☐ False   Polling the jurors after a verdict has been entered provides feedback about what worked in a case and what did not and assists in deciding whether to appeal the decision of the court. (p. 10.23)

30. Defense counsel and the claim representative should review the case and analyze whether an appeal is warranted. Complete the list of the factors that should be considered in this analysis. (p. 10.24)

    • The expense of an appeal, including appeal bonds and legal fees, and the time spent by the claim representative that will detract from his or her attention to other claim files

31. Court reform has changed laws to promote fairness and add predictability and efficiency to the civil justice system. List issues that most of these laws affect. (pp. 10.24–10.25)

32. List two procedures in which the judge seeks agreement and compromise between the parties to a suit in an effort to effect an out-of-court settlement of a case. (pp. 10.24–10.25)

33. Identify the traits of practices that have helped bring efficiency to the legal system as status conferences or pretrial procedural deadlines. (pp. 10.25–10.26)
    a. Best suited to relatively uncomplicated cases
    b. Best suited for cases that are somewhat complicated and require hands-on supervision by the court
    c. Called by judges to inform litigants of the status of the litigation and to establish deadlines for matters such as discovery, joinder of additional parties, and motions for summary judgement
    d. Less expensive caseflow management device
    e. Provides that cases are deemed ready for trial within a specified period of time after the case has been filed, unless the party moves and shows cause to establish a different schedule

34. Give two reasons an insurer might benefit from hiring only expensive, top trial lawyers. (p. 10.26)

35. Complete the lists of benefits of good litigation management for each of the following parties. (p. 10.27)

    Insurers:

    - Reduced administrative costs and processes because of better understanding of the roles of all parties and clear direction and authority
    - Reduced and more consistent and predictable legal fees

    Defense Firms:

    - Higher volume of work by making the client's work easier

    Insureds:

    - Resultant lower premiums from insurers

Writing notes as you read your materials will help you remember key pieces of information.

36. Complete the list of ten principles of good litigation management. (p. 10.27)

 (1) Avoid litigation through effective negotiation or alternative dispute resolution.

 (2)

 (3)

 (4) Establish attorney/law firm performance measures and track performance.

 (5)

 (6)

 (7)

 (8)

 (9) Understand attorneys' needs and make sure attorneys understand company's needs.

 (10)

37. Why are litigation files audited? (10.28)

38. List several common performance metrics insurers use to help manage litigation. (p. 10.28)

39. Ideally, insurers establish performance metrics, then collect data to determine performance. Often, insurers use management by visible numbers instead. What is meant by "management by visible numbers"? (pp. 10.28–10.29)

40. Complete the list of information that could be helpful in assessing legal defense needs. (pp. 10.28–10.29)

    - Amount spent on outside legal counsel
    - Amount spent on each type of claim
    - Amount law firms charge for specific tasks

41. Defense attorneys often perceive litigation guidelines as interference in their professional obligations and attacks on their professional integrity. How can claim representatives counter this impression? (p. 10.30)

42. List issues to be considered in evaluating case factors. (p. 10.31)

43. Complete the table to show factors in each plan in a detailed case budget. (p. 10.31)

Discovery Plans	Pretrial Motion Plans	Trial Plan
Check insured's version of accident	Case review	Pretrial conferences

44. Explain how a billing threshold that an insurer sets for a case helps control litigation costs. (p. 10.32)

45. How can insurers defuse legal counsel's complaints about billing guidelines? (p. 10.32)

46. Of the following, identify those that are suggested billing standards for legal counsel. (p. 10.33)

    a. Establish written billing guidelines.

    b. Ask lawyers to include insured and plaintiff names and claim or file numbers on bills.

    c. Bill full cost of a task that benefits multiple clients.

    d. Bill activities by tenths of an hour.

    e. Indicate the time spent on each task.

    f. Insist on minimal details for less complicated billing.

    g. Include the name of the lawyer or paralegal who performed the task.

    h. Itemize expenses.

47. ☐ True   ☐ False   Third-party auditors, often former claim representatives or practicing lawyers, claim the ability to accurately analyze lawyers' bills and help insurers reduce the excess in them. Use of these auditors is highly accepted in the legal field. (p. 10.33)

48. What is the most significant concern about using third-party auditors on defense counsel bills? (p. 10.35)

49. What document can insurers send out to seek alternative billing
    arrangements to hourly billing? (pp. 10.35–10.36)

50. Match each of the alternative billing arrangements with its
    description. (pp. 10.36–10.37)

    ___ a.   Yearly retainer arrangement

    ___ b.   Flat fee schedule

    ___ c.   Modified flat fee

    ___ d.   Capped fee arrangement

    ___ e.   Blended hourly rates

    ___ f.   Defense contingency fee

    ___ g.   Volume discount

    1. Parties establish a fixed fee to be paid for work on an
       entire case file, regardless of the number of hours devoted
       to it. (p. 10.39)

    2. The insurer agrees to pay an hourly rate for the work
       performed on the case, but a maximum amount limits the
       total cost for the case.

    3. If the defense lawyer succeeds in keeping awards as low as
       or lower than agreed on in advance, the lawyer is reward-
       ed with a higher fee. This provides an incentive for the
       lawyer to achieve a favorable verdict or settlement.

    4. Billing is charged on an hourly basis, but at a fixed hourly
       rate, whether a senior partner in the firm or the newest
       associate performs the work.

    5. The defense lawyer or law firm agrees to handle every
       case (within certain guidelines) for the insurer in return
       for a fixed lump-sum payment. The fee is renegotiated at
       the end of each year.

    6. The defense lawyer charges a lower hourly rate in consid-
       eration for a large volume of work. Complex work might
       warrant a higher rate than routine work.

    7. A flat fee is charged for a defined segment of the case.
       This generally includes the common, basic legal work to
       be completed. An hourly rate is charged for additional
       work such as trial preparation and trial activity.

51. Explain some general ways that an insurer can be a good client.
    (pp. 10.37–10.38)

52. Identify all of the following that are ways in which the claim representative can meet his or her end of the litigation management bargain. (p. 10.38)

    a. Provide timely coverage analysis.

    b. Research the legal issues and share findings with the attorney.

    c. Promptly review the case when a suit is filed and determine the best actions and alternatives.

    d. Complete factual investigations.

    e. Establish a list of specific items to accomplish with realistic due dates.

    f. Promptly communicate analysis of actions with the attorney.

53. ☐ True   ☐ False   Claim representatives do not require special training or assertiveness for handling litigation because they typically give the entire claim file to their attorney. (p. 10.39)

54. Identify all of the following that represent ethical issues in litigation management. (pp. 10.39–10.40)

    a. An attorney who represents an insured cannot represent the insurer on a coverage issue in a claim.

    b. Legal auditors have a duty to base insurer savings on true billing abuses and not to invent abuses to increase their own contingency fees.

    c. Defense fees must be reasonable, and the fee arrangement must be communicated to the insured client.

    d. Insurers must ensure that their guidelines do not require an attorney to benefit one client to the detriment of another.

    e. Alternative fee arrangements must contain safeguards so that any significant disparity between the actual fee and the equivalent hourly rate does not suggest that the attorney failed to adequately defend the insured's interests.

    f. Law firms should be selected based on professional criteria, not on how well the lawyers promote the firm through social events.

Answers to Assignment 10 Questions

NOTE: These answers are provided to give students a basic understanding of acceptable types of responses. They often are not the only valid answers and are not intended to provide an exhaustive response to the questions.

Review Questions

1. a, b, d, e, f

   c—The inflation rate in the 90s was low but didn't affect the increase in lawsuits.

2. a. 4
   b. 2
   c. 3
   d. 7
   e. 5
   f. 1
   g. 6

3. May need independent legal counsel for insured

4. If a complaint alleges facts that, if proven true, would obligate the insurer to indemnify the insured against the damages recovered by the claimant

5. Through a reservation of rights letter or a nonwaiver agreement

6. False—Independent counsel must be retained at the insurer's expense.

7. A spirit of cooperation and mutual respect will accomplish more than will such tactics.

8. False—The claim value should not be linked to the policy limits in any way.

9. By keeping the insured advised and seeking the insured's point of view

10. The claim representative; this will reduce the litigation expense.

11. Expectations and service needs must be met:
    - By promptly returning telephone calls and answering correspondence
    - By providing timely periodic reports
    - By taking time to make time and cost entries as they are incurred
    - By contacting the claim person in advance whenever changes necessitate revised fees and costs

12. Technological abilities that promote litigation management and customer service:
    - Compatible software formats to exchange data
    - Project management systems
    - Time tracking and billing software that the insurer can access
    - E-mail
    - Groupware for sharing case files and status reports
    - Availability of computerized legal research

13. Allows the claim representative direct access to the case file and the status at any time; avoids the need for lengthy correspondence between them

14. Small law firms:
    - High-touch customer service
    - Customized litigation management
    - Specialization in areas of law

    Large law firms:
    - Larger pool of experts
    - Better computer research facilities
    - Greater nonlawyer assistance

15. Issues for expectations:
    - Procedures
    - How litigation activities should be shared and coordinated
    - How and when lawyers should report
    - How cost and billing issues should be addressed
    - Accountability for results

16. a, c

17. False—Legal counsel consults the claim representative, who provides additional details and makes a recommendation to claim management supporting the request to increase the settlement authority.

18. The claim representative

19. Because the defendant generally has only twenty days to appear and answer or a default judgement could be rendered against the plaintiff (insured) – the insurer would have to pay that judgment

20. True

21. Claim files can be subpoenaed in court proceedings or viewed by insurance examiners. There should be nothing in the file that could form a basis for an action against the company or the claim representative for defamation or bad faith.

22. True

23. True

24. a. Motions
    b. Subpoenas
    c. Interrogatories
    d. Requests for admissions
    e. Deposition

25. False—Depositions are costly, so claim representatives should ask legal counsel whether they are necessary.

26. a, b, d, e, f, h

    c—A clerk of the court or an attorney acting as an officer of the court issues subpoenas.

    g—The claim representative should attend only key depositions in significant cases.

27. Considerations to settle or try a case:

    - The settlement value or potential jury verdict value of similar claims
    - The practices and predilections of the trial judge
    - The makeup of jury panels and the general characteristics of jurors in the community
    - The strengths and weaknesses of defense counsel

28. This provides an incomparable opportunity to advance the claim representative's professional knowledge. He or she can assist at trial by providing information that defense counsel may need at a moment's notice or by helping with a recalcitrant witness. A settlement opportunity may present itself during the trial to an observant claim representative.

29. True

30. Analysis factors for appeals:

    - The likelihood of a successful appeal in light of the law of the jurisdiction
    - The strength of the defense case
    - The views of the appellate judiciary and potential for setting favorable or unfavorable appellate precedents

31. Court reform issues:

    - Setting caps on punitive damages
    - Replacing joint and several liability with proportionate liability
    - Increased penalties against those who bring frivolous lawsuits
    - Modifying product liability laws

32. Procedures that can effect out-of-court settlements:

    - Mandatory settlement conferences
    - Pretrial conferences

33. a. Pretrial procedural deadlines

    b. Status conferences

    c. Status conferences

    d. Pretrial procedural deadlines

    e. Pretrial procedural deadlines

34. The reputation of top trial lawyers keeps plaintiff attorneys from filing frivolous suits and helps obtain lower settlements because plaintiff attorneys might not want to face them. The higher rates reflect greater efficiency in the work they do.

35. Insurers' benefits:
    - Better case assignment to appropriate legal experts
    - Better relationship with legal counsel

    Defense firms' benefits:
    - Less administrative expense
    - Less friction with clients
    - Development of legal expertise

    Insureds' benefits:
    - Better customer service (reduced time away from work and family)

36. (2) Select appropriate legal counsel.

    (3) Work with legal counsel as a team.

    (5) Establish litigation guidelines.

    (6) Establish litigation case plans and budgets.

    (7) Perform legal audits.

    (8) Develop alternative billing arrangements.

    (10) Do not permit unethical practices and avoid conflicts of interest.

37. Avoid litigation, contain costs

38. Performance metrics:
    - Average costs per case
    - Average hours per case
    - Ratio of attorney to nonattorney costs
    - Win/loss ratio at trials
    - Ratio of cases that settle to those that go to trial

39. Management bases measurements on the information that they can capture with their current systems.

40. Assessing legal defense needs:
    - Amount spent at each law firm
    - Average settlement per type of claim
    - Average outside counsel fee per type of claim
    - Budgeted versus actual figures

41. By treating attorneys with respect, making only reasonable demands, and deferring to defense counsel on legal matters when they provide a reasonable explanation for deviating from established guidelines

42. Issues in evaluating case factors:
    - The uniqueness of the case
    - The publicity the case might bring
    - The claimant's willingness and ability to spend a lot of money

43. Discovery Plan:
    - Prepare court documents.
    - Check opponent's facts.
    - Make a discovery plan.

    Pretrial Motion Plan:
    - Legal research
    - Initial pleadings
    - Discovery
    - Expert witnesses
    - Motions
    - Settlement and negotiation conferences and drafting settlement agreements

    Trial Plan:
    - Compulsory settlement meetings
    - Trial preparation
    - Jury or judge deciding the case

44. If the threshold is exceeded early on, then the case budget may be inadequate. If the threshold amount is not exceeded after several months, then the case may not be getting adequate attention.

45. They can make sure their legal counsel understands that if any question is raised, defense counsel need only explain why certain tasks are necessary and permission will be granted readily.

46. a, b, d, e, g, h

47. False

48. This might breach attorney-client confidentiality and the legal protection of attorney-client privilege.

49. Requests for proposals

50. a. 5
    b. 1
    c. 7
    d. 2
    e. 4
    f. 3
    g. 6

51. By acting professionally, treating lawyers with respect, communicating, encouraging teamwork, and meeting promises made to the firm

52. a, c, d, f

    b—The lawyer is responsible and has the expertise to complete this.

    e—This list should be completed with the lawyer in a team effort.

53. False

54. a, c, d, e, f

    b—Insurers have a duty to monitor the behavior of legal bill auditors.

Direct Your Learning

Auto Liability Claims

Educational Objectives

After learning the content of this assignment, you should be able to:

1. Explain how liability is assessed in auto claims.

2. Describe some of the common "rules of the road."

3. Explain how liability is assessed with claims involving parked or disabled vehicles.

4. Explain the liability issues involving passengers in insureds' cars.

5. Explain the effect that seat belt laws have on liability.

6. Explain how liability is assessed for claims involving pedestrians and bicyclists.

7. Explain how vicarious liability occurs in auto liability claims.

8. Describe the thresholds and benefits of personal injury protection (PIP) or limited tort plans.

9. Explain how claim representatives investigate auto liability claims by describing:

   • What activities are involved in auto liability investigations.

   • How proximate cause is determined in auto liability cases.

   • How experts might be used.

   • The type of evidence gathered in auto liability claims.

10. Given an auto liability case, be able to analyze liability issues and investigate auto liability claims.

11. Define or describe each of the Key Words and Phrases for this assignment.

Study Materials

Required Reading:
▶ Liability Claim Practices
  • Chapter 11

Study Aids:
▶ SMART Online Practice Exams
▶ SMART Study Aids
  • Review Notes and Flash Cards—Assignment 11

Outline

▶ **The Initial Phase of the Claim**

▶ **Analyzing Auto Law and Liability**
  A. Rules of the Road for Motorists
  B. Liability Involving Parked Vehicles
  C. Liability Involving Disabled Vehicles
  D. Liability Involving Passengers
  E. The Effect of Seat Belt Laws on Auto Liability
  F. Pedestrians and Bicyclists—Rights and Duties
  G. Commercial Vehicles

▶ **Vicarious Liability in Auto Claims**
  A. Vicarious Liability of Vehicle Owners
  B. Negligent Entrustment of Auto

▶ **Personal Injury Protection (PIP) and Limited-Tort Laws**
  A. Thresholds for Exempting Tort Claims
  B. Benefits Provided Under PIP
  C. Claim Administration and Subrogation Under PIP

▶ **Auto Liability Claim Investigations**
  A. Proximate Cause and Auto Liability
  B. The Use of Experts in Auto Liability Claims
  C. Evidence in Auto Liability Claims

▶ **Case Study—The Auto Liability Accident**
  A. Twenty-Two Tattoos
  B. Insurance Coverages
  C. The Liability Investigation
  D. Analyzing the Loss Exposures
  E. Cassandra's Claim
  F. Lenny's Injuries and Damages
  G. The Accident Reconstruction Expert
  H. Case Conclusion

▶ **Appendix—Automobile Accident Statement Guideline**

Before starting a new assignment, briefly review the Educational Objectives of those preceding it.

Key Words and Phrases

Define or describe each of the words and phrases listed below.

Clear, assured distance (p. 11.3)

Displayed (p. 11.3)

Guest statute (p. 11.5)

Seat belt defense (p. 11.6)

Negligent entrustment of an automobile (p. 11.8)

Threshold (PIP and limited tort) (p. 11.9)

Verbal threshold (p. 11.9)

Death benefits to survivors (p. 11.10)

Medical expense benefits (p. 11.10)

Monetary threshold (p. 11.10)

Replacement services benefits (p. 11.10)

Last clear chance doctrine (p. 11.13)

Unavoidable accident defense (p. 11.13)

Road defects (p. 11.14)

Forensic engineer (p. 11.14)

Biomechanics (p. 11.14)

Review Questions

1. Describe three rules of the road that motorists must obey.
   (pp. 11.3–11.4)

2. Explain whether a motorist who has illegally parked a car is
   liable when someone else collides with his parked car. (p. 11.4)

3. What would be a viable defense for a motorist who left a disabled vehicle in a traveled portion of the road? (pp. 11.4–11.5)

4. Describe two situations in which an insured driver might not be liable for injuries sustained by passengers even if the insured driver was guilty of ordinary negligence. (p. 11.5)

5. Describe how not wearing a seat belt is viewed differently by different states as a defense against injury claims. (p. 11.6)

6. Explain how liability would be assessed against a driver who struck a child who darted from behind parked cars. (p. 11.7)

7. Describe two circumstances in which owners of vehicles may be found liable for the negligence of others who are using the owners' vehicles with permission. (pp. 11.7–11.8)

8. Explain the purpose of PIP and limited tort laws.
   (pp. 11.8–11.9)

9. Explain the criticism of monetary thresholds in PIP states.
   (p. 11.10)

10. Describe some of the different activities that would be included in a typical auto liability investigation. (pp. 11.11–11.14)

Application Questions

1. An insured reports the following accident information to the claims office:
   - The accident involved one car and happened in a rural area.
   - The insured vehicle was forced off the road by an unknown party.
   - The insured was injured.
   - The accident occurred at 1:00 AM on a Saturday morning.

   The state where this accident occurred is a PIP state. What should the claim representative consider regarding coverages, damages, and possible investigative issues?

2. Bill is traveling on a country road and approaching an intersection. Bill has a stop sign, but it is obscured by tall weeds. Bill does not stop or slow down at the intersection and collides with a vehicle that comes from his right side on the intersecting road. Explain how liability should be assessed in this situation, given that the stop sign was not visible.

3. Mary is driving in her car when a bee flies in her car window. Mary is allergic to bee stings to the extent that a bee sting could threaten her life. Mary panics and tries to get the bee to fly back out the window. While doing this, she veers into the oncoming lane of traffic and strikes another vehicle. Mary claims that this was an unavoidable accident and an act of nature beyond her control. Is this a valid and appropriate defense for this claim?

Answers to Assignment 11 Questions

NOTE: These answers are provided to give students a basic understanding of acceptable types of responses. They often are not the only valid answers and are not intended to provide an exhaustive response to the questions.

Review Questions

1. Answers may vary.
   - Obey traffic controls
   - Conform to highway regulations
   - Keep vehicles under control
   - Do everything possible to avoid accidents
   - Keep a clear, assured distance behind other vehicles
   - Comply with displayed traffic signs
   - Yield the right-of-way to traffic on main roads, and oncoming traffic, emergency vehicles, school buses, pedestrians in crosswalks, etc.

2. If the illegal parking caused or contributed to the accident, then the motorists would be held liable; otherwise, not.

3. Proving that (1) there was an emergency that caused the vehicle to be disabled and (2) the driver took every precaution possible in leaving the car (emergency flashers, flares, etc.)

4. Possible answers include the following:
   - If the passenger assumed the risk by getting into the car with an obviously intoxicated driver
   - If the accident occurs in a state that has a guest statute

5.
   - States that don't recognize this as a defense
   - States that set strict limitations on this defense
   - States that permit defendants to use this defense

6. In theory, the defendant driver would not be liable. Juries are sympathetic to young children and might assess some liability if the driver should have foreseen the possibility of such an incident because of the number of children playing near or around the street. Depending on the child's age (older than seven years), the child might be held negligent as well.

7. Owners can be held liable for the negligence of permissive users when (1) they negligently entrust the autos to incompetent drivers, (2) the driver is an agent of the owner, or (3) state law (usually statutes) imposes liability on the owner regardless of negligence.

8. Under PIP or limited tort laws, claimants are permitted to sue only when they have serious injuries. They cannot sue for minor injuries; for less serious injuries, they may collect benefits (such as for medical expenses and wage loss) only from their own insurance carrier.

9. Critics argue that monetary thresholds only encourage claimants to build up higher expenses in order to meet the threshold and sue the negligent driver.

10.
- Taking statements from insureds, claimants, and witnesses
- Investigating and diagramming the accident scene
- Obtaining police reports
- Photographing the accident scene and damage
- Gathering evidence
- Determining the proximate cause of the accident

(Among other liability investigation activities and damage evaluation activities such as obtaining medical documents)

Application Questions

1. The question of an uninsured motorist is probably the most important. As mentioned in Chapter 2, accidents caused by "phantom vehicles" are problematic. Is this going to be a hit-and-run vehicle? Is there evidence of contact with the other vehicle?

   As mentioned in Chapter 11, one-car rural accidents tend to be serious. Therefore, the claim representative should be prepared to set substantial reserves and investigate this thoroughly. Such an investigation should establish where the insured was coming from and going at this hour in the morning.

   As part of the documentation of the medical benefits under PIP, the claim representative should find out whether a blood test was performed to determine whether the insured was intoxicated at the time of the accident.

2. For a motorist to be held liable for violating a traffic sign, the sign must be properly displayed. Two criteria of "properly displayed" are that the sign must be visible and readable. This sign was not.

   This does not relieve Bill from negligence though. If this was an uncontrolled intersection, then he should have slowed down, especially if he could not see the cross-traffic. Also, in an uncontrolled intersection, Bill would have had to yield the right-of-way to the vehicle on his right side. Thus, Bill is negligent for this accident.

3. The bee flying into the car would be unexpected, but Mary's reaction was not prudent. Her panic was understandable, but she should have immediately stopped the vehicle. The unavoidable accident defense would not be viable in this claim.

▶▶

Direct Your Learning

Premises Liability Claims

Educational Objectives

After learning the content of this assignment, you should be able to:

1. Explain the duties land possessors owe to each of the following:
   - Trespassers (and the types of trespassers, including children)
   - Licensees
   - Business invitees

2. Explain how the concepts of actual and constructive notice determine the duty to business invitees.

3. Given a premises liability claim, determine whether a land possessor has breached its duty to an individual by identifying the claim factors that would affect liability.

4. Explain the investigative issues involving the following types of claims:
   - Slip-and-fall claims in stores
   - Slip-and-fall claims involving ice and snow

5. Explain the legal and investigative issues involving dog-bite claims.

6. Explain how liability is assessed in premises security liability claims under the following theories:
   - Negligent hiring of employees
   - Negligent retention of employees

7. Explain how liability is assessed in premises security liability claims under the theory of inadequate security. Be able to identify and explain how the following affect this theory:
   - Special relationships
   - Special circumstances
   - Voluntary assumption of liability
   - Statutory duty to provide security

8. Given a premises liability claim scenario, explain whether liability exists by analyzing the duty owed, whether there has been a breach of the duty owed, and whether the breach was the proximate cause of a claimant's injuries.

9. Define or describe each of the Key Words and Phrases for this assignment.

Study Materials

Required Reading:
- ▶ Liability Claim Practices
  - Chapter 12

Study Aids:
- ▶ SMART Online Practice Exams
- ▶ SMART Study Aids
  - Review Notes and Flash Cards—Assignment 12

Outline

▶ **Negligence in Premises Liability Claims**
  A. General Duties Owed in Premises Liability
  B. Breach of Duty Owed
  C. Causation
  D. Damages
  E. Investigating Premises Liability Claims
  F. Slip-and-Fall Claims With Ice and Snow

▶ **Dog-Bite Claims**
  A. Investigating Dog-Bite Claims
    1. Dangerous Dogs
    2. Extenuating Circumstances
    3. Claimant Legal Status
  B. Misrepresentations on Insurance Applications

▶ **Premises Security Liability Claims**
  A. Liability for Crimes Committed by Employees
  B. Liability for Criminal Attacks Committed by Third Parties

▶ **Case Study One—Premises Liability Claim**
  A. Case One—Conclusion

▶ **Case Study Two—Premises Security Liability Claim**
  A. Case Two—Conclusion

▶ **Appendix A—Statement Guideline for Premises Liability Claim (Claimant)**

▶ **Appendix B—Statement Guideline for Dog-Bite Claim (Insured)**

Perform a final review before your exam, but don't cram. Give yourself between two and four hours to go over the course work.

Key Words and Phrases

Define or describe each of the words and phrases listed below.

Trespasser (p. 12.2)

Attractive nuisance doctrine (p. 12.2)

Limited trespasser (p. 12.3)

Known trespasser (p. 12.3)

Licensee (p. 12.3)

Business invitee (p. 12.3)

Actual notice (p. 12.4)

Constructive notice (p. 12.4)

Vicious propensities (p. 12.12)

Leash law (p. 12.14)

Premises security liability (p. 12.15)

Negligent hiring (p. 12.16)

Negligent retention (p. 12.16)

Inadequate security liability claims (p. 12.17)

Special relationship (p. 12.17)

Statutory duty to provide security (p. 12.17)

Special circumstances (p. 12.17)

Voluntary assumption of a duty to provide security (p. 12.18)

Review Questions

1. In general, a trespasser assumes the risks inherent in entering someone else's property. Identify some exceptions to this general rule. (pp. 12.2–12.3)

2. Explain how constructive notice differs from actual notice. (p. 12.4)

3. What are four factors that affect the foreseeability of injuries related to a hazardous condition on a premises? (p. 12.7)

4. Explain how warnings of dangerous conditions on a premises affect the liability of the property owner. (p. 12.8)

5. Explain how a grocery store's inspection records can affect premises liability. (p. 12.10)

6. Explain the defenses that an insured homeowner might have against a person who slipped and fell on the insured's driveway during a snowstorm. (p. 12.11)

7. Identify at least three investigative issues that a claim representative should consider in investigating a dog-bite claim. (p. 12.12)

8. Explain how a school might be held liable for negligent hiring or negligent retention. (pp. 12.15–12.16)

9. Explain how a motel might be held liable for the assault and battery of a guest by an unknown assailant who entered the motel room through a door with a broken lock. (pp. 12.16–12.18)

Application Questions

1. Fred's Nursery has a greenhouse where it grows and sells flowers. Customers go directly to the greenhouse where the plants are grown and choose their own flowers. The greenhouse often has water on the floor because of an automated sprinkler system that sprays water on the flowers. Mud is also on the floor because customers occasionally spill potting soil on the floor when they make their selection of flowers. Fred regularly cleans the floor at the end of each day. One customer injures herself when she slips and falls on some mud located in a poorly lit area of the greenhouse. Analyze liability by examining each of the elements of negligence. Consider how Fred's method of merchandising (self-service, directly from the greenhouse) affects liability. What liability defenses, if any, might Fred have?

2. Bob goes into a men's clothing store at the mall and finds a pair of pants on sale. He decides to buy the pants, but when he goes to check out, the overworked cashier doesn't ring up the discounted sales price, but instead rings up a higher price. When Bob questions her, she agrees in a surly manner and says, "Fine, whatever. That's not the price that's in the computer." Bob feels that she is questioning his integrity and walks out of the store. He drives ten miles to another store to buy the pants. En route to the other store, Bob is still fuming over the incident with the cashier, and his mind is not on his driving. Bob drives into the path of a bus and is injured. Is the first clothing store negligent and responsible for Bob's injuries?

3. Pam and Kevin own a home with a swimming pool. They
   have learned from experience that insurance companies charge an
   additional premium for people who have swimming pools. After
   some searching, they found one insurance company that sold
   insurance over the Internet that did not require an agent to come
   to their home. The company sent them an application to fill out,
   which asked whether they had a swimming pool. Pam and Kevin
   answered "No" on the application. They obtained insurance from
   the company even though the company would not have insured
   them had it known about the pool. The pool was elaborate with
   slides and diving boards. Pam and Kevin had erected a privacy
   fence on one side of the pool to prevent the next-door neighbors
   from seeing the pool, but the other three sides of the pool were
   open. One day while Kevin and Pam were on vacation, a three-
   year-old neighbor child wandered over to the pool, climbed up
   on a slide, and slid into the pool. The child could not get out and
   sank to the bottom of the pool. By the time the child was discovered and resuscitated by his parents, he had been under water for
   so long that he suffered brain damage. Explain how liability would
   be assessed in this situation. What liability defenses, if any, would
   Pam and Kevin have? What coverage defenses would Pam and
   Kevin's insurance company have?

4. Kim parks her new car in the parking lot of the grocery. She
   notices several shopping carts around the parking lot and tries to
   avoid them because it is a windy day. She parks her car and goes
   into the store to shop. When she returns an hour later, she finds
   a shopping cart pressed against the side of her new car. The wind
   had blown the cart into her car door and scratched the paint. Kim
   makes a claim against the grocery store for the cost to repaint the
   car door. Assess the grocery store's liability for this damage based
   on the four factors of foreseeability often considered by courts.

5. Cindy, a claim representative with Common Insurance, receives the following loss notice:

> Insured owns two pit bulls which are kept chained in insured's back yard. One of the insured's dogs broke loose and chased and killed a neighbor's dog. Neighbor making claims for loss of dog and emotional injury to children, who witnessed the event.

What are some liability issues that Cindy should investigate?

Answers to Assignment 12 Questions

NOTE: These answers are provided to give students a basic understanding of acceptable types of responses. They often are not the only valid answers and are not intended to provide an exhaustive response to the questions.

Review Questions

1. • When young children are lured onto the premises by attractive nuisance
    • When trespassing is known and tolerated
    • When trespassing is on specific, isolated areas known to land possessor

2. • Actual notice means the land possessor knew of a hazard.
    • Constructive notice means the land possessor should have, through reasonable inspection, known of the hazard.

3. (1) The probability of harm occurring as a result of the condition
    (2) How serious the harm would likely be
    (3) What precautions the land possessor could have taken to prevent harm
    (4) How burdensome these precautions would have been to the land possessor

4. Warnings reduce the likelihood of injuries and may be the only reasonable action that a land possessor can take in some circumstances. Therefore, warnings of danger can reduce or eliminate liability.

5. Well-kept records can establish that the grocery store made regular, periodic inspections. This helps document that the grocery store met its duty owed to patrons, so that even if a patron is injured, liability might not exist.

6. • The insured did not have a duty to clear the snow.
    • The claimant was comparatively at fault.
    • The snow was a general condition of the community and no worse at the insured's house.

7. Possible answers include the following:
    • Whether the dog has previously bitten any other people or animals.
    • Whether the dog has shown vicious propensities to people or animals.
    • Whether the dog was in violation of a leash law when it bit the claimant.
    • Were there extenuating circumstances that would have provoked the dog to attack?
    • What is the legal status of the claimant (trespasser, licensee, business invitee)?
    • What is the dog's breed?

8. A school has a "special relationship" with its students that requires it to take more precautions to ensure the safety of students than would be required of businesses. If the school hired a person with a history of violent criminal behavior, then the school could be held liable for injuries suffered by children harmed by this person. If the school failed to exercise care in doing a background check, it could be guilty of negligent hiring. If the person's behavior was found out after hiring and the employee was retained, then the school could be held liable for negligent retention. The school might defend itself by showing that the person worked hours when the children were not in school.

9. The motel might be held liable under two theories: special relationship and special circumstances. Under the special relationship theory, the motel owes a high duty to its guests. Having faulty locks would probably not meet that high level of care owed. Also, most municipal ordinances require hotels and motels to have functioning locks. Failure to comply with the ordinances would be negligence per se.

    The motel might also be liable if the motel premises (or even surrounding premises) have been sites of violent criminal activity. Such activity would have made this incident more foreseeable and may have required the motel to take further precautions in terms of lighting or hiring security personnel.

Application Questions

1. First, Fred owes a duty to his customers. The duty owed for business invitees is to warn of known, hidden hazards and to make periodic inspections of the premises to clean up potential hazards. Allowing customers to come into the greenhouse and pick out flowers on their own places an even higher burden on Fred to take precautions to ensure the safety of customers. Cleaning the floor only once during the day would not likely meet the standard of care owed for this type of operation. Failing to make more regular inspections and failing to take precautions to prevent slippery floors were the causes of the customer's fall and subsequent injury. Fred would be liable for these injuries.

    Depending on what facts are gathered, the customer might have seen the mud on the floor and still continued to walk over it. This would raise the possibility of an assumption of risk defense, and comparative or contributory negligence. Given the circumstances of the operation and the poorly lit area of the greenhouse, these defenses would be weak.

2. The cashier is an agent of the men's clothing store, which is liable if the cashier is negligent, but there is no negligence on the part of the cashier. The store (and its employees) owes a duty (1) not to harm customers; (2) to warn customers of known, hidden hazards; and (3) to make periodic inspections. It doesn't have a legal duty to provide courteous sales staff, even though that would make good business sense. Also, the proximate cause of Bob's damages is not the cashier's surly attitude, but instead the bus accident. This accident is too far removed from the cashier's actions and too unforeseeable to make the store liable. Thus, the store did not violate any duty owed to Bob, and even if it did, the breach of the duty did not cause his injuries. The intervening bus accident caused his injuries.

3. Normally, the child would be considered a trespasser and the only duty the homeowner would owe to the trespasser would be the duty to not intentionally harm the trespasser. However, this swimming pool is a classic example of an attractive nuisance. The land possessors (Pam and Kevin) would be liable under this doctrine because:

    *   Pam and Kevin had reason to know the swimming pool is in an area where children are likely to trespass.

    *   The pool poses a risk of serious harm.

    *   The child who trespassed was too young to recognize the danger.

    *   The benefit of the item is slight compared to its risk.

    *   Pam and Kevin did nothing to eliminate the danger or protect children (such as putting a fence completely around the pool).

Pam and Kevin's failure to safeguard the pool was the proximate cause of the child's injury.

They would have few defenses because the child was too young (age three) to assume the risk or to be comparatively liable. The parents might also be liable for negligent supervision, but that is not going to eliminate Pam's and Kevin's liability.

Pam's and Kevin's insurer has a defense of material misrepresentation. Pam and Kevin lied on their application about a material (significant) risk.

4.
- The probability of harm in not gathering shopping carts—fairly high
- How serious the harm would likely be—very low
- The precautions that could be taken to prevent harm—such as sending more workers outside more frequently to gather carts
- The burden of sending more workers outside more frequently—fairly substantial

Looking at these factors, courts would likely consider the financial burden too great to justify preventing such minor damage. (Note: Disputes over these types of claims often end up in small claims courts.)

5.
- Where did the attack occur (on the insured's premises, a neighbor's, or public property)?
- Is there a leash law that applies to this municipality?
- How did the insured's dog break loose? (Was there anything that the insured could reasonably have done to prevent this?)
- Has the dog shown any vicious propensities before?
- What provoked the dog to attack?
- What type of dog was killed? (How much does it cost to replace this dog?)

The issue with the children's emotional injury claim is a "red herring." Emotional injury claims for loss of property damage (in this case, dogs) are still not permitted. Some trial courts have permitted pure emotional injury claims for damage to homes because of the emotional attachment that people have to their homes, but to date, these cases have been overruled on appeal. It would be unlikely that courts would open up a Pandora's box and allow pure emotional injury claims for property damage because every fender bender would then have the potential for an emotional injury claim.

Direct Your Learning

Product Liability

Study Materials

Required Reading:
▶ Liability Claim Practices
  • Chapter 13

Study Aids:
▶ SMART Online
  Practice Exams
▶ SMART Study Aids
  • Review Notes and
    Flash Cards—
    Assignment 13

Educational Objectives

After learning the content of this assignment, you should be able to:

1. Identify and describe situations in which specific theories of negligence would make product manufacturers, suppliers, distributors, and retailers liable for harm caused to product users. In support of this objective, you should be able to explain how the following theories apply:

   - Negligent design
   - Negligent inspection
   - Negligent assembly
   - Failure to properly warn
   - Negligent sales or sales in violation of a statute

2. Identify and describe situations in which the defenses to the theories of negligence would apply. In support of this objective, you should be able to explain how the following defenses apply:

   - No defect
   - Misuse or alteration of the product
   - Duty not breached
   - Harm was unforeseeable
   - Intervening cause
   - Act of God
   - Contributory or comparative negligence
   - Assumption of risk by product user
   - Statute of limitation
   - No causation (defendant's actions did not cause the injury)

3. Identify and describe situations in which sellers can be liable for the harm caused by their products based on warranty laws. In support of this objective, you should be able to explain the following:

   - Implied warranty of title
   - Implied warranty of merchantability
   - Implied warranty of fitness for a particular purpose
   - Expressed warranty
   - Uniform Commercial Code (UCC)

4. Identify and describe situations in which the defenses to warranty would apply. In support of this objective, you should be able to explain how the following defenses apply:

   - The warranty was fulfilled
   - The "expressed warranty" was just exaggerated sales talk
   - Disclaimers
   - Assumption of risk

5. Identify and describe situations in which sellers could be held liable for harm caused by their products based on strict liability.

6. Identify and describe situations in which defenses to strict liability for products would apply. In support of this objective, you should be able to explain how the following defenses apply:

   - The circumstances do not meet the criteria for strict liability
   - Contributory/comparative negligence
   - Assumption of risk
   - Misuse of the product
   - State of the art (at the time the product was made)
   - Government specifications

7. Explain what defenses and rights to recovery retailers might have against a manufacturer in product liability claims.

8. Define or describe each of the Key Words and Phrases for this assignment.

Outline

▶ **Product Liability Laws and Concepts**

▶ **Negligence and Product Liability**

   A. Supplier's Negligence

   B. Retailer's Negligence

   C. Sales in Violation of a Statute

   D. Negligence Defenses for Product Liability

▶ **Warranty and Product Liability**

   A. Implied Warranty of Title

   B. Implied Warranty of Merchantability

   C. Warranty of Fitness for a Particular Purpose

      1. Expressed Warranties

   D. Uniform Commercial Codes

   E. Warranty Defenses

▶ **Strict Liability for Products**

   A. Market-Share Liability

   B. Strict Liability Defenses for Product Liability

▶ **Retailer Defenses and Recoveries**

▶ **Application of Product Liability**

▶ **Product Liability—Case Study**

   A. The Notice of Loss

   B. The Investigation

   C. Analyzing Liability

      1. Duty To Warn

   D. Assessing Defenses

      1. Improper Use

      2. Comparative Negligence

      3. Assumption of Risk

   E. Other Responsible Parties

   F. Evaluating the Damages

      1. Damages

      2. Defense-Cost Issues

   G. Case Conclusion

▶ **Appendix—Checklist for Product Liability Investigations**

When reviewing for your exam, remember to allot time for frequent breaks.

Key Words and Phrases

Define or describe each of the words and phrases listed below.

Product liability (p. 13.2)

Negligent design (p. 13.2)

Failure to warn (p. 13.3)

Product warning label (p. 13.3)

Negligent misrepresentation (p. 13.6)

Implied warranties (p. 13.8)

Breach of warranty (p. 13.8)

Implied warranty of title (p. 13.9)

Implied warranty of merchantability (p. 13.9)

Implied warranty of fitness for a particular purpose (p. 13.9)

Expressed warranty (p. 13.9)

Seller (p. 13.11)

Market-share liability (p. 13.13)

State of the art defense (p. 13.14)

Indemnification (p. 13.14)

Review Questions

1. Identify whether each of the following theories of product liability would likely apply to manufacturers, retailers, or both. (pp. 13.2–13.13)
   a. Negligent design
   b. Negligent labeling or packaging
   c. Negligent inspection
   d. Negligent assembly
   e. Breach of warranty of merchantability
   f. Breach of warranty of fitness for a particular purpose
   g. Strict liability
   h. Market-share liability
   i. Negligent misrepresentation

2. Explain how foreseeability affects product liability as it relates to product design and product warning labels. (pp. 13.2–13.3)

3. Explain whether warranties can pay for costs beyond the cost to repair or refund the purchase price of the defective item. (pp. 13.8–13.9)

4. Explain whether exaggerations about a product's qualities (puffery) subject the seller to product liability based on expressed warranty. (p. 13.11)

5. Explain how the term "seller" is defined in strict liability claims. (pp. 13.11–13.12)

6. Explain the advantage to the claimant of making a claim under strict liability over making a claim based on some theory of negligence. (13.12)

7. What constitutes a product "defect"? (p. 13.12)

8. Describe the criteria that must be met in order to establish a product liability claim under strict liability. (p. 13.13)

9. Identify whether the following defenses are available for claims made under negligence, warranty, or strict liability. (Write all that apply.) (pp. 13.7–13.14)

    a. Comparative negligence

    b. Disclaimer

    c. State of the art

    d. Seller exercised due care

    e. Statute of limitation

    f. Assumption of risk

10. Explain how retailers may be able to recover damages and legal defenses paid on product liability claims. (pp. 13.14–13.15)

Application Questions

1. At an intersection, Norman Hughes was involved in an accident with a car that entered the intersection from his right. Hughes claimed that because he saw a stop sign for the other car, he did not brake until it was too late. Hughes further claimed that the anti-lock feature of his brakes did not work, causing him to spin out of control.

   Hughes and the other driver want to sue the manufacturer of Hughes' car for an alleged defect in the brakes. What must be proven to succeed in an action based on each of the following?

    a. Negligence

b. Breach of expressed warranty

c. Strict liability

2. Tom bought a bottle of fruit juice from Connor's Market. Connor's Market bought the juice already bottled from the manufacturer and did nothing except resell it. The label on the bottle stated, "Warranty of Purity: Guaranteed to contain 100% fruit juice, without preservatives, pesticides, or other harmful substances." When Tom opened the bottle, he discovered a dead mouse inside. Although Tom never drank any of the juice, he became very upset.

a. Explain whether Connor's Market may be liable to Tom on the basis of negligence.

b. Explain one basis, other than negligence, on which Connor's Market may be liable to Tom.

c. Explain the options Tom may have if it is determined a breach of warranty occurred.

3. High-Flyer is a well-known glue used for assembling model airplanes. Unfortunately, High-Flyer is equally well known among teenagers who inhale the glue fumes as a cheap way to get high. Recently, a number of teenagers have died or suffered brain damage from inhaling (known as "huffing") the glue. These facts are brought to the attention of management, but they are loath to add any warning labels specifically stating that death or serious injury could arise from inhaling the glue fumes. Management argues that the warning label is adequate because it tells users to use the product in a well-ventilated area. Research on their product shows that no user has died or even been injured from inhaling glue fumes when the product is used as intended.

   a.   Explain whether the manufacturer could be held liable for users' deaths or injuries under the theory of strict liability.

   b.   Explain whether the product warning label is adequate as it currently exists (that is, without the specific warning of the potential for death or serious injury if the product is intentionally inhaled for a prolonged time period).

   c.   What defenses would High-Flyer raise against strict liability claims made against the manufacturer by claimants who inhaled the glue?

▶▶

d. A product engineer for High-Flyer shows the company that by adding one noxious-smelling ingredient to the glue, it could prevent people from inhaling the fumes because they would become sick before inhaling enough to be seriously injured. This ingredient would add 8 cents to the cost of a tube of glue. Management declines the engineer's suggestion even though a competitor is adding a similar ingredient to its product. Management argues that by deliberately adding a noxious ingredient to the glue, they are setting themselves up for a product liability claim, and they point out that they have never lost a lawsuit made against them by a person who had "huffed" their product. Explain how this new possibility for adding an ingredient to prevent serious injury could affect liability.

Answers to Assignment 13 Questions

NOTE: These answers are provided to give students a basic understanding of acceptable types of responses. They often are not the only valid answers and are not intended to provide an exhaustive response to the questions.

Review Questions

1. a. Manufacturers
   b. Manufacturers
   c. Usually manufacturers, especially if item is in a sealed container
   d. Both
   e. Both
   f. Most likely retailer because of need to know buyer's intent
   g. Both
   h. Manufacturer
   i. Most likely retailer

2. Product design: Manufacturer must anticipate dangers of the product and try to build in reasonable safeguards, such as making a car that does not explode when it is struck in the rear.

    Warning labels: Must not only explain dangers associated with use of product but also with foreseeable misuse of product.

3. Warranty law can also require sellers to pay for personal injuries and property damage caused by the product.

4. Some exaggerations are considered to be "sales talk" and not warranties. Sales representative opinions such as, "This is the most comfortable car on the road" or "This is the world's friendliest computer program," are not likely to be considered warranties.

5. Sellers can be retailers, manufacturers, suppliers, or any party in the sales chain.

6. Under strict liability, the seller can be liable even if the seller exercised all possible care.

7. Any weakness or flaw in the product that causes harm (Even inadequate warning labels have been considered defects.)

8. The product must have had a defect when it left the manufacturer.

    The defect is unreasonably dangerous to the user or consumer.

    The seller is somehow engaged in getting the product.

    The product is expected to reach the consumer without substantial changes in the condition in which it was sold.

    The product was used in a manner reasonably anticipated by the manufacturer.

9. a. Applies to all three.

   b. Applies mainly to warranties.

   c. Applies to strict liability or negligent design.

   d. Applies to negligence.

   e. This applies to negligence and strict liability. Technically, warranties are contracts, and therefore the statutes of repose apply to them.

   f. Applies to all three.

10. Retailers may have indemnity action against the manufacturer to recover damages and even legal fees paid out on a claim. The retailer is supposed to notify the manufacturer of the claim as soon as the claim is made against the retailer. Contracts between retailers and manufacturers often govern this indemnification process.

Application Questions

1. a. To succeed under a theory of manufacturer negligence, the claimant must prove:
   - There was truly a problem with the anti-lock brake system.
   - The failure of the anti-lock brake system caused the accident.
   - The anti-lock brake system was improperly designed, or
   - The anti-lock brake system was improperly installed or made of inferior materials, or
   - The manufacturer failed to give adequate warning about the anticipated uses or misuses of the anti-lock brake system.

   b. To succeed under a breach of an expressed warranty, the claimant must prove:
   - A representation (warranty) was expressly made about the capability of the anti-lock brake system.
   - The anti-lock brake system did not meet the capabilities stated in the warranty.
   - Not meeting the capabilities stated was the cause of the accident.

   c. To succeed under strict liability, the claimant must be able to prove:
   - There was a defect in the anti-lock brake system, and the defect would be dangerous to the consumer. (The claimant would not have to prove negligence in the design or installation.)
   - The defective brakes caused the accident.

2. a. Negligence would not be an effective theory of liability because of the sealed container. Retailer has no duty to check inside.

   b. The retailer would be liable under strict liability, but only if the emotional upset is compensable. Pure emotional injury damages may not be compensable in many states.

   The most viable theory is breach of warranty of merchantability.

   c. Under breach of warranty, Tom would be entitled to the cost of the product and personal injury. Again, this is a very questionable injury and may not be compensable.

3. a.   To be held liable under strict liability, the claimants would have to establish the following:

- The glue was defective.

- The glue was unreasonably dangerous to the claimants.

- The glue caused harm to the user.

- The glue was used in a manner reasonably anticipated by the manufacturer.

Users (or more appropriately misusers) were harmed by the products. Proving that the glue was unreasonably dangerous would be somewhat difficult unless there was evidence that a number of people were harmed by the glue, which seems to be the situation in this case. Proving that the product was defective would be very difficult for a plaintiff. The tactic that a plaintiff might take is that the product was defective because of an inadequate warning label. It would not be easy for a plaintiff to convince a jury of High-Flyer's liability.

b.   A proper warning label should convey the potential dangers of the product. Management is aware of the misuse of the product, and it is now foreseeable (and perhaps was foreseeable before now) that the product will be misused. The warning should convey the dangers of this foreseeable misuse.

c.   The most obvious and most viable defense would be the misuse of the product.

Contributory or comparative negligence would also be viable.

In addition, if the claimants were somehow aware of the risks involved (even though there was no warning label to make them aware), then the assumption of risk defense would apply. This would be a difficult defense to prove because the claimants would not be able to give a statement that they knew of the dangers.

d.   Manufacturers are supposed to build reasonable safeguards in their products that anticipate foreseeable uses and misuses of their products. High-Flyer's management fails to recognize that the state of the art for the product has changed. By not incorporating the new ingredient into their product, they are exposing themselves to liability. In the same way that automakers must continue to keep up with new safety features that are invented to prevent injuries, High-Flyer must do the same, especially if the cost to do so is not overly burdensome.

Exam Information

About Institutes Exams

Exam questions are based on the Educational Objectives stated in the course guide and textbook. The exam is designed to measure whether you have met those Educational Objectives. The exam does not test every Educational Objective. Instead, it tests over a balanced sample of Educational Objectives.

How to Prepare for Institutes Exams

What can you do to prepare for an Institutes exam? Students who pass Institute exams do the following:

▶ Use the assigned study materials. Focus your study on the Educational Objectives presented at the beginning of each course guide assignment. Thoroughly read the textbook and any other assigned materials, and then complete the course guide exercises. Choose a study method that best suits your needs; for example, participate in a traditional class, online class, or informal study group; or study on your own. Use The Institutes' SMART Study Aids (if available) for practice and review. If this course has an associated SMART Online Practice Exams product, you will find an access code on the inside back cover of this course guide. This access code allows you to print (in PDF format) a full practice exam and to take additional online practice exams that will simulate an actual credentialing exam.

▶ Become familiar with the types of test questions asked on the exam. The practice exam in this course guide or in the SMART Online Practice Exams product will help you understand the different types of questions you will encounter on the exam.

▶ Maximize your test-taking time. Successful students use the sample exam in the course guide or in the SMART Online Practice Exams product to practice pacing themselves. Learning how to manage your time during the exam ensures that you will complete all of the test questions in the time allotted.

Types of Exam Questions

The exam for this course consists of objective questions of several types.

The Correct-Answer Type

In this type of question, the question stem is followed by four responses, one of which is absolutely correct. Select the *correct* answer.

> Which one of the following persons evaluates requests for insurance to determine which applicants are accepted and which are rejected?
>
> a. The premium auditor
>
> b. The loss control representative
>
> c. The underwriter
>
> d. The risk manager

The Best-Answer Type

In this type of question, the question stem is followed by four responses, only one of which is best, given the statement made or facts provided in the stem. Select the *best* answer.

> Several people within an insurer might be involved in determining whether an applicant for insurance is accepted. Which one of the following positions is primarily responsible for determining whether an applicant for insurance is accepted?
>
> a. The loss control representative
>
> b. The customer service representative
>
> c. The underwriter
>
> d. The premium auditor

The Incomplete-Statement or Sentence-Completion Type

In this type of question, the last part of the question stem consists of a portion of a statement rather than a direct question. Select the phrase that *correctly* or *best* completes the sentence.

> Residual market plans designed for individuals who are unable to obtain insurance on their personal property in the voluntary market are called

a. VIN plans.

b. Self-insured retention plans.

c. Premium discount plans.

d. FAIR plans.

"All of the Above" Type

In this type of question, only one of the first three answers could be correct, or all three might be correct, in which case the best answer would be "All of the above." Read all the answers and select the *best* answer.

> When a large commercial insured's policy is up for renewal, who is likely to provide input to the renewal decision process?

a. The underwriter

b. The loss control representative

c. The producer

d. All of the above

"All of the following, EXCEPT:" Type

In this type of question, responses include three correct answers and one answer that is incorrect or is clearly the least correct. Select the *incorrect* or *least correct* answer.

> All of the following adjust insurance claims, EXCEPT:

a. Insurer claim representatives

b. Premium auditors

c. Producers

d. Independent adjusters